Line spacing	Layout (Shift-F8) Line Line Spacing	Repeat	Esc
Lines	Graphics (Alt-F9) Lines	Replace	Search Replace (Alt-F2)
Macro, define	Tools Macro Define (Ctrl-F10)	Reveal codes	Edit Reveal Codes (Alt-F3)
Macro, repeat	Tools Macro Execute (Alt-F10)	Save and quit	File Exit (F7) Yes Yes
Margins, left and right	Layout (Shift-F8) Line Margins	Save and continue	File Save (F10)
Margins, top and bottom	Layout (Shift-F8) Page Margins	Search backward	Search Backward (Shift-F2)
		Search forward	Search Forward (F2)
Move text	Edit Select or Move (Ctrl-F4)	Select printer	File Print (Shift-F7) Select Printer
Normal print	Font (Ctrl-F8) Normal	Shadow printing	Font (Ctrl-F8) Appearance Shadow
Outline print	Font (Ctrl-F8) Appearance Outline	Small print	Font (Ctrl-F8 S) Small
Page break	Ctrl-↵	Small capital printing	Font (Ctrl-F8) Appearance Small Cap
Page numbering	Layout (Shift-F8) Page Page Numbering	Spell	Tools Spell (Ctrl-F2)
Page size	Layout (Shift-F8) Page Page Size	Strikeout printing	Font (Ctrl-F8) Appearance Strikeout
Print		Subscript	Font (Ctrl-F8 S) Subscript
document	File Print (Shift-F7) Full	Superscript	Font (Ctrl-F8 S) Superscript
from disk	File Print (Shift-F7) Document on Disk	Switch documents	Edit Switch Documents (Shift-F3)
page	File Print (Shift-F7) Page	Tab set	Layout (Shift-F8) Line Tab Set
multiple copies	File Print (Shift-F7) Number of Copies	Tables	Layout Tables (Alt-F7 T)
multiple pages	File Print (Shift-F7) Multiple Page	Thesaurus	Tools Thesaurus (Alt-F1)
		Typeover mode	Ins
Quit	File Exit (F7)	Underline	Font Appearance Underline (F8)
Recall document	File Retrieve (Shift-F10)	Very large print	Font (Ctrl-F8 S) Very Large
Redline printing	Font (Ctrl-F8) Appearance Redline	View document	File Print (Shift-F7) View Document
		Window Size	Edit Window (Ctrl-F3)

The ABC's of
WordPerfect 5.1

The ABC's of WordPerfect® 5.1

Alan R. Neibauer

San Francisco • Paris • Düsseldorf • London

Acquisitions Editor: Dianne King
Editor: Peter Weverka
Technical Editor: Maryann Brown
Word Processors: Deborah Maizels and Chris Mockel
Series Design: Jeffrey James Giese
Chapter Art and Layout: Ingrid Owen
Screen Graphics: Delia Brown
Typesetter: Elizabeth Newman
Production Editor: Carolina Montilla
Indexer: Ted Laux
Cover Designer: Thomas Ingalls + Associates
Cover Photographer: Michael LaMotte
Screen reproductions produced by XenoFont

To Barbara,
for her support,
understanding, and love

Acknowledgments

It takes more than an author to produce a book such as this, and I owe thanks to many others who helped complete this project. Foremost are Peter Weverka, who edited the manuscript and kept up the constant flow between Philadelphia and Alameda, Joanne Cuthbertson, supervising editor, and Maryann Brown, technical reviewer.

Special recognition must also go to those who finally translated all our notes into the finished product—word processors Deborah Maizels and Chris Mockel, typesetter Elizabeth Newman, and production editor Carolina Montilla. The superb design of the book is the contribution of Jeff Giese.

The foundation of this edition was laid some time ago, thanks to the efforts of editor Eric Stone and others at SYBEX. So thank you again to David Kolodney, Brian Atwood, David Clark, Jocelyn Reynolds, Olivia Shinomoto, Kristen Iverson, Paula Alston, Ingrid Owen, Jeff Giese, and Michelle Hoffman.

Thanks also to Dianne King and Dr. Rudolph S. Langer.

Finally, my sincere appreciation to Barbara Neibauer.

Contents
at a Glance

Table of Contents

Introduction

1 *Creating Your First Document*

2 *Improving and Correcting Your Document*

3 More Efficient Revision Techniques

4 Enhancing the Appearance of Your Documents

5 Formatting Characters for Emphasis and Variety

6 Aligning Text and Creating Tables

7 Right and Left Indents and Other Paragraph Formats

11 Streamlining Your Editing with Search and Replace

12 Creating Multicolumn Layouts

13 Creating Personalized Form Letters

14 Adding Footnotes and Endnotes

15 Advanced Printing and Setup

16 Automating Keystrokes with Macros

Word Tools: The Speller and Thesaurus

 Enhancing Your Documents with Graphics

 Printing Special Characters and Equations

 How to Make Backups

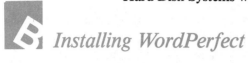

Introduction

If you've never used WordPerfect before and want to learn how, or have tried an older version of WordPerfect, then this book is for you. You will learn how to create and print documents in short, easy-to-understand lessons. Each lesson takes only a few minutes, so you can complete several lessons in one session, learning a complete and useful task easily and quickly.

As your skills increase, the lessons will start to cover more sophisticated functions of this remarkable word processing tool—including the powerful graphics and desktop publishing functions. But even these "advanced" lessons are clear and concise. They were designed to get you working in just minutes without the need to refer constantly to manuals.

WordPerfect comes in several versions for a variety of computers. This book covers Version 5.1 for the IBM family of personal computers and those compatible to them. The program is basically the same whether you're using DOS or OS/2 as your disk operating system. So if you're using an IBM PC/XT, AT, PS/2, or similar computer, you can just follow the instructions in this book.

Of course, WordPerfect comes in versions for other computers that use other operating systems. While the differences are too numerous to be covered adequately in an introductory book, once you've learned the elements of WordPerfect presented here, it will be easy to apply what you've learned to other versions if the need arises.

Why use this book when you already have the manual that came with WordPerfect? The manual is a well-written and complete reference to WordPerfect, but it is designed as a reference, not as a learning aid. Its primary function is to explain in detail—in over 800 pages—every technicality that even the most advanced user needs.

This book, on the other hand, is designed for the beginning Word-Perfect user. It can be used even if you are just learning how to use your computer system. It shows you how to copy and install WordPerfect, and to create, edit, and print documents of all types. If you are already using WordPerfect's basic functions, then the advanced lessons later in the book will teach you more difficult tasks. And even if you're an expert on older versions of the program, you'll quickly learn the major differences needed to stay productive with the new version.

How to Use this Book

Each chapter is made up of several lessons. Most of the lessons include a series of easy-to-follow numbered steps. To learn how to use WordPerfect, just sit down at your computer and do what each step instructs. You'll be amazed how easy it is.

If you just purchased WordPerfect, the first two appendices will be invaluable. There you'll learn how to make a copy of your disks, install WordPerfect on your computer, and tell WordPerfect what printer you're using. Go directly to these appendices if you have not yet used the program or are not sure that you've set it up correctly.

The lessons in the first chapter show you how to start WordPerfect and how to type, print and save a simple document in the fewest key-strokes possible. Not every detail of editing, saving, or printing is given in these beginning lessons, just the basics. This is to demonstrate how easy WordPerfect really is, and to test your hardware and printer before going any further. Chapter 1 also teaches you to type and print those simple documents that you need right away.

The chapters that follow include lessons covering every aspect of WordPerfect. In Chapters 2 and 3 you'll learn about editing your text; in Chapters 4 to 8 about formatting it for printing, including creating boxed spreadsheet-like tables using the remarkable new table feature. In Chapter 9 you'll learn how to add headers and footers to your documents and number pages. Chapter 10 shows you how to work with blocks of text, and in Chapter 11 you'll learn how to search for and replace words or groups of words automatically.

The remaining chapters cover WordPerfect features that are more specialized and are useful in a great variety of applications. In Chapter 12 you'll learn how to create columns of text, which you'll need if you produce newsletters, and Chapters 13 and 14 show you how to produce form letters and add footnotes to your documents. In Chapter 15 you'll learn how to use some advanced printing features, and in Chapter 16 I'll show you how to create labor-saving "macros." You'll learn about WordPerfect's powerful Speller and Thesaurus in Chapter 17, and how to add lines, boxes, and drawings to documents in Chapter 18, taking full advantage of WordPerfect's desktop publishing features. Chapter 19 shows you how to work with special characters and symbols, and how to format and print even the most complex equations.

While there is a normal progression in learning a program such as this, you can jump ahead to more advanced lessons if you need that information to complete your work. For example, while following an earlier lesson you might have the need to move an entire section of text from one location to another. This is called a Block function. Just look in the table of contents or index and go directly to that lesson. Follow the steps and, when done, return to the earlier chapter and continue.

However, this is only recommended when absolutely needed. Because the lessons are short and designed to teach you quickly, you'll reach the advanced chapters before you realize it.

The WordPerfect Keyboard

For typing, the computer keyboard is really no different than a regular typewriter. It doesn't matter if you have the original IBM/PC keyboard (Figure I.1), the keyboard first sold with IBM PC/ATs (Figure I.2), or the newer "enhanced" keyboard now shipped with most IBMs including the PS/2s (Figure I.3). The middle section of the keyboard includes the keys for letters, numbers, and punctuation marks needed to enter your text.

But the keyboard also includes special keys not found on a typewriter. These keys allow you to harness the power of the computer for word processing. During the lessons that follow, you will be instructed to press these special keys, and even combinations of them.

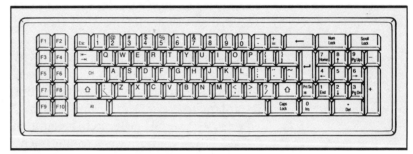

Figure I.1: Original IBM keyboard

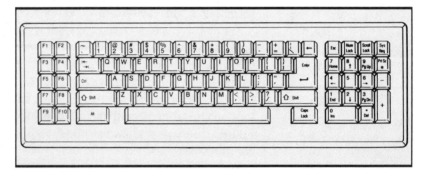

Figure I.2: Older IBM PC/AT keyboard

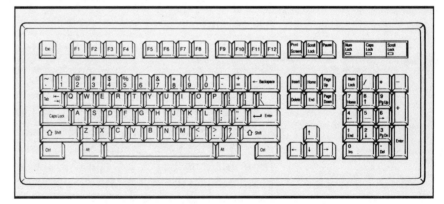

Figure I.3: Enhanced IBM keyboard

Special Keys

Look at your keyboard for the following keys:

 This is the Tab key. When an instruction says to press Tab, press this key.

 This is the Shift key. When an instruction says to press Shift, press this key. You can press either of the two Shift keys on the keyboard.

 This is the Enter key—one of the most important keys you will be using. You use the Enter key to end paragraphs or insert blank lines into the text. The Enter key is also called Return. To avoid confusion, we'll use the symbol ◄─┘ throughout this book. So when an instruction says to press ◄─┘, press this key.

 This is the Backspace key. It is used to delete unwanted characters.

 When an instruction says to press Esc, press this key, the Escape key. This key is used to repeat characters and commands automatically.

 When an instruction says to press Ins, press this key. This is the Insert key, which switches between the Insert and Typeover modes. In the Insert mode, existing characters will move over to make room for new ones. In the Typeover mode, new characters will replace existing ones.

 When an instruction says to press Del, press this key. This is the Delete key, used to erase characters from the screen.

When an instruction says to press Alt, press this key, the Alternate key. It is used with the function keys described below.

 When an instruction says to press Ctrl, press this key, the Control key. It is also used with the function keys.

Function Keys

Most of WordPerfect's features can be accessed using either the keyboard or the mouse. Appendix C discusses the mouse in detail. If you don't have a mouse, or if you want to learn all the ways to use Word-Perfect, then you should become familiar with your computer's function keys.

Depending on your computer, you may have 10 or 12 special keys, labelled F1 to F10 or F12. They are either on the left side of the keyboard or above the top row, as on the "enhanced" IBM keyboard. They operate exactly the same in either location.

These keys have been "programmed" by WordPerfect for special functions and provide quick and easy methods for performing complex tasks. Certain functions are performed by pressing a function key by itself. Other functions are accomplished by pressing them in combination with the Alt, Shift, or Ctrl keys.

At first, you might be overwhelmed by the large number of function keys available. But keep in mind that WordPerfect can also be controlled by a comprehensive series of pull down menus—lists of options that let you select features without having to memorize keystrokes or refer to a keyboard template.

Two templates describing the use of function keys are supplied with your WordPerfect manual. The square template with the cutout in the middle is designed for keyboards with the function keys on the right. Place it over the keys and refer to it as you type. The long template is for the enhanced keyboard—place it above the keys so you can refer to it when you want to use the function keys.

Notice that both templates give four different uses for each of the function keys. Some uses are printed in black, others in red, green, or blue. The task in black is accomplished by pressing the function key by itself. The other colors represent combining the key with either the Ctrl, Shift, or Alt key.

Color	Key + function key
Red	Ctrl
Green	Shift
Blue	Alt

If you have misplaced your template, see the inside cover of this book for a recap of the function keys.

Numeric Keypad

On the right side of the keyboard is a group of keys that serve as both the numeric keyboard and the cursor-movement keys. These keys have both numbers and arrows printed on them. Normally, they act as the cursor-movement keys, as explained in Chapters 1 and 2. But if you do a lot of numeric typing you might find it convenient to use these keys rather than the numbers on the top row of the middle section. To use the keypad for numbers you have to press the Num Lock key above the keypad. With the Num Lock key off, these keys are cursor-movement keys. With Num Lock on, they are numbers. You can tell when NumLock is on because the characters *Pos* blink at the bottom right of the screen (as will be explained fully in Lesson 2). With some keyboards, a small light in the Num Lock key itself will be on when the Num Lock key is on. Press the key to turn off the light and the key.

Some keyboards have separate cursor keys and a separate numeric keypad. If you have this type of keyboard, then use the keypad for entering numbers and the arrow keys to the left of the keypad for cursor movement.

Communicating with WordPerfect

Special instructions for using the mouse appear in margin notes such as this, and in Appendix C.

There are two ways to communicate with WordPerfect: through pull down menus or by the function keys. If you've used an earlier version of WordPerfect, then you are already familiar with the way the function keys operate.

Both pull down menus and function keys, however, let you select WordPerfect options for editing, formatting, and printing documents. In fact, in many cases, the function keys and pull down menus will result in displaying the same menu, prompt line, or message. They are just two ways of achieving the same end.

Pull Down Menus

There are three steps to using the pull down menus:

1. Display the menu bar.

2. Pull down the menu desired.

3. Select from the pull down menu, then from any additional menus that may appear.

Displaying the Menu Bar

When in WordPerfect, press *Alt-* = (hold down the Alt key, then press =) to display the main menu bar, as shown in Figure I.4.

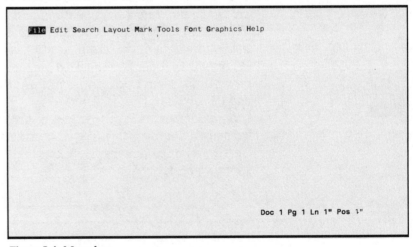

File Edit Search Layout Mark Tools Font Graphics Help

Doc 1 Pg 1 Ln 1" Pos 1"

Figure I.4: Menu bar

If you have a mouse, click the right button to display the menu bar.

The first option—**F**ile—is already highlighted and all of the options have one character in boldface. Notice that the boldfaced character is not always the first, as in **F**ont.

Pulling Down a Menu

The next step is to "pull down" a menu of options. You can do this in three ways.

- Press the letter that appears in boldface, such as *O* for F**o**nt, or *G* for **G**raphics.

- Press the → or ← keys to highlight the choice, then press the ↓ key or ⏎.

- Place the mouse pointer on the option, then click the left button.

A pull down menu of additional options will appear on the screen, as shown in Figure I.5. Like the menu bar, each option has one character in boldface.

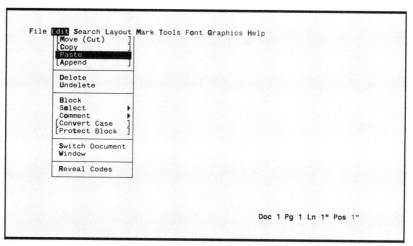

Figure I.5: Edit pull down menu

Some options, such as Select and Comment, have a small triangle at the right. These options have their own pulldown menus that will appear when selected.

Options in brackets are unavailable and cannot be selected. Most of these are options that first require sections of text to be selected, or blocked before you can activate them. Until you block text, as you'll learn how to do later, you cannot select that option from the menu.

If you see that you've pulled down the wrong menu, press the → or ← keys. The cursor moves to the next option on the menu bar and the pull down menu automatically appears. To cancel any selection just press the Esc key.

Selecting Options

Now select one of the options on the pull down menu using one of these methods:

- Press the letter that appears in boldface.
- Press the ↓ or ↑ keys to highlight the choice, then press the ↓ key or ←⟂.
- Place the mouse pointer on the option, then click the left button.

What happens now depends on the option you selected. If you select an option with a small triangle, another menu appears, as in Figure I.6. Make your selection from this new menu.

Other choices will either perform some action immediately, such as inserting a code in the document, or display a prompt, selection line, or menu. In most cases, this will be the same prompt, selection line, or menu that would appear if you used the function keys.

Prompts

A prompt is a brief message at the bottom of the screen asking you to make a selection. For instance, if you select Exit from the File pull-down menu, the selection line will read

Save Document? Yes (No)

```
    File Edit Search Layout Mark Tools Font Graphics Help
         [Move (Cut)      ]
         [Copy            ]
          Paste
         [Append          ]

          Delete
          Undelete

          Block
          Select          ▶
          Comment           Sentence
         [Convert Case      Paragraph
         [Protect Block     Page

          Switch Document [Tabular Column]
          Window          [Rectangle     ]

          Reveal Codes




                                                Doc 1 Pg 1 Ln 1" Pos 1"
```

Figure I.6: *Edit Select submenu*

This is the Save prompt asking if you want to save the current text or not. The **Yes** at the end of the prompt is the *default* value. Default values usually represent the most common choice and appear automatically for your convenience. You can just press ⟵ to accept the default value shown. If you do not want that value, make another choice—in this case, select **No** or press the F1 key to cancel the command. (F1, by the way, can always be used to cancel the effect of the last function key pressed.)

To select a choice from the prompt line, press the boldfaced letter or click it with the mouse.

Whether it displays a prompt, a series of choices, or information about the status of your document, the line at the bottom of the screen is generally called the status line. We'll discuss it in more detail in Chapter 1.

Selection Lines

Other options reveal a number of choices in a selection line, such as

Columns: **1** On; **2** Off; **3** Define:0

This particular selection line is used to format text in more than one column. Notice that each choice is numbered and that one character of the choice, not always the first, appears in boldface. Press either the number of the desired choice or the boldfaced letter (such as **2** or **f** to turn off multiple columns), or click it with the mouse, to select that option. Or, press the ⟵ key by itself to select the default option shown at the end of the line. In this case, the default 0 will cancel the action. Your selection might perform some action immediately or lead to additional selection lines. Continue picking the desired options.

You can always press the F1 key to cancel the selection line and return to the document.

Menus

A *menu* is a list of choices too long to fit on just one selection line at the bottom of the screen, such as the Format menu shown in Figure I.7. Even though the menu takes up the entire screen, the document will return when you have completed making your selections.

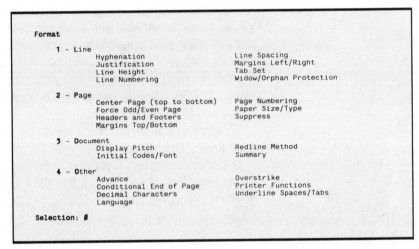

Figure I.7: *Format menu*

Notice that the menu has four options, numbered 1 to 4, and that one letter of each choice appears in boldface. At the bottom of the screen is a prompt:

Selection: 0

This is used to determine which of the four options you wish to select. As with selection lines, press the number or boldfaced letter to select the menu option.

You can use the default 0 value to quickly "escape" from the menu. Press ← to accept the default value (or press the F1 key) to return to the document.

What happens when you select an option other than 0 depends on the selection. In this case, selecting any choice will show a new menu of additional options. With other menus, however, some settings will automatically change or you may have to type in a new setting.

Changing Your Mind

No matter what menu is displayed, you can press the Esc key to remove it and return to the previous level. For example, if you are on the Edit Select submenu shown in Figure I.6, press Esc to display just the Edit menu shown in Figure I.5, Esc again to display just the menu bar, and Esc once more to clear the screen and return to the document.

Get to Know Your Hardware

Now that you are familiar with the keyboard, make sure you understand the rest of your IBM PC or compatible computer.

Monitors

You may have either a monochrome, color, or composite monitor. A monochrome monitor displays "black and white" images. The color monitor can display at least 16 different colors. The composite monitor is also considered "black and white" because it is not in color. However, shades of gray (or green or amber depending on your monitor) are substituted where colors would appear. For instance, yellow would be displayed as a lighter shade, red a darker one.

Display Cards

The display card is the part of your computer that puts an image on the monitor. It matches your monitor in terms of having monochrome or color (including composite) capabilities. But the display card also determines the *resolution* of your image and the number of colors that can be displayed at one time. Resolution refers to the quality of the displayed image, how sharp and clear the characters and graphics will appear.

WordPerfect automatically determines the type of display card and monitor you have when it starts.

Disk Drives

To use WordPerfect you must have a hard disk or two disk drives, in any combination of floppy (either high-density 5¼ or 3½-inch, but not 5¼-inch 360K).

If you have two floppy disk drives, they may be either side by side, or stacked on top of each other. The drive on the left hand side, or on top, is called drive A. The other drive is called B. When you insert a disk into the drive, you must first open the drive door. With horizontally mounted drives, insert the disk with the label facing up and the small write-protect notch toward the left. (With 3½-inch disks, the write-protect notch is the small square window with the red tab that can be moved back or forth.) For vertically mounted drives, the label faces toward the left and the write-protect notch on the bottom. Never bend the disk, expose it to magnetic fields, extremes of heat or cold, or cigarette smoke. Store your disks in plastic or cardboard storage boxes.

Always hold 5¼-inch disks on the edge with the label. Never touch the areas exposed by the long oval slot, which goes into the drive first.

A hard disk is normally called drive C. So if you have a hard disk and only one floppy, you have drives A and C in your system. Your hard disk should already contain the disk operating system and you can "boot" or start your computer without a floppy disk. The instructions in this book assume that if you have a hard disk, it is already set up with DOS.

Printer

In Appendix B you will set up WordPerfect for your printer. WordPerfect is designed to work with hundreds of different printers, so this will be an easy task. Just make sure you know the name and model number of your printer before continuing.

Conventions Used in this Book

Special notes and tips will appear in the margin like this.

Throughout this book, we'll show the exact steps required to select options and control WordPerfect. Many steps will start with the word "Select." When referring to a menu bar option, this means to press Alt-= (or click the right mouse button). This will be followed by the command words in the menu bar and pull down menu, such as this:

Select F**o**nt **A**ppearance **B**old.

Using the keyboard, this instruction means to do one of the following things:

- Press *Alt-= O A B*. Notice that the instruction includes the keys you should press in italics.

- Press *Alt-=* , then use the arrow keys to select the menus and options shown—first the Font option on the menu bar, then the Appearance option on the pull down menu, then the Bold option on the submenu. Then press ↵.

- Click the right mouse button, then left on Font, then on Appearance and Bold as they appear in the menus.

You can also use combinations of techniques. For example, you can press *O* for the F**o**nt option, and then use the arrow keys to make further selections.

In some cases, a menu command may consist of more than one word—and the boldfaced character may be in either one, such as

Select **M**ark Cross **R**eference.

This means to press *Alt-= M R*. Be careful to note which characters are boldfaced—don't automatically press the first character in each word.

Instructions for selecting from menus and prompt lines will be given the same way, such as

Select **J**ustification **L**eft

In cases such as this, press the boldfaced letters in the sequence given—*J*, then *L*—or click the words with the mouse.

In the text itself, the actual instructions will appear like this:

Select Font (Ctrl-F8) **A**ppearance **B**old.

The items in parentheses are meant for readers using the function keys, rather than the pull down menus, to work with WordPerfect. Just ignore them if you are using the pull down menus.

Using Function Keys

All of the tasks that can be performed by the pull down menus can be activated by function keys and combinations of keys. These are the "traditional" keystrokes that earlier versions of WordPerfect required.

Many WordPerfect commands require more than one keystroke to activate. These key combinations can be of two types. You might have to press two or more keys at the same time, or you might have to press several keys in sequence.

Keys that should be pressed together are separated with a hyphen. For example, if an instruction says to press Shift-F7, this means that you should press and *hold down* the Shift key, then press the F7 key. The sequence is this:

1. Press and hold down the first key listed.

2. Press and release the second key.

3. Release the first key.

Other key combinations must be pressed in sequence, one after the other. These are always separated by blank spaces. For instance, if an instruction says to press F7 **No No**, this means you should

1. Press and release the *F7* key.

2. Press *N*.

3. Press *N* a second time.

The instruction Shift-F7 **No** combines both types of instructions. First do Shift-F7 by pressing and holding the Shift key while you press F7. Then let go of them both and press the *N* key.

This might seem to be a great number of keystrokes for one command. However, as you learn commands such as these, you'll find they become almost automatic. In most cases, you don't have to pause between keystrokes, so pressing three keys will not slow your progress.

We'll include these keystrokes in parentheses, immediately after the pull down menu instructions, such as

Select File **P**rint (Shift-F7) **F**ull.

This instruction means that pressing Shift-F7 is the same as selecting the **File P**rint options from the pull down menus. So if you want to use the more traditional keystrokes, you would press Shift-F7, then the F key.

Likewise, the instruction

Select File Exit (F7) **N**o **N**o.

means that you should press *F7*, then *N* twice.

Following the Instructions in this Book

Most lessons in this book take you step by step through a specific task. Just follow each instruction to master the technique discussed. You will see several types of instructions. So to differentiate between the instructions, the things you type, and things that WordPerfect displays on the screen, here are a few rules.

- When you are asked to type something in from the keyboard, what you are to type will appear in italics, like this: Type *myfirst* or *b:myfirst*

- Sometimes you will be asked to type several lines of text, or even entire paragraphs. These lines will be indented and set off from the instruction, and will be in colored type, like this:

1. Type the following:

> WordPerfect allows the creation, editing, and printing of all types of documents. They can be saved at any time.

- When WordPerfect shows something on the screen in response to something you have done, that information will also be shown in colored type, like this:

> Save document? Yes (No)

- When you are to actually do something on your computer, I will give you a series of numbered steps to follow:

1.

2.

3.

Read and perform each step in the order given. But be sure to read all of the text that is in the step, because in a few cases some optional instructions may be given, such as:

> If you want to accept the default value, press ←, then skip to step 18.

In this case, you'd press the ← key, then go directly to step 18, skipping any steps in between. If you don't want to accept the default value, don't press ←, but continue reading and following instructions.

You're now ready to start WordPerfect. If you have not yet used the program, begin at Appendix A, B, and, if you plan on using the mouse, C.

Creating Your First Document

Featuring

Starting WordPerfect

The WordPerfect screen

Typing characters

Moving the cursor

Inserting characters

Printing documents

Saving documents

Getting help

You're probably anxious to use WordPerfect. Good. But before using this powerful program for the first time you must do the three things that are explained in the appendices:

1. Make a copy of WordPerfect solely for your own backup.

2. Make a working set of floppy disks or install the program on a hard disk.

3. Let WordPerfect know what printer or printers you'll be using for your documents.

If you've already followed the installation instructions in the Word-Perfect manual, you are ready to start Lesson 1 right now. Otherwise, carefully follow the instructions in Appendices A, B, and C, then come back to this chapter.

Now that WordPerfect is ready, let's begin!

*L*esson 1—How to Start WordPerfect

When you start a program, you are actually transferring it from the disk into the computer's memory. Then the control of your program is passed from the disk operating system (DOS or OS/2) to the program itself.

With WordPerfect, only the functions that you'll use most often are loaded into your computer. Other segments of the program remain on the disk and are loaded only when you need them. So when you select certain more advanced commands, you'll hear your disk spin while these instructions are loaded. WordPerfect uses this technique so you'll have as much memory as possible available for your own documents.

How you start WordPerfect depends on whether you are using a computer with a hard disk or two floppy disk drives.

Hard Disk

To start WordPerfect on the hard disk,

1. Turn on your computer. Respond to the date and time prompts if they appear. The *C>* prompt will appear.

2. Type *CD\WP51* and press ←. (If you called your subdirectory something other than WP51, type that name instead.)

3. Type *WP* and press ←.

Floppy Disks

If you are using floppy disks, you should have all of the WordPerfect disks handy when you are typing. Use the backup disks you made in Appendix A, not the original WordPerfect disks. These should be stored in a safe location in case your copies become damaged.

To start WordPerfect with a floppy disk system,

1. Place the WordPerfect 1 program disk in drive A and turn on your computer. Respond to the date and time questions. The *A>* prompt will appear.

2. Place the blank formatted disk in drive B.

3. Type *WP* and press ←.

   An alternative method of starting WordPerfect will automatically save your documents on the document disk in drive B. After starting your computer and inserting your disks as described in steps 1 and 2, type *B:* then press ← to "log onto" drive B. The prompt changes to *B>*. Now start WordPerfect by typing *A:WP* and pressing ←.

If you are not ready to go on to the next lesson, press Alt-= F X to select Exit from the File pull down menu (F7), then press **No Yes** (*N* to the *Save Document?* **Y**es (No) prompt, and *Y* to the *Exit WP?* No (**Y**es) prompt). This exits the program quickly without saving the text on the screen.

*L*esson 2—The WordPerfect Screen

If you are not already in WordPerfect, start the program as you did in Lesson 1.

When you start WordPerfect, the screen is entirely blank except for the blinking cursor and a small *status line* on the bottom of the screen:

Doc 1 Pg 1 Ln 1″ Pos 1″

This line lets you know where the cursor is located in the document. Since you can work on two different documents at a time, the status line also tells you which document you are currently editing.

The four elements that are always on the status line are:

Doc   The document number, which can be either 1 or 2, depending on which document you are editing.

Pg   The number of the page you are currently viewing on the screen.

Ln   The distance of the cursor from the top of the page. With the default settings, a new page will start at 9.83".

Pos   A number indicating where the cursor is on the line in relation to the left margin. For example, using the default values, the text has a 1-inch, or 10-character left margin. So when you are starting a line, the cursor will be in position 1" and the status line will show Pos 1". (If you're using a laser printer and certain typestyles, your position indicator at the left margin might show something other than 1". You'll see why in Chapter 5.) If *Pos* is blinking, then Num Lock is turned on and certain keys will display numbers instead of moving the cursor. If *POS* is all uppercase, then the Caps Lock is on and you'll get all uppercase letters.

The lower-left corner of the screen will usually be blank or contain the name of the current document. This indicates that you are in the *Insert* mode. If you enter characters within existing text, words to the right will move over and down to make room for the new characters. If you press the Ins key (the *0* key on the keypad), the word *Typeover* will appear in the lower-left corner. New characters typed will now replace existing ones.

Typeover   Doc 1 Pg 1 Ln 1″ Pos 1″

Insert and Typeover are two basic typing modes that will be explained in Chapter 2.

Ins, by the way, is called a *toggle* key. You press it once to turn on a function; press it again to turn off the same function. So to get back into the Insert mode, press Ins again so the word *Typeover* disappears from the status line.

When you are word processing, various other messages and prompts will appear on the status line.

Scrolling Text on the Screen

The most obvious difference between the screen and the printed page is the number of lines they hold. The WordPerfect screen can display only 24 lines of text at one time. But don't worry—your documents can be as long as you want thanks to the scrolling and auto-pagination features.

As you type, the cursor will move down the page and the Ln indicator in the status line will change. As you pass the last line on the screen, the lines at the top will *scroll* up out of view into the computer's memory. You'll be able to scroll the text back down into view, as explained in Lessons 7 and 12.

As your text grows even longer, you don't have to worry about ending one page and starting another—just continue typing. After you type the 54th line on a page, a line of dashes will appear across the screen to mark the end of the page, and the Pg indicator in the status line will increase by one. This is *auto-pagination*. If you later add or delete lines from a page, the page breaks will change so the default value of 54 typing lines will appear on each page. You can manually end a page at any time by pressing Ctrl-⏎.

*L*esson 3—How to Type in WordPerfect

If you've ever used a typewriter, you can start using WordPerfect. All of the letter, number, and punctuation keys on the four middle rows of the keyboard work just the same. You just type, letting the text scroll up and start new pages automatically. But don't worry if you've never typed a word in your life. I type using only three fingers, but I was still able to use WordPerfect to write this entire book.

Now let's look at one of the best features of word processing—word-wrap. Follow these steps:

1. Type the text below. *Do not* press the ⏎ key when the cursor reaches the right edge of the screen, just continue typing. If you make a mistake, press the Backspace key. This will move the cursor back through your text, erasing characters.

> WordPerfect allows the creation, editing, and printing of all types of documents.

Depending on your printer, word-wrap may occur at a different location—that is, your line may break at a different location than mine did in Figure 1.1.

When you typed the word *types*, it automatically moved to the next line (see Figure 1.1); this is called *word-wrap*. (If you're using a laser printer or some other printer with proportional spacing, your sentence may word-wrap at some other location.) WordPerfect senses when the word you are typing

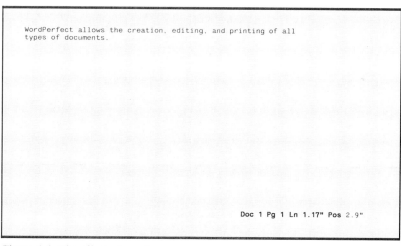

Figure 1.1: The effect of word-wrap

will not fit within the right margin. So it moves the word to the next line and lets you continue typing without having to listen for the margin bell and press ← at the end of every line, as you would do on a typewriter.

2. Complete the paragraph, noticing how word-wrap works at each line.

    WordPerfect allows the creation, editing, and printing of all types of documents. They can be saved on a disk and recalled at any time.

3. Press the ← key. The cursor will move to the next line, under the last sentence typed.

4. Press the ← key again to insert a blank line between paragraphs.

5. Type the following:

    Because WordPerfect is designed to use the full powers of your computer, you can format and manipulate text in ways unimaginable with a typewriter.

6. Press the ← key and your screen will look like Figure 1.2. You can use the ← key to end the paragraph, as in steps 3 and 6, or to insert a blank line in the document, as in Step 4.

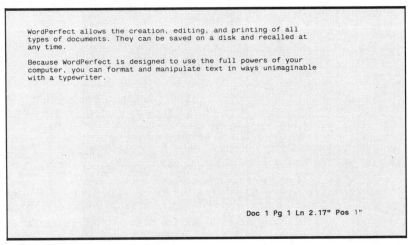

Figure 1.2: The completed example

*L*esson 4—How to Move the Cursor

Place the mouse pointer where you want the cursor to appear, then click left.

The cursor is that small blinking line on the screen that shows where the next character you type will appear. If the cursor is at the end of your document, characters you type will be added to the end of your text. But you can move the cursor anywhere in your document. If you want to add words to the middle of a paragraph, move the cursor to that spot and start typing.

Most of the cursor movement keys are located on the right side of the keyboard, either combined with the numeric keypad or to its left. If they are combined and a number appears on the screen when you try to move the cursor, press the key marked Num Lock.

The four most basic cursor movement keys are the directional arrows.

To scroll the screen, move the mouse pointer to the top or bottom edge of the screen, press the right button, and then move in the direction you want to scroll.

↑   This is the up arrow key. When you press this key the cursor moves up one line. If you press it while the cursor is on the first line of the screen, lines not shown will scroll down into view and you will see the text above the previous cursor position. Pressing the key has no effect if you are on the first line of the document.

↓   This is the down arrow key. When you press this key the cursor moves down one line, unless you are on the last line of the document. (To move beyond the last line, press ←⏎.) If the cursor is on the last line of the screen, any lines not shown will scroll up into view and you will see the text below the previous cursor position.

→   This is the right arrow key. It moves the cursor one character to the right. When you reach the right margin, the cursor will move to the first character of the next line.

←   This is the left arrow key. It moves the cursor one character to the left. When you reach the left margin, the cursor will move to the last character of the line above.

To move more than one line or character at a time, hold down the directional arrow key.

L esson 5—How to Insert Text

Let's use the arrow keys to change your document on the screen. First make sure that the word *Typeover* does not appear in the status line. If it does, press the Ins key.

1. Press the ↑ and ← keys to place the cursor at the start of the first sentence, the *W* in *WordPerfect*.

2. Press the Tab key. The first sentence is indented five spaces (Figure 1.3).

```
      WordPerfect allows the creation, editing, and printing of all
types of documents. They can be saved on a disk and recalled at
any time.

Because WordPerfect is designed to use the full powers of your
computer, you can format and manipulate text in ways unimaginable
with a typewriter.
```

Figure 1.3: A tab inserted to indent a sentence

3. Press any one of the arrow keys. The word *all* is wrapped to the next line and the entire paragraph adjusts to accommodate the tab (Figure 1.4). Moving the cursor adjusts text to the format settings.

```
      WordPerfect allows the creation, editing, and printing of
all types of documents. They can be saved on a disk and recalled
at any time.

Because WordPerfect is designed to use the full powers of your
computer, you can format and manipulate text in ways unimaginable
with a typewriter.
```

Figure 1.4: The adjusted paragraph after moving the cursor

4. Now insert a tab at the beginning of the next paragraph.

   a. Move the cursor to the beginning of that paragraph.

b. Press the Tab key.

c. Move the cursor in any direction to adjust the paragraph.

The text is shown in Figure 1.5.

```
        WordPerfect allows the creation, editing, and printing of
all types of documents. They can be saved on a disk and recalled
at any time.

        Because WordPerfect is designed to use the full powers of
your computer, you can format and manipulate text in ways
unimaginable with a typewriter.
```

Figure 1.5: *The text with both paragraphs indented*

Let's insert some other text into your document just to see how it works.

5. Move the cursor to the letter *d* in *disk*, in the first paragraph.

6. Type

    floppy or hard

7. Press the spacebar after the word *hard* to insert a space between this word and the word *disk*.

8. Now press any arrow key to adjust the paragraph (Figure 1.6).

```
        WordPerfect allows the creation, editing, and printing of
all types of documents. They can be saved on a floppy or hard
disk and recalled at any time.

        Because WordPerfect is designed to use the full powers of
your computer, you can format and manipulate text in ways
unimaginable with a typewriter.
```

Figure 1.6: *Words inserted into the text*

As you see, text or tabs can be inserted anywhere in the document. The paragraph will automatically adjust when the cursor is moved.

Lesson 6—How to Print Documents

The introduction of this book explains pull down menus and how to use them in detail.

Click right, drag down the File menu, and then click on Print.

WordPerfect has many powerful printing features. For the impatient, let's print the text that is now on the screen. Make sure your printer is turned on and paper is ready. Since this is the first time you've used pull down menus in this book, let's go over the steps you need to take to use a pull down menu. In this case we'll be dealing with the File pull down menu.

1. Press Alt-= to display the main menu across the top of your screen.

2. Press F or press the ↓ key to display the File menu (Figure 1.7).

3. To choose **Print**, either press P or press ↓ until Print is highlighted, and then press ←— (Shift-F7) (Figure 1.8).

4. Select **Full Document**. Since your document is only one page long, you could also have selected **Page**.

If your printer is set for either *Sheet Feeder* or *Continuous*, the document will now be printed.

If you set your printer for Manual, you'll hear a short beep telling you to load the paper into the printer. When the paper is ready, select

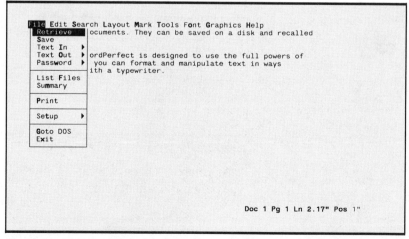

Figure 1.7: The File pull down menu

Control Printer to display the Printer Control menu (Figure 1.9), then the **G**o option.

```
Print

      1 - Full Document
      2 - Page
      3 - Document on Disk
      4 - Control Printer
      5 - Multiple Pages
      6 - View Document
      7 - Initialize Printer


Options

      S - Select Printer                    IBM PC Graphics Printer
      B - Binding Offset                     0"
      N - Number of Copies                   1
      U - Multiple Copies Generated by       WordPerfect
      G - Graphics Quality                   Medium
      T - Text Quality                       High




Selection: 0
```

Figure 1.8: The Print menu

```
Print: Control Printer

Current Job

Job Number: 1                             Page Number:   1
Status:      Printing                     Current Copy: 1 of 1
Message:     None
Paper:       Standard 8.5" x 11"
Location:    Manual feed
Action:      Insert paper
             Press "G" to continue

Job List

Job  Document              Destination           Print Options
 1   (Screen)              LPT 1


Additional Jobs Not Shown: 0



1 Cancel Job(s); 2 Rush Job; 3 Display Jobs; 4 Go (start printer); 5 Stop: 0
```

Figure 1.9: Printer Control menu

When printing with hand-fed, or manual paper, you'll hear the beep after each page. Insert the next sheet of paper into the printer, then issue the Go command. If the Printer Control menu is already displayed, select **G**o. From the Print menu select Control Printer, then

Go. If you've already returned to the document, select **File** **P**rint from the pull down menu (Shift-F7) as in Step 2, then select **C**ontrol Printer, then **G**o.

Press F1 until you clear the menus and return to the document.

*L*esson 7—*How to Save Your Document*

When you are done typing your document, you must save it on the disk if you want to edit or print it later. How you save it depends on what you want to do next—whether you want to work on another document or stop using WordPerfect.

In this lesson, you'll learn how to save a document that you have just worked on for the first time. Later I'll show you how to save a document after you've recalled it from the disk to make revisions.

You need to save a document after printing it only if you think you'll need it later.

*S*aving New Documents and Quitting WordPerfect

Save the document you just created under the name *MYFIRST*.

1. Select **F**ile **E**xit from the pull down menu (F7). To do this,

   a. Press Alt-=.

   b. Press *F X* or press the ↓ key to highlight *Exit*, then press ←.

Click right, click left on File for the File menu, then click on Exit.

The prompt

   Save Document? Yes (No)

will appear.

2. Press ←. If you change your mind about saving the document, just press **No**. You have not yet given this document a name, so the prompt

   Document to be saved:

appears.

3. Type *MYFIRST* if you have a hard disk system, or *B:MY-FIRST* if you have a floppy disk system and you did not log onto drive B in Lesson 1, then press ⏎.

Document names can be from one to eight characters long and should start with a letter. Remember to begin the name with B: to store it on drive B unless you are using a hard disk or you logged onto drive B.

Finally, the prompt

Exit WP? No (Yes)   (Cancel to return to document)

appears.

4. Select **Yes** to return to the disk operating system.

If you change your mind at any step in this process, just press the F1 key until no prompts appear at the bottom of the screen.

Lesson 8—How to Get Help

WordPerfect is so powerful that there may be functions you use rarely, and between uses it is easy to forget how they work. So for just those times, WordPerfect has a Help function that you can reach quickly from with the pull down menus or keyboard.

If you are using floppy disks, make sure you have the Learning diskette handy. Hard disk users should have already installed the WPHELP.FIL file into the WP subdirectory containing WordPerfect. Here's how to get help:

1. Restart WordPerfect as you learned in Lesson 1.

2. Select the **Help** pull down menu to display these options:

    Help

    Index

    Template

In a few moments, floppy disk users will see the following message on the status line:

WPHELP.FIL not found. Insert Learning Diskette and press drive letter:

From the keyboard, press F3 to select the Help function. When menus other than pull down menus are on-screen, pressing F3 displays information on those menu items. Otherwise, a screen appears explaining how to use Help.

Remove the document disk in drive B and replace it with the Learning Diskette. Close the drive door and press *B*.

You can now get three types of help:

- Help explains how to use the Help function.

- Index displays the first page of help topics, in alphabetical order.

- Template displays the template.

Once you've accessed the Help functions, you can take these actions:

- Press F3 to display the template on the screen.

- Press any function key or key combination for a description of its uses.

- Press any letter for an alphabetical index of functions and corresponding keystrokes.

- Press the spacebar or ⏎ to return to the document.

Shift-PrtSc may not work if you are on a network.

3. Select any of the help options, then press the F3 function key. A copy of the template will appear. You will see functions that are unfamiliar to you, but don't worry. You will learn about all of them in the upcoming lessons.

 If you have lost your template, and your printer is on and ready, press Shift-PrtSc to get a printed copy of the one displayed on the screen.

 As long as you are still in the help function, let's explore the help explanations of function keys.

4. Press several function key combinations, and several letters, to see the type of help provided. When you are done, press the spacebar or ⏎ to return to the typing window.

5. If you are not ready to continue with the next lesson, select **File Exit** from the pull down menu (F7) and answer **No** (since you don't need to save what's on the screen), and then **Yes** to exit WordPerfect.

*Improving
and Correcting
Your Document*

Featuring

Recalling documents

Advanced cursor movement

Deleting text

Undeleting text

Typeover

Resaving edited documents

Lesson 9—How to Recall a Document from Disk

We all make mistakes. Errors in spelling and grammar or accidental keystrokes somehow find their way into documents. Surely at times you've spent a great deal of time changing—or correcting—what you had already typed. With a typewriter, this often means throwing away the page and starting over.

Well, one of the most important features of word processing is how easy it is to edit your documents, correcting errors without retyping the rest of the text.

Editing can be done on new documents as you type them, or on documents already saved on the disk. Of course, to edit a saved document you must first load it into the typing window.

Let's recall the document MYFIRST, which you created in the last chapter.

Recall by Name

Since you know the name of the document you wish to recall, just follow these steps:

1. Start WordPerfect.

2. Select **File R**etrieve from the pull down menu (Shift-F10). The message

    Document to be retrieved:

    appears on the status line.

3. Type *MYFIRST* or *B:MYFIRST* (if you're using two floppy disk drives) and press ⏎.

The document will appear on the screen, with its name in the lower-left corner.

Recall by Directory

You've already recalled the document MYFIRST. But if you were not sure of the document's name, you could also recall it by first displaying the directory from within WordPerfect.

1. Select List Files from the File pull down menu (F5). The letter of the current drive will appear on the status line.

2. Press ⏎ if that is the disk containing the document, or type the letter of another drive followed by a colon and press ⏎. A directory of the disk will appear on the screen (Figure 2.1). If there are more files on the disk than can be displayed, you'll see a small arrow at the bottom of the center line that separates the columns.

```
10-03-89  06:21p              Directory C:\WP51\*.*
Document size:         0   Free:  3,031,040 Used:  3,367,081      Files:      61

.         Current   <Dir>                  ..      Parent     <Dir>
8514A    .VRS      4,797   09-22-89 10:48a   ATI      .VRS      4,937   09-22-89 10:48a
CHARACTR.DOC     41,968   09-22-89 10:35a   CONVERT  .EXE    104,689   09-22-89 10:35a
CURSOR  .COM      1,452   09-22-89 10:35a   EGA512   .FRS      3,584   09-22-89 10:48a
EGAITAL .FRS      3,584   09-22-89 10:48a   EGASMC   .FRS      3,584   09-22-89 10:48a
EGAUND  .FRS      3,584   09-22-89 10:48a   FIXBIOS  .COM         50   09-22-89 10:35a
GENIUS  .VRS     15,473   09-22-89 10:48a   GENOA    .VRS     10,972   09-22-89 10:48a
GRAB    .COM     15,602   09-22-89 10:35a   GRAPHCNV .EXE    105,472   09-22-89 10:35a
HPLAS500.PRS      6,517   10-03-89 11:27a   HRF12    .FRS     49,152   09-22-89 10:48a
HRF6    .FRS     49,152   09-22-89 10:48a   IBPCGRPR .PRS      7,657   10-03-89 01:12p
INSTALL .EXE     58,720   09-22-89 11:03a   KEYS     .MRS      4,800   09-22-89 10:09a
MACROCNV.EXE     26,021   09-22-89 10:35a   MYFIRST  .            613   10-03-89 12:12p
NEC     .VRS      4,682   09-22-89 10:48a   NWPSETUP .EXE     27,648   09-22-89 10:35a
PARADISE.VRS     14,492   09-22-89 10:48a   SPELL    .EXE     53,760   09-22-89 10:35a
STANDARD.CRS      2,557   09-22-89 10:35a   STANDARD .IRS      4,373   09-22-89 10:09a
STANDARD.PRS      1,942   09-22-89 10:09a   STANDARD .VRS     28,426   09-22-89 10:09a
VERTICOM.VRS      4,945   09-22-89 10:48a   VGA512   .FRS      4,096   09-22-89 10:48a
VGAITAL .FRS      4,096   09-22-89 10:48a   VGASMC   .FRS      4,096   09-22-89 10:48a
VGAUND  .FRS      4,096   09-22-89 10:48a ▼ VIDEO7   .VRS      4,943   09-22-89 10:48a

1 Retrieve; 2 Delete; 3 Move/Rename; 4 Print; 5 Short/Long Display;
6 Look; 7 Other Directory; 8 Copy; 9 Find; N Name Search: 6
```

Figure 2.1: File Listing

Click right on the file name to select a document. Double-click left to display it.

3. Press the arrow keys. Notice that the "highlighting" moves from document name to document name, scrolling the listing up if there are more files than can be seen at one time. Highlight the name of the document you wish to retrieve.

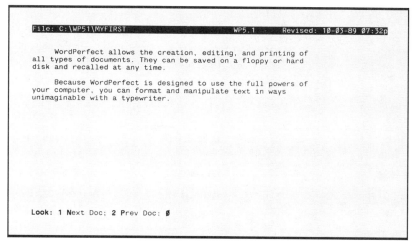 If you display nondocument files, such as executable programs, you'll just see nonsensical characters and symbols.

If you're not sure what you called the document, you can temporarily display its contents. Highlight one of the possible names, then select the **L**ook option. The document will appear on the screen as shown in Figure 2.2.

```
File: C:\WP51\MYFIRST                          WP5.1        Revised: 10-03-89 07:32p

        WordPerfect allows the creation, editing, and printing of
    all types of documents. They can be saved on a floppy or hard
    disk and recalled at any time.

        Because WordPerfect is designed to use the full powers of
    your computer, you can format and manipulate text in ways
    unimaginable with a typewriter.




    Look: 1 Next Doc; 2 Prev Doc: 0
```

Figure 2.2: Displaying a document in Look mode

You can't edit the document while in this mode; you can just use the ↑ and ↓ cursor movement keys to look at its contents. Select **N**ext to display the file listed after the one on the screen; or **P**revious for the one before it. Press F7 to return to the directory listing—the last file displayed will be selected.

4. When you've highlighted the correct document, select **R**etrieve, but don't do this now or you'll get two copies of MYFIRST on the screen. Just press F7 to return to the editing window.

L esson 10—How to Move the Cursor More Efficiently

While the arrow keys can be used to move the cursor anywhere in the document, there are faster ways of moving more than one line or character at a time.

*M*oving Down through a Document

Press the following keys or key combinations to move down through a document. As you move down past the last displayed line, the text will scroll up, displaying additional text if it exists.

Home Home ↓	Moves the cursor to the end of the document.
PgDn	Moves the cursor to the top of the next page in the document. For example, pressing this key while editing page 5 will place the cursor at the top of page 6.
Home ↓ or + (on the numeric keypad)	Moves the cursor to the bottom of the screen or, if already there, displays the next 24 lines of text.
Esc *n* PgDn	Moves the cursor down *n* pages. Press Esc, enter the number of pages to move, then press PgDn.
Esc *n* ↓	Moves the cursor down *n* lines. Press Esc, enter the number of lines to move, then press the down arrow.
Ctrl-Home ↓	Moves the cursor to the bottom of the current page. The Ctrl-Home combination is called GoTo.

*M*oving Up through a Document

Press the following keys or key combinations to move up through a document. As you move up past the topmost displayed line, the text will scroll down, displaying additional text if it exists.

Home Home ↑	Moves the cursor to the top of the document.
PgUp	Moves the cursor to the top of the previous page. For example, if you are editing page 3, press this key to place the cursor at (and to display) the top of page 2.

Home ↑ or − (on the numeric keypad)	Moves the cursor to the top of the screen or, if already there, displays the previous 24 lines of text.
Esc *n* PgUp	Moves the cursor up *n* pages.
Esc *n* ↑	Moves the cursor up *n* lines.
Ctrl-Home ↑	Moves the cursor to the top of the current page.

*M*oving Left

Press the following key combinations to move the cursor toward the left margin:

Home ←	Moves the cursor to the beginning of the line.
Esc *n* ←	Moves the cursor *n* characters to the left.
Ctrl-Home ←	Moves the cursor to the next column when typing multicolumn documents.
Ctrl-Home Home ←	Moves to the first column on a multi-column page.
Ctrl-←	Moves to the next word on the left.

*M*oving Right

Press the following keys or key combinations to move the cursor toward the right margin:

End	Moves the cursor to the end of the current line.
Home →	Moves the cursor to the right edge of the screen.
Esc *n* →	Moves the cursor *n* characters to the right.
Ctrl-Home →	Moves the cursor to the previous column when typing multicolumn documents.

Ctrl-Home	Moves to the last column on a multi-
Home →	column page.
Ctrl-→	Moves to the next word on the right.

Moving to Specific Locations

Finally, the GoTo combination (Ctrl-Home) can be used to place the cursor at a specific page or character.

Ctrl-Home *n*	Moves the cursor to the top of page *n*.
Ctrl-Home *x*	Moves the cursor to the first occurrence of the character *x* (it must occur within the nearest 2000 characters). For example, press Ctrl-Home M to place the cursor on the first letter *M* within 2000 characters of the cursor. The character can be any single keystroke—a letter, number, or punctuation mark.

Lesson 11—How to Delete Text

Inserting text is easy. Just move the cursor and type. But how do you delete text that you no longer want in the document? You already know that you can press the Backspace key to delete characters to the left of the cursor. Here are other ways of deleting.

To complete the exercises below, display the MYFIRST document on your screen, as shown in Figure 1.6.

Deleting Characters

Let's delete the words *floppy or hard* that you inserted in the last chapter.

1. Place the cursor on the letter *f* in *floppy*.

2. Press the Del key. When you do, the character above the cursor is erased and the remaining text moves to the left.

Keep in mind the difference between Backspace and Del. Backspace deletes characters to the left; Del deletes the character at the cursor position.

3. Now press the Del key 14 more times until the rest of the words have been deleted and the text readjusts, as shown in Figure 2.3.

```
    WordPerfect allows the creation, editing, and printing of
all types of documents. They can be saved on a disk and recalled
at any time.

    Because WordPerfect is designed to use the full powers of
your computer, you can format and manipulate text in ways
unimaginable with a typewriter.
```

Figure 2.3: *The MYFIRST document after deletions*

When deleting other groups of words you might have to press an arrow key to readjust the text.

Just as there are advanced cursor movement commands, there are advanced deletion commands. These let you erase text faster than one character at a time.

Deleting Words

1. Place the cursor on the word *full* in the second paragraph. The cursor can be on any character of the word.

2. Press Ctrl-Backspace. The entire word is deleted.

3. Press an arrow key to adjust the text. It should now look like this:

```
    WordPerfect allows the creation, editing, and
printing of all types of documents. They can be saved
on a disk and recalled at any time.

    Because WordPerfect is designed to use the powers of
your computer, you can format and manipulate text in
ways unimaginable with a typewriter.
```

Deleting Lines

1. Place the cursor in the space before the word *on* in the first paragraph.

2. Press Ctrl-End. This command deletes every character on the line to the right of the cursor. Your screen should now read

> WordPerfect allows the creation, editing, and printing of all types of documents. They can be saved at any time.
>   Because WordPerfect is designed to use the powers of your computer, you can format and manipulate text in ways unimaginable with a typewriter.

Mass Deletion

Finally, you can delete the entire last paragraph.

1. Place the cursor in the blank line following the first paragraph.

2. Press Ctrl-PgDn. The prompt

> Delete Remainder of page? No (Yes)

appears. Select No because you'll be using this document later. Ctrl-PgDn deletes all of the text from the position of the cursor to the end of the page.

Deleting Parts of Words

You can quickly delete from the cursor position to either the beginning or the end of a word in which the cursor is placed. Type

> repercussion

and place the cursor on the *c*. Press Home Backspace (one after the other, not together) to delete from the cursor position to the start of the word. This results in *cussion*.

Or press Home Del (one after the other, not together) to delete from the cursor position to the end of the word. In this example, *reper* would remain.

A *Summary of Deletion Commands*

COMMAND	WILL DELETE
Backspace	the character to the left of the cursor
Del	the character above the cursor
Ctrl-Backspace	the entire word under which the cursor is placed
Ctrl-End	from the cursor to the right margin
Ctrl-PgDn	from the cursor to the end of the document
Home Backspace	from the cursor to the beginning of the word
Home Del	from the cursor to the end of the word

L*esson 12—How to Restore Deleted Text*

Oops! By accident, you just deleted an entire paragraph. Select **Edit Undelete (F1)**, as in Figure 2.4, to display the prompt

Undelete: 1 Restore: 2 Previous Deletion: 0

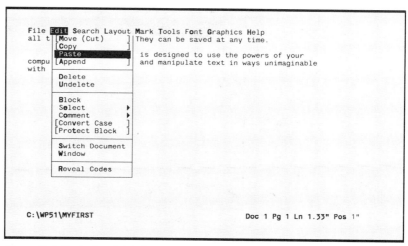

Figure 2.4: *Restoring deleted text*

The last characters you deleted, whether a single character, a word, or an entire page, will reappear highlighted at the position of the cursor. Select **R**estore to restore the character(s) at that location on the screen. Since WordPerfect "remembers" the last three deletions made, select **P**revious Deletion to reveal the one before, and **P**revious Deletion again for the deletion before that. Whatever text is highlighted will be restored at the cursor position when **R**estore is selected at the Undelete prompt.

Undelete can also be used as a quick way of moving words or phrases. Delete the text, move the cursor, then just select **U**ndelete and then Retrieve whenever you want the text to appear.

Let's try using the Undelete key. If you quit WordPerfect after the last lesson, start the program and load the MYFIRST document.

1. Place the cursor at the start of the second paragraph.

2. Press Ctrl-PgDn Y to delete all the text starting at the position of the cursor.

3. Select **E**dit **U**ndelete (F1). The text you just deleted reappears highlighted on the screen with the Undelete prompt in the status line (Figure 2.5). The highlighted text is not yet restored, however.

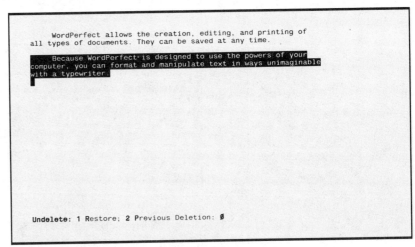

Figure 2.5: Deleted text ready to be restored

4. Select **R**estore to restore the deleted text.

Now let's see how Undelete can move text from one position to another.

5. Place the cursor again at the start of the second paragraph.

6. Press Ctrl-PgDn Y to delete the paragraph.

7. Place the cursor at the start of the first paragraph.

8. Select **U**ndelete (F1). The deleted paragraph appears high-lighted at the new position.

9. Select **R**estore to restore the paragraph.

You'll learn some even more efficient ways to move text in Chapter 10. First, let's see how you can save a new copy of this edited document.

Lesson 13—How to Save a Document after Revisions

In Lesson 7 you saved MYFIRST on your disk. Now let's save the edited version. How you save a document depends on what you want to do afterward—exit WordPerfect, continue working on the same document, or start a new one.

Saving the Edited Document and Quitting WordPerfect

To save an edited document, then quit WordPerfect, follow these steps:

1. Select **F**ile E**x**it from the pull down menu (F7) to display the prompt

   Save Document? Yes (No)

   If you did not change the document since the last time you saved it, the message *(Text was not modified)* will appear at the bottom right of the status line.

2. Press ⏎.

3. Since the document already has a name, it will appear in the next prompt:

Document to be saved: C:\WP51\MYFIRST

To keep the same name, press ←⏎. If you want to change the document's name, just type another name and you will have both the old and the new versions of the document saved on disk.

If you did not change the name, the prompt would change to

Replace C:\WP51\MYFIRST? No (Yes)

Select **Yes** to replace the original version with the new text. If you select **No** or press ←⏎, the *Document to be saved* prompt will again appear so you can give the revised document a new name.

You cannot have two different documents with the same name on the same disk, so if you give a new document the name of an existing one and select **Yes** to the Replace prompt, the original will be erased.

4. To quit WordPerfect, select **Yes** at the prompt

Exit WP? No (Yes)

Saving and Starting a New Document

To start a new document when one is already on the screen, save the current document first. Follow the steps above to do this, but select **No** at the prompt

Exit WP? No (Yes)

The current document will be stored on the disk and the screen will clear.

If you change your mind and want to remain in WordPerfect with the same document displayed, press F1.

Saving and Continuing with the Same Document

As a precaution, get into the habit of saving your work every 15 minutes or so, even when you're not finished working on a document.

If anything goes wrong with your computer (such as a pulled plug or an accidental reset) you won't lose a great deal of work. Saving the current document in this way leaves you in the WordPerfect program.

Select File Save (F10). Since the document already has a name, it will appear in the next prompt:

Document to be saved: C:\WP51\MYFIRST

To keep the same name, press ⏎. If you want to change the document's name, just type another name and you will have both the old and the new versions of the document saved on disk.

If you did not change the name, the prompt would change to

Replace C:\WP51\MYFIRST? No (Yes)

Select **Yes** to replace the original version with the new text. If you select **No**, the *Document to be saved* prompt will again appear so you can give the revised document a new name.

You cannot have two different documents with the same name on the same disk, so if you give a new document the name of an existing one and select **Yes** to the Replace prompt, the original will be erased.

Quitting WordPerfect without Saving the Document

There are times when you write a document but do not want to save it. For example, you might type a brief note and print it immediately. Once printed, it may not be important enough to save. Or you may make some changes to a document and then decide they should not have been made. In these cases, select File **Exit** from the pull down menu (F7) to display the *Save Document?* prompt, but select **No**. Then select **Yes** to exit WordPerfect or select **No** to clear the screen and remain in the program.

3

*More Efficient
Revision
Techniques*

Featuring

Typeover

Revealing codes

Combining and splitting paragraphs

Repeating commands

Multiple documents

Inserting the date

*L*esson 14—How to Use Typeover

One way to change characters is to delete the incorrect ones and then insert new ones in their place.

But there is also a *Typeover* mode, entered by pressing Ins, that can be used to change characters quickly. With Typeover, the new characters you type replace existing ones. Each new character takes the place of one already there.

While Typeover is a fast way to change mistakes, it has limited value. Use Typeover when you are replacing characters with the same number of new ones. This way you will not erase words accidentally as you continue typing. I can't tell you how many times I've mistakenly deleted text by trying to insert while in Typeover mode.

You can use either Typeover or Insert to add characters to the end of a paragraph.

Let's try using Typeover.

1. Start WordPerfect.

2. Using the Tab key to indent the paragraphs, type the letter shown in Figure 3.1.

3. Press the Ins key so the word *Typeover* appears in the status line.

4. Place the cursor on the *t* in the word *two*.

5. Type

   ten

   The new characters simply took the place of the existing ones.

6. Place the cursor at the start of the word *class* in the first paragraph.

7. Type

   September class.

```
March 12, 1990

Mr. Robert Williams
53 Kinder Lane
Willow Grove, PA. 18985

Dear Mr. Williams:

    The admissions committee has reviewed your application and I
am pleased to offer you a place in our class of 1996.

    However, it is imperative that you notify this office within
two days to reserve your place. If we do not hear from you by that
time, we will award your place in the class to another student.

    We are looking forward to hearing from you. We are confident
the next year will be an exciting one for you.

                        Sincerely,

                        Wilfred Magatel
                        Admissions Director
```

Figure 3.1: The sample letter

Even though you typed more new characters than were in the line, they did not affect the carriage return at the end of the line.

If you are not ready to continue, save your document under the name LETTER. Select **F**ile **E**xit (F7), answer **Y**es to the Save prompt, type *LETTER* (or *B:LETTER* if you have floppy drives), press ←, and select **Y**es to leave WordPerfect.

If you're staying in WordPerfect, press Ins to return to Insert mode. The word Typeover will disappear from the status line.

L esson 15—How to Work with Codes

Keys like Tab and ← do not display any characters on the screen although they affect the format of the text. They do, however, insert "invisible" codes that can be deleted just like any other character. While you don't have to see these codes to delete them, making them visible simplifies the editing of complex documents.

If you quit WordPerfect after the last lesson, start WordPerfect again and recall the LETTER document.

Revealing Codes

1. Place the cursor at the start of the second paragraph.

2. Select **Edit Reveal** Codes (Alt-F3) to reveal the codes (Figure 3.2).

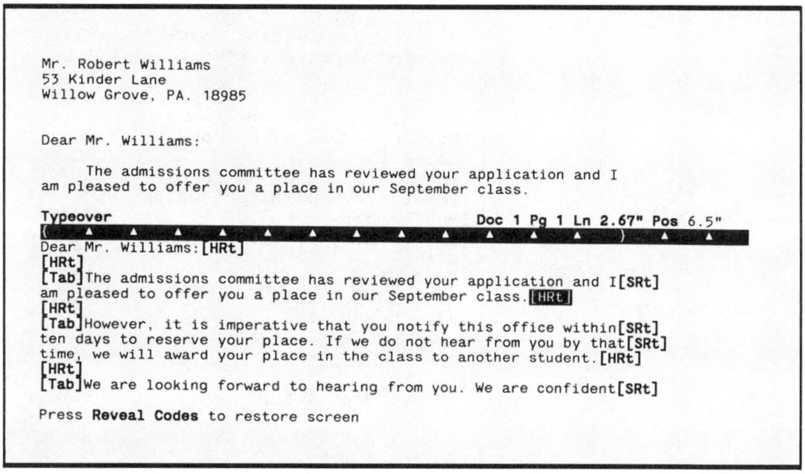

```
Mr. Robert Williams
53 Kinder Lane
Willow Grove, PA. 18985


Dear Mr. Williams:

    The admissions committee has reviewed your application and I
am pleased to offer you a place in our September class.

Typeover                                          Doc 1 Pg 1 Ln 2.67" Pos 6.5"
▲    ▲    ▲        ▲      ▲      ▲      ▲      ▲      ▲      ▲     )   ▲      ▲
Dear Mr. Williams:[HRt]
[HRt]
[Tab]The admissions committee has reviewed your application and I[SRt]
am pleased to offer you a place in our September class.[HRt]
[HRt]
[Tab]However, it is imperative that you notify this office within[SRt]
ten days to reserve your place. If we do not hear from you by that[SRt]
time, we will award your place in the class to another student.[HRt]
[HRt]
[Tab]We are looking forward to hearing from you. We are confident[SRt]

Press Reveal Codes to restore screen
```

Figure 3.2: *WordPerfect screen with codes revealed and scale line*

You can adjust the placement of the scale line using the Window option, which is discussed in Lesson 18.

A *scale line* near the middle of the screen shows the positions of the tabs (with little triangles) and the left and right margins. Above the scale line are eleven lines of text. Beneath the scale line are ten lines, but with symbols showing the invisible codes. The position of the cursor is shown highlighted, or *in reverse video*.

Hard carriage returns (created by pressing the ⏎ key) are represented by [HRt], soft carriage returns (added by word-wrap) are shown as [SRt], and tabs are [Tab]. Figure 3.3 lists the most common codes. Don't try to memorize the codes or worry about them. As you use the program you'll become familiar with the important ones. In most cases, you can work with WordPerfect without even thinking about the codes themselves.

3. Use the arrow keys to move the cursor in all four directions. Notice that the cursor changes position both above and below the scale line.

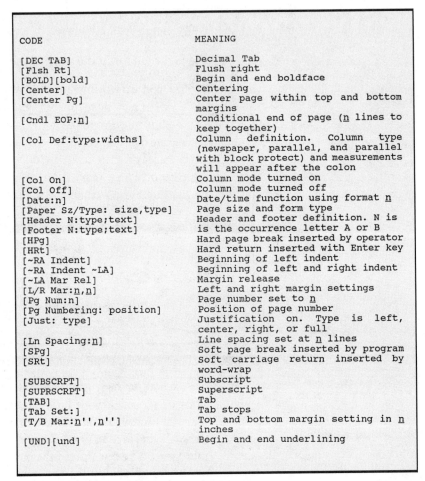

```
CODE                              MEANING

[DEC TAB]                         Decimal Tab
[Flsh Rt]                         Flush right
[BOLD][bold]                      Begin and end boldface
[Center]                          Centering
[Center Pg]                       Center page within top and bottom
                                  margins
[Cndl EOP:n]                      Conditional end of page (n lines to
                                  keep together)
[Col Def:type:widths]             Column   definition.   Column  type
                                  (newspaper, parallel, and parallel
                                  with block protect) and measurements
                                  will appear after the colon
[Col On]                          Column mode turned on
[Col Off]                         Column mode turned off
[Date:n]                          Date/time function using format n
[Paper Sz/Type: size,type]        Page size and form type
[Header N:type;text]              Header and footer definition. N is
[Footer N:type;text]              is the occurrence letter A or B
[HPg]                             Hard page break inserted by operator
[HRt]                             Hard return inserted with Enter key
[~RA Indent]                      Beginning of left indent
[~RA Indent ~LA]                  Beginning of left and right indent
[~LA Mar Rel]                     Margin release
[L/R Mar:n,n]                     Left and right margin settings
[Pg Num:n]                        Page number set to n
[Pg Numbering: position]          Position of page number
[Just: type]                      Justification on.  Type is left,
                                  center, right, or full
[Ln Spacing:n]                    Line spacing set at n lines
[SPg]                             Soft page break inserted by program
[SRt]                             Soft carriage return inserted by
                                  word-wrap
[SUBSCRPT]                        Subscript
[SUPRSCRPT]                       Superscript
[TAB]                             Tab
[Tab Set:]                        Tab stops
[T/B Mar:n'',n'']                 Top and bottom margin setting in n
                                  inches
[UND][und]                        Begin and end underlining
```

Figure 3.3: Common WordPerfect codes

With the codes revealed, you can delete either text or the codes themselves by pressing Del or Backspace. The text both above and below the scale line will change accordingly.

4. Place the cursor to highlight the [Tab] code in the first paragraph.

5. Press Del. The text will readjust on both sides of the scale line.

6. Select **Edit Reveal** Codes again (Alt-F3). The scale line and bottom display area disappear.

7. The cursor should still be at the beginning of the first paragraph. Press Tab to indent the paragraph again.

You'll learn more about deleting codes in later lessons. For now, remember that you do not have to reveal codes to delete them. For example, you could also have deleted the tab by placing the cursor at the start of the line and pressing Del.

Take advantage of these codes when you're working. For instance, I recommend displaying the codes whenever the text on the screen just doesn't appear correct. Sometimes you may enter a format code by accidentally pressing the wrong function key. By revealing the codes, you can tell where these incorrect functions were added and easily delete them.

Working with Codes Revealed

Displaying the codes at the bottom of the screen simply gives you two views of the same document. You can leave the codes revealed and continue writing or editing in the upper portion. However, you'll see fewer lines of text at one time.

So it's much easier to reveal the codes when needed and then select **Edit Reveal Codes** (Alt-F3) again to return the screen to normal for writing and editing.

Lesson 16—How to Split and Combine Paragraphs

You press the ⬅ key to begin a new paragraph. This inserts the Hard Carriage Return code [HRt] at the end of a line. It follows, then, that if you press ⬅ when the cursor is within a paragraph, an [HRt] code will be inserted, dividing the paragraph into two. And by deleting an [HRt] code between two paragraphs, they will be combined into one.

Combining Two Paragraphs

To combine two paragraphs into one, position the cursor immediately after the first paragraph you want to combine and press Del. The paragraph below will move up one line. (If one delete doesn't do the trick, there might be some extra spaces between the end of the sentence and the [HRt] code. Keep pressing Del until the paragraphs come together.) If you double-spaced between paragraphs by pressing ← twice, you must press Del twice.

If the codes are revealed, place the cursor on the [HRt] code before pressing Del. We'll use this technique to readjust the letter on the screen.

1. Place the cursor at the end of the first paragraph.

2. Press → to move past the last word in the sentence. The cursor didn't move into the blank spaces after the sentence, but down to the next line. That's because there are *no* blank spaces after the sentence, just the [HRt] code. Let's confirm this by looking at the codes again.

3. Select **E**dit **R**eveal Codes (Alt-F3). Look at the end of the first paragraph. There's the [HRt] code. When you moved the cursor with the → key, the cursor first moved past the [HRt] code and then to the next line.

4. Select **E**dit **R**eveal Codes (Alt-F3) to clear the displayed codes.

5. Now, again place the cursor at the end of the first paragraph.

6. Press the spacebar. This inserts the space that will separate the two sentences.

7. Press Del three times. While no codes were revealed, you deleted first the [HRt] code after the sentence, then the [HRt] code that created the blank line between paragraphs, and finally the [Tab] code that indented the second paragraph (Figure 3.4).

Splitting a Paragraph into Two

To split one paragraph into two, position the cursor at the beginning of the sentence that will start the new paragraph and press ←.

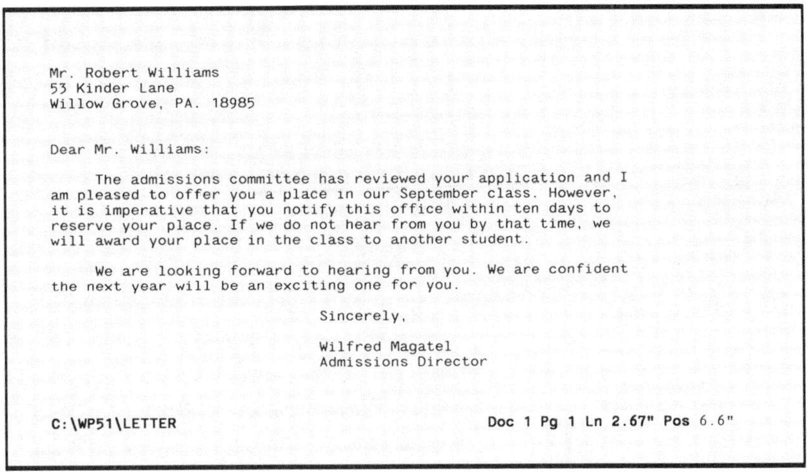

```
┌─────────────────────────────────────────────────────────┐
│                                                           │
│   Mr. Robert Williams                                     │
│   53 Kinder Lane                                          │
│   Willow Grove, PA. 18985                                 │
│                                                           │
│   Dear Mr. Williams:                                      │
│                                                           │
│       The admissions committee has reviewed your application and I │
│   am pleased to offer you a place in our September class. However, │
│   it is imperative that you notify this office within ten days to │
│   reserve your place. If we do not hear from you by that time, we │
│   will award your place in the class to another student. │
│                                                           │
│       We are looking forward to hearing from you. We are confident │
│   the next year will be an exciting one for you.          │
│                                                           │
│                          Sincerely,                       │
│                                                           │
│                          Wilfred Magatel                  │
│                          Admissions Director              │
│                                                           │
│                                                           │
│   C:\WP51\LETTER                    Doc 1 Pg 1 Ln 2.67" Pos 6.6" │
└─────────────────────────────────────────────────────────┘
```

Figure 3.4: Two [HRt] codes and a tab deleted

The text of that paragraph from the cursor position down will move down to the next line. Press ↵ again if you want to double-space between paragraphs, then Tab to indent the first line.

1. Place the cursor on the word *If*, which begins the third sentence of the first paragraph.

2. Press ↵ twice—the first time to separate the paragraphs, and again to insert the blank line between paragraphs.

3. Press Tab to indent the new paragraph.

4. Press an arrow key to adjust the text.

5. If you are not ready to continue with Lesson 17, resave the document.

Lesson 17—How to Repeat Keystrokes

Sometimes you want to repeat a certain keystroke a specific number of times. For example, you might want to place a line of 64 dashes across the screen, or move the cursor a specific number of spaces or lines. You also might need to repeat a certain command more than once—to delete the next five words or seven lines, for instance.

In each of these examples, you would have to press the appropriate keystroke repeatedly, counting the strokes and watching the screen carefully. However, with WordPerfect you can use the Esc key to perform repeated actions easily and quickly.

In a moment we'll use Escape to edit the LETTER document. Here's how it works: Press Esc to show the

Repeat Value = 8

prompt on the status line. The default value of 8 indicates that the next nonnumeric keystroke that follows will be executed eight times. If you want a different number of repetitions, type a new number. Type the keystroke, or press the command, to be repeated. You can only press one keystroke or one command. Because the number of repetitions is specified, you don't have to count each one.

For example, to print a line of dashes across the screen, press Esc, type *64* (the number of characters in a line), then press –. To delete the next ten words, press Esc, type *10*, then press Ctrl-Backspace. To delete five lines, place the cursor at the start of the first line, press Esc, type *5*, then press Ctrl-End.

Now we'll use the Esc key with the LETTER document. If you quit WordPerfect after Lesson 16, start the program and recall LETTER.

1. Press Home Home ↑ to place the cursor at the start of the letter.

2. Press Esc 10 ↓. The cursor moves down ten lines.

3. Press Esc 4 Ctrl-Backspace to delete the first four words.

4. Type

   have the pleasure of offering

5. Press ↓ to adjust the text. Your screen should now look like Figure 3.5.

Adjusting the Screen after Editing

Several times now you've been instructed to press an arrow key to adjust the text after adding or deleting characters. This forces the document to realign itself.

```
March 12, 1990

Mr. Robert Williams
53 Kinder Lane
Willow Grove, PA. 18985


Dear Mr. Williams:

      The admissions committee has reviewed your application and I
have the pleasure of offering you a place in our September class.
However, it is imperative that you notify this office within ten
days to reserve your place.

      If we do not hear from you by that time, we will award your
place in the class to another student.

      We are looking forward to hearing from you. We are confident
the next year will be an exciting one for you.

                        Sincerely,


                        Wilfred Magatel
                        Admissions Director
C:\WP51\LETTER                          Doc 1 Pg 1 Ln 2.83" Pos 4"
```

Figure 3.5: The sample letter revised using the Escape key

In these instances, or when the text on the screen fails to conform to any changes you've made, you can also use the Rewrite command. Here's how:

1. Press Ctrl-F3 to display the prompt

   1 Window; **2** Line Draw; **3** Rewrite: 3

2. Press *R*, *3*, or ◄─┘ to rewrite the screen so it adjusts to recent editing or format changes.

In the next lesson, you'll learn how to use the Window option in this prompt line to display and edit more than one document at a time.

L esson 18—How to Work with Multiple Documents

You're working feverishly on a document and want to refer to another on the same disk. You may have come up with an idea for a change to the other document, or it may have a section of text that can be used to make your work easier. But it will just take too long to save the current document and then load the other.

Fortunately for times like this, WordPerfect allows you to work with two documents at one time. You can recall the second document without saving or exiting the first. By selecting **E**dit **S**witch Document from the pull down menu (Shift-F3), you can switch back and forth between the two, even copying text from one to the other.

Try this with the document already on the screen:

1. Select **E**dit **S**witch Document (Shift-F3). The screen will clear and the status line will change to

   Doc 2 Pg 1 Ln 1″ Pos 1″

   You are now in the second document window. Anything you type, or any commands used, will have no effect on the text displayed in document 1, which is safely stored in memory. Each document can be edited or saved separately.

   You could now start typing the second document, or retrieve an existing one from the disk. (With the Document 2 window displayed, load a saved document using the exact same techniques you've already learned.) To switch back and forth between the two documents, just select **E**dit **S**witch Document (Shift-F3) again. Think of this as a toggle between document 1 and document 2.

2. Type

   I am pleased to accept the position in the September class.

3. Select **E**dit **S**witch Document (Shift-F3) to switch back to the first document. It's still there, unchanged.

4. Select **E**dit **S**witch Document (Shift-F3) to return to document 2. Now let's save this document and return to the first.

5. Select **F**ile **E**xit (F7), answer **Y**es to the Save prompt, type *ACCEPT* (or *B: ACCEPT*), and press ←⏎. In a few moments the prompt will change to

   Exit doc 2? No (Yes)

6. Select **Y**es. The first document reappears.

Displaying Two Documents

Working with two documents is easier if you can see them both on the screen at the same time. For this, use the WordPerfect Window command. Try this now with the document already on the screen.

1. Select **Edit Window** (Ctrl-F3 W) to show

   Number of lines in this Window: 24

   The default 24 indicates that the current document will use all 24 lines of the screen (the status line uses the 25th).

2. Type *12*, then press ←. The screen is divided at the twelfth line, as shown in Figure 3.6.

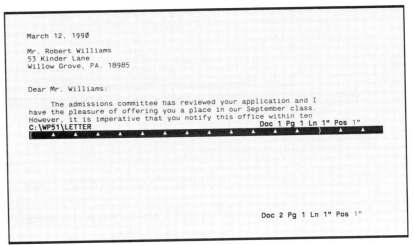

Figure 3.6: The screen divided into two document areas

Instead of typing the number of lines, you could also have pressed the ↑ or ↓ keys instead of typing a number. The scale line would have appeared and moved in the direction of the arrow key being pressed. Press ← when the scale line reaches the desired position.

3. Select **Edit Switch Document** (Shift-F3). The cursor moves to the document in the bottom window and the triangular tab markers now point down.

4. Recall the ACCEPT document. Select **File** **R**etrieve (Shift-F10), type *ACCEPT*, then press ↵. Parts of both documents are now displayed (Figure 3.7). Scrolling in one document window will not affect the other.

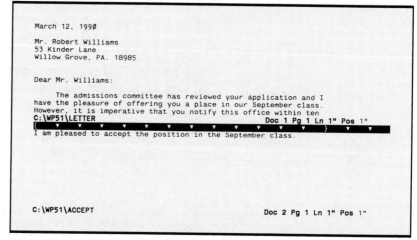

```
    March 12, 1990

    Mr. Robert Williams
    53 Kinder Lane
    Willow Grove, PA. 18985


    Dear Mr. Williams:

        The admissions committee has reviewed your application and I
    have the pleasure of offering you a place in our September class.
    However, it is imperative that you notify this office within ten
C:\WP51\LETTER                                    Doc 1 Pg 1 Ln 1" Pos 1"
    ▼     ▼     ▼     ▼     ▼     ▼     ▼     ▼     )     ▼     ▼
    I am pleased to accept the position in the September class.




    C:\WP51\ACCEPT                                Doc 2 Pg 1 Ln 1" Pos 1"
```

Figure 3.7: *Two documents on the screen with the cursor in the second document*

*C*learing Windows

1. Still in the bottom window, select **File** **E**xit (F7) **N**o **Y**es to exit document 2. In this case, even though you did exit from document 2, the screen is still divided into two windows. The cursor is in the first document, however.

    To remove the bottom window, make the other one fill the entire screen.

2. Select **E**dit **W**indow (Ctrl-F3 W) to change the window size.

3. Type *24* and press ↵. The second document window disappears.

*D*isplaying the Scale Line

In some word processing programs, the scale line is always displayed as a point of reference for margins and tabs. WordPerfect gives you a choice. If you want the scale line displayed, follow these steps:

1. Select **Edit Window** (Ctrl-F3 W) for the Window option.

2. Type *23* and press ⏎ to set the window at 23 lines.

When you size a window at 23 lines, the scale line dividing windows appears at the bottom of the screen. When you switch windows, the scale line stays at that position but changes to reflect the format of the other document, which now appears on the screen. To delete the scale line, resize the window to a full 24 lines. The 25th screen line is used by the status line.

Lesson 19—How to Add the Date to Documents

The LETTER document contains the date you typed on the first line. If you don't print and mail the letter until some time later, the date will be incorrect. So you would have to delete the incorrect date and type the current one just before printing.

Instead, you can use WordPerfect's Date function to automatically insert the date when the letter is printed. To use this function you must enter the correct date when starting DOS, or have a built-in clock in your computer.

1. Delete the date at the top of the letter.

    a. Press Home Home ↑ to place the cursor at the start of the letter.

    b. Press Ctrl-End to delete the date.

2. Select **Tools Date Code** (Shift-F5 C), as in Figure 3.8.

    The line will disappear and the date code will be inserted into the text, with the current date maintained by DOS displayed on the screen. When the document is printed, that day's date will appear on the finished copy. Thus, you can complete a letter on another day and have the date on which it is printed appear in the letter. But keep in mind that if you later recall the letter, the current date will appear, not the date

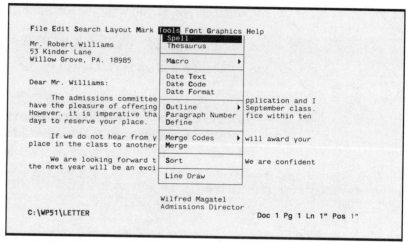

Figure 3.8: Tools pull down menu

it was written or printed. You cannot use the function to remind you when the letter was mailed.

The Date Text option would also insert the system date. However, this inserts the current date as text into the document. No matter when the document is printed or recalled, the date when the function was originally entered will appear. Use this if you type and print a letter the same day, since the date will serve as a reminder of when it was mailed. You can also use this when writing a diary or log. Select Date Text (Shift-F5 T) to display the date, then type the entry for that day.

3. Select **E**dit **R**eveal Codes (Alt-F3) to reveal the codes. The date appears in the top part of the screen, with the Date code in the bottom part (Figure 3.9). If you have selected Date **T**ext, the same date appears in both areas.

4. Select **E**dit **R**eveal Codes (Alt-F3) to clear the displayed codes.

5. Resave the document and exit WordPerfect. Select **F**ile Exit, select **Y**es, and press ↵ to save the document with the same name. Select **Y**es to confirm the replacement, and then select **Y**es again to exit the program.

One word of caution if you do not have a built-in clock: unless you enter the date when you start your computer, the system date could be

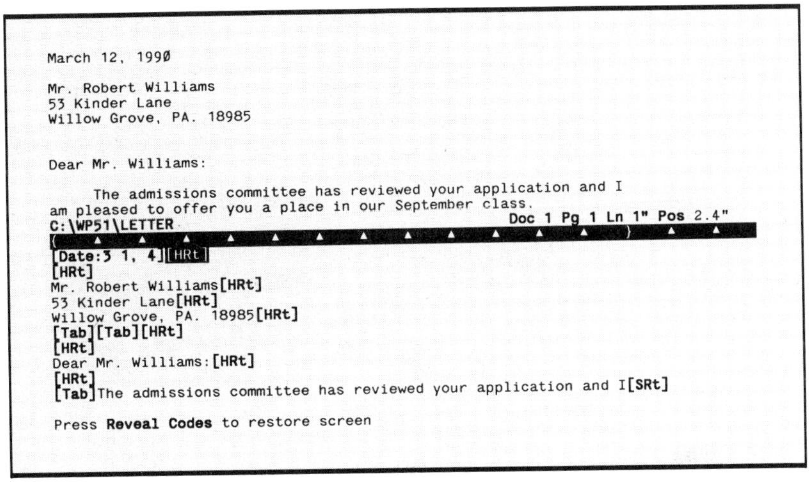
March 12, 1990
Mr. Robert Williams
53 Kinder Lane
Willow Grove, PA. 18985
Dear Mr. Williams:
The admissions committee has reviewed your application and I
am pleased to offer you a place in our September class.
C:\WP51\LETTER
Doc 1 Pg 1 Ln 1" Pos 2.4"
[Date:3 1, 4][HRt]
[HRt]
Mr. Robert Williams[HRt]
53 Kinder Lane[HRt]
Willow Grove, PA. 18985[HRt]
[Tab][Tab][HRt]
[HRt]
Dear Mr. Williams:[HRt]
[HRt]
[Tab]The admissions committee has reviewed your application and I[SRt]
Press Reveal Codes to restore screen

Figure 3.9: *The Date code causing the current date to be displayed in the typing window*

something like January 1, 1980. If you enter the date one day and use the Date function, be sure to enter the date again if you later restart the computer to print the document. Otherwise, *January 1, 1980* could appear on your letter.

Changing Date Formats

The **T**ools Date **F**ormat option allows you to change the format in which the date and time appear. Follow these steps to change the format:

1. Start WordPerfect and select **T**ools Date **F**ormat (Shift-F5 F). The Date Format menu appears (Figure 3.10).
2. Enter the numbers and any punctuation to correspond to the format you wish to appear. These examples will help you:

KEYSTROKES	RESULTING FORMAT
3 1, 4	December 25, 1988
2/1/5 (6)	3/5/84 (Tuesday)
8:9 0	2:55 am
6, 3 1, 4	Tuesday, December 25, 1988
7:9 (0)	23:30 (pm)

```
Date Format

    Character    Meaning
        1        Day of the Month
        2        Month (number)
        3        Month (word)
        4        Year (all four digits)
        5        Year (last two digits)
        6        Day of the Week (word)
        7        Hour (24-hour clock)
        8        Hour (12-hour clock)
        9        Minute
        Ø        am / pm
        %,$      Used before a number, will:
                 Pad numbers less than 1Ø with a leading zero or space
                 Abbreviate the month or day of the week

    Examples:  3 1, 4        = December 25, 1984
               %6 %3 1, 4    = Tue Dec 25, 1984
               %2/%1/5 (6)   = Ø1/Ø1/85 (Tuesday)
               $2/$1/5 ($6)  =  1/ 1/85 (Tue)
               8:9Ø          = 1Ø:55am


Date format: 3 1, 4
```

Figure 3.10: Date Format menu

You can also insert leading zeros or spaces in front of date and time numbers or abbreviate the names of days and months by using the percent (%) and dollar sign ($) key. For example:

KEYSTROKES	RESULTING FORMAT
%2/%1/5 (%6)	03/05/84 (Tue)
$2/$1/5 ($6)	3/ 5/84 (Tue)

3. Press ⏎ twice to return to the typing window.

4

*Enhancing
the Appearance
of Your Documents*

Featuring

Default values

Left and right margins

Line spacing

Ending pages

Document comments and summary

It's an unfortunate fact of life, but first appearances often mean the difference between success and failure. How your document looks can be as important as what it says. Just picture how you look through your own mail. If you're like me, you open the envelopes that look important first, leaving ones that appear to be junk mail until the end.

Arranging the appearance of your text on the page is called *formatting*. An attractive format is almost a guarantee that your document will be read.

With a typewriter, formatting can be like jumping into a bottomless pit. But with WordPerfect, you can arrange and rearrange your document as often as you like until it's just right.

L esson 20—Default Values and Format Changes

Each time you start WordPerfect, standard default settings are provided automatically to let you type and print documents without worrying about page size, line spacing, and other details of format. The default settings are

Page Size:	8 by 11 inches
	66 lines per page
	54 typed lines
Top Margin:	1"
Bottom Margin:	1"
Left Margin:	1" (10 character positions from the left)
Right Margin:	1" (character position 74)
Page Numbering:	None
Line Spacing:	Single space, 6 lines per inch

Font:	Standard single-strike, 10 pitch (10 characters per inch)
Tabs:	Every 5 spaces (inch)
Full Justification:	On (when printed; not displayed)

These settings result in a page with 54 lines of text, each line 65 characters (or about 6 inches) wide. The text will appear neatly arranged when printed on standard business stationery, with text aligned on both the left and right margins.

You don't have to change a thing if you like these settings and want to use them for every page of your document. But you can change any of these settings easily if you want other formats.

Most often you'll make temporary format changes that affect only the document in which they are made. Every other document will follow the default values, or the format changes you make within that document. In fact, page format changes need not affect the entire document. They just control the text from the cursor position where the change was made to either the next format change or the end of the document, whichever comes first. Finally, format changes can be inserted within existing text, just like any other code. They then automatically change the original format with which the text was typed, so that the previously typed text now conforms to the new format. Say you have already typed a document single-spaced. If you place the cursor midway through the text and insert a double-space code, all text from that position on will become double-spaced.

The ability to change the format of text at any time is one of the greatest features of word processing. You can type the document using the default settings, then adjust the margins, line spacing, and other dimensions until they appear the way you desire. In fact, you'll do just that in the next lesson.

Lesson 21—How to Change Left and Right Margins

There are many ways to adjust the final format of a printed document. This lesson explains how to change the right and left margins—of either an entire document or just parts of it.

In determining the right and left borders of a page, margin settings also set the length of the printed line, adjust for different widths of paper, and affect the amount of text that will fit on a page. For example, to make a document appear longer, make the margins a little wider.

The default left margin is 1 inch, or 10 character positions. In this lesson you will learn how to change the margins. Follow these steps:

1. Start WordPerfect.

2. Pull down the **Layout** menu (Shift-F8), as in Figure 4.1.

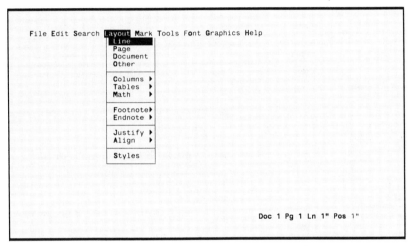

Figure 4.1: *Layout menu*

This is the menu that you'll use to adjust the format of your document. In this case, you're interested in setting the left and right margins, which are set with the Line option. You'll see in a moment what format options are available in each of these categories.

3. Select **Line** to show the Format Line menu (Figure 4.2).

The current settings, the default formats being used by Word-Perfect, are shown next to each type of format. You select which option to change by typing either the number next to the option or the letter that is highlighted.

Notice that option 7 is used to change the left and right margins. So you can change margins by selecting **Margins** (*7* or *M*).

```
Format: Line

   1 - Hyphenation                        No

   2 - Hyphenation Zone - Left            10%
                          Right           4%

   3 - Justification                      Full

   4 - Line Height                        Auto

   5 - Line Numbering                     No

   6 - Line Spacing                       1

   7 - Margins - Left                     1"
                 Right                    1"

   8 - Tab Set                            Rel: -1", every 0.5"

   9 - Widow/Orphan Protection            No


Selection: 0
```

Figure 4.2: Format Line menu

4. Select **Margins**. The cursor moves to the default 1" left margin setting.

5. Type *2*, then press ←—. Word Perfect automatically adds the inches sign (") after the entry and moves the cursor to the right margin setting.

6. Type *2*, then press ←—. The new settings are stored on the menu.

   At this point, you could press F7 to save the changes and return to the document. But let's take a look at the Format menu first.

7. Press Esc (←— works also) to save the changes and display the main Format menu (Figure 4.3).

This menu appears when you press Esc or ←— from the Line, Page, Document, or Other menus, all of which are reached from the Layout pull down menu. Take a moment to review the options under each of the four major categories.

8. Now, press F7 to return to the document.

9. Type the following proposal. The lines will be about 45 characters wide.

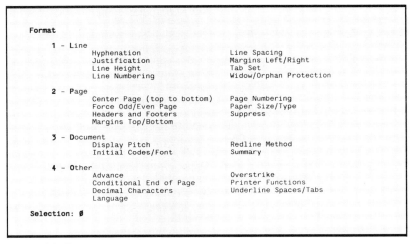

```
Format

   1 - Line
            Hyphenation                    Line Spacing
            Justification                  Margins Left/Right
            Line Height                    Tab Set
            Line Numbering                 Widow/Orphan Protection

   2 - Page
            Center Page (top to bottom)    Page Numbering
            Force Odd/Even Page            Paper Size/Type
            Headers and Footers            Suppress
            Margins Top/Bottom

   3 - Document
            Display Pitch                  Redline Method
            Initial Codes/Font             Summary

   4 - Other
            Advance                        Overstrike
            Conditional End of Page        Printer Functions
            Decimal Characters             Underline Spaces/Tabs
            Language

   Selection: 0
```

Figure 4.3: *Format menu*

Fox and Associates, Inc. is happy to bid on your proposal for data processing training. We have been professional trainers for over 15 years. Fox and Associates, Inc. has earned an outstanding reputation and we will be pleased to provide references upon request.

In consideration for the amount of $800.00, Fox and Associates will perform the following services:

Provide two days of training in word processing for two operators at 6543 Fifth Avenue, Boston.

Fox and Associates will guarantee this price only for the next 60 days. We maintain the authority to adjust the bid if contracts are not formalized in that period.

This bid is submitted pursuant to the laws of New York State and, if accepted, its terms shall be binding on both parties.

Fox and Associates greatly appreciates the opportunity to bid on this project.

This proposal represents an estimate of the cost of materials and labor. While every effort has been made to accurately compute all costs involved, the actual price of services, binding on both parties, will be stated in the final contract.

10. Save the document now under the name CONTRACT. You will use it in a later lesson.

    a. Select **File Save** (F10).

    b. Type *CONTRACT.*

    c. Press ←—.

Saving the document in this way will not exit the WordPerfect program.

11. Press Home Home ↑ to reach the start of the text.

12. Select **Edit Reveal Codes** (Alt-F3) to reveal the codes. The [L/R Mar:2",2"] code is in the text (Figure 4.4).

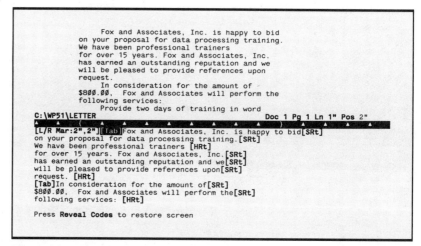

Figure 4.4: A Margin Set code in the text

Let's experiment with the margin setting to see what happens. First you will insert a new margin code to the right of the current one. The new code should reformat all of the text on the screen.

13. Select **Edit Reveal Codes** (Alt-F3) to remove the code display.

14. Select **Layout Line Margins** (Shift-F8 L M) for the margin prompt. Now let's set ½" margins.

15. Type *.5*, press ◄──┘, type *.5*, press ◄──┘, then F7 to return to the document. Notice that the text will not be aligned properly at the new margins.

16. Press Ctrl-F3 **R** to select the **R**ewrite option and adjust the text to the new margins. You could also adjust the text by moving the cursor down through the text. Use Ctrl-F3 R if you want to adjust the text without moving the cursor, so you can edit or add text at the current location.

17. Reveal the codes again by selecting **E**dit **R**eveal Codes (Alt-F3). Notice that both Margin Set codes are still in the text (Figure 4.5).

```
        Fox and Associates, Inc. is happy to bid on your proposal for data
processing training. We have been professional trainers
for over 15 years. Fox and Associates, Inc. has earned an outstanding
reputation and we will be pleased to provide references upon request.
     In consideration for the amount of $800.00,  Fox and Associates will
perform the following services:
     Provide two days of training in word processing for two operators at
6543 Fifth Avenue, Boston.
     Fox and Associates will guarantee this price only for the next 60 days.
We maintain the authority to adjust the bid if contracts are not formalized
in that period.
C:\WP51\LETTER                                      Doc 1 Pg 1 Ln 1" Pos Ø.5"
(   ▲   ▲   ▲   ▲  ▲   ▲   ▲   ▲   ▲   ▲   ▲   ▲   ▲   ▲   ▲   ▲  )
[L/R Mar:2",2"][L/R Mar:Ø.5",Ø.5"][Tab]Fox and Associates, Inc. is happy to bid
on your proposal for data[SRt]
processing training. We have been professional trainers [HRt]
for over 15 years. Fox and Associates, Inc. has earned an outstanding[SRt]
reputation and we will be pleased to provide references upon request. [HRt]
[Tab]In consideration for the amount of $800.00,  Fox and Associates will[SRt]
perform the following services: [HRt]
[Tab]Provide two days of training in word processing for two operators at[SRt]
6543 Fifth Avenue, Boston. [HRt]
[Tab]Fox and Associates will guarantee this price only for the next 60 days.[SRt

Press Reveal Codes to restore screen
```

Figure 4.5: Two Margin Set codes in the text

Text is always formatted by the code immediately before it, so the second Margin Set code is now used to format the document. However, the first code does not disappear, so you can return to the previous margins by simply deleting the new code.

18. Select **E**dit **R**eveal Codes (Alt-F3) to return to the typing window.

19. Place the cursor on the left side of the screen at the fifth paragraph.

20. Change both margins to 1¹/₂ inches.

    a. Select **Layout Line** (Shift-F8 L).

    b. Select **Margins**.

    c. Type *1.5.*

    d. Press ↵.

    e. Type *1.5.*

    f. Press ↵.

    g. Press F7.

    h. Press Ctrl-F3 R.

The text from the cursor position down adjusts to the new margins, but the text above the cursor remains unchanged (Figure 4.6). The margins of the text will appear in the appropriate relative positions on your screen. So the paragraphs with 1 ¹/₂-inch margins are indented from those above having just ¹/₂-inch margins. If you set very small margins, the resulting lines will be too long to fit on the screen, so they'll scroll off the side. When this happens, use the → and ← keys to scroll the text into view.

```
        Fox and Associates, Inc. is happy to bid on your proposal for data
processing training. We have been professional trainers
for over 15 years. Fox and Associates, Inc. has earned an outstanding
reputation and we will be pleased to provide references upon request.
        In consideration for the amount of $800.00, Fox and Associates will
perform the following services:
        Provide two days of training in word processing for two operators at
6543 Fifth Avenue, Boston.
        Fox and Associates will guarantee this price only for the next 60 days
We maintain the authority to adjust the bid if contracts are not formalized
in that period.
                This bid is submitted pursuant to the laws of New
        York State and, if accepted, its terms shall be binding
        on both parties.
                Fox and Associates greatly appreciates the
        opportunity to bid on this project.
                This proposal represents an estimate of the cost of
        materials and labor.  While  every effort has been made
        to accurately compute all costs involved, the actual
        price of services, binding on both parties,  will be
        stated in the final contract.


C:\WP51\CONTRACT                                    Doc 1 Pg 1 Ln 2.83" Pos 1.5"
```

Figure 4.6: Not all text may appear after a margin change.

All formatting codes affect only the text from the position where they are inserted to the end of the document—or to the next similar formatting code.

21. To delete the margin setting, press Backspace, then **Yes** in response to the prompt

   Delete [L/R Mar: 1.5″, 1.5″]? No (Yes)

22. Select **File Exit (F7) No No** to clear the document from the screen without saving the changes.

Deleting Margin Set Codes

Margin Set codes can also be deleted from the text. With codes revealed, just place the cursor on the [L/R Mar] code and press Del. When the codes are not revealed, the message

   Delete [L/R Mar:]? No (Yes)

appears. Select **Yes** to delete the code, or **No** or ◄─┘ to leave it as is.

Prompts like this appear so you can confirm the deletion of most codes.

Lesson 22—How to Adjust Line Spacing

Like right and left margins, line spacing also changes the overall appearance of the document.

Like margins, line spacing can be changed for the entire document, or just for sections within it. Spacing is allowed in half-line increments, although text will appear on the screen in the nearest integer. For example, lines spaced at 1.5 will be double-spaced on the screen, although they will be printed at 1.5.

Because only 24 lines can be displayed on the screen at one time, it is wise to type documents single-spaced. This reduces the amount of scrolling you'll have to do during the editing process. Then, before printing, change the line spacing where desired and make any adjustments.

We will now use the Line Spacing function to adjust the appearance of the document that you called CONTRACT in the last lesson. If you exited WordPerfect after the last lesson, start the program.

1. Recall CONTRACT. The text has 2-inch margins.

2. Select **Layout Line** (Shift-F8 L) to display the Format Line menu, then **Line Spacing** (S) to select line spacing.

3. Press *2* for double-spacing, press ←┘, then F7. The paragraphs, and the spaces between them, will become double-spaced.

4. Select **Edit Reveal Codes** (Alt-F3) to reveal the codes. Notice the [Ln Spacing:2] code in the text.

   Each time you press the ↑ or ↓ key, the Ln indicator will change in two-line increments.

5. Select **File Exit** (F7) **No No** to clear the document from the screen without saving the changes. The original CONTRACT remains unchanged as you saved it in Lesson 21.

So far we have concentrated on documents of just one page. Longer documents will automatically be divided into pages by auto-pagination. The next lesson explains how to manually end a page before the ending point established by auto-pagination.

L esson 23—How to Control Page Breaks

You already know that WordPerfect paginates documents as you type. Using the default settings, a new page starts after every 54 lines. A dashed line will appear across the screen and the Pg indicator will increase by one. These are called *soft page breaks* and are marked with the [SPg] code.

However, you might want to end a page before it is filled, as when typing a short cover memo or title page. This calls for a new page or *hard page break*—[HPg].

To insert a hard page break, press Ctrl-◄┘. A double row of dashes (=) appears, so you can tell whether page breaks are soft or hard.

Like all codes, the hard page break can be inserted in existing text and deleted.

1. Type the following:

   MEMORANDUM

   TO: All Department Chairpersons
   FROM: Rose Savage
   RE: Reserved Equipment List

   Attached is a list of Class 2 equipment that must be re-served at least two weeks before needed.

2. Press ◄┘.

3. Press Ctrl-◄┘.

   A double line of dashes will appear on the screen, with the cursor underneath. The Pg indicator will read *2* (Figure 4.7).

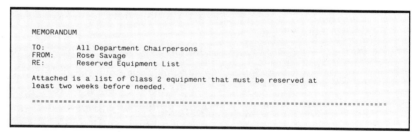

Figure 4.7: A hard page break inserted

There are only eight lines above the page break line. But when printed, the first page will roll out and the second, if there is one, will begin printing.

4. Select **Edit Reveal** Codes (Alt-F3) to reveal the codes. Instead of a page break line there is an [HPg] code.

5. Select **Edit Reveal** Codes (Alt-F3) to return to the document, then type the text of the second page. In Chapter 6 you'll learn

how to center text automatically. But for now, press Tab five times to center the title.

> Class 2 Equipment
>
> Electron Microscopes
> Fluorescent Microscopes
> Cryostat
> Serum Glutamic Pyruvic Transaminase Analyzer
> Flow Cytometer
> Nuclear Magnetic Resonance Scanner

6. Select **F**ile **P**rint **F**ull (Shift-F7 F) to print the two-page document. The memorandum is printed at the top of the first page. When WordPerfect encountered the Hard Page Break code, it ejected the first page before printing the next.

Deleting Page Breaks

Soft page breaks can only be changed by adding or deleting text. But hard page breaks, which are manually inserted, can be deleted just like any other code.

7. Place the cursor on the line just above the page break line.

8. Press Del. The page break line will disappear.

    When you delete a Hard Page code, any text that was on the page below will be added to the one above. Soft page breaks following will adjust automatically.

9. If you are not ready to continue with the next lesson, save the document and exit WordPerfect.

    a. Select **F**ile **E**xit (F7).

    b. Select **Y**es.

    c. Type *MEMO*, then press ←⏎.

    d. Select **Y**es to exit WordPerfect.

Margins, line spacing, and page endings are three of the most useful formatting techniques. In later lessons you will learn how to format individual characters, paragraphs, and pages. The next lesson is really not about document formats. But it will be an invaluable aid, not only when you are creating a document but also if you ever need to refer to that document again.

*L*esson 24—*How to Add Document Comments and Summary*

As you write, you're going to keep adding documents to your disk. It will get harder to remember what you've named each document and just as difficult to distinguish one from the other on the directory listing. After all, an 11-character name (eight characters plus the extension) can't fully identify every different document you write.

My own directory is so full of useless listings (such as *MEMO1* and *MEMO2*) that it's like reading a menu in some obscure foreign language.

Luckily, WordPerfect allows us to add a document summary to each document and to insert comments within the text itself. Neither the summary nor the comments are printed along with the text. But they can be displayed on the screen or printed separately to help identify the document or to serve as reminders and messages.

You can have only one summary per document, and it is stored in a special area with the file.

Comments, however, can be inserted anywhere in the document, and you can have as many as you wish. Use them to write notes and reminders that you'll need when working on the document but that you do not want printed with it.

If you are not in WordPerfect, start the program and recall the MEMO document.

*D*ocument Summary

1. Select **L**ayout **D**ocument (Shift-F8 D) to display the Format Document menu shown in Figure 4.8. Most of the options on this menu are for more complex formatting tasks. But a document summary is created using option 5.

```
Format: Document

    1 - Display Pitch - Automatic  Yes
                         Width      Ø.1"

    2 - Initial Codes

    3 - Initial Base Font          Courier 1Øcpi

    4 - Redline Method             Printer Dependent

    5 - Summary




Selection: Ø
```

Figure 4.8: Format Document menu

2. Select Summary to display the Document Summary screen shown in Figure 4.9.

   Let's look at this screen for a moment.

   • Revision Date shows the last time the document was revised.

   • Document Name and Document Type let you add a descriptive document name (up to 88 characters) and document type (up to 20 characters).

```
Document Summary

         Revision Date   Ø3-12-9Ø Ø4:1Øp

    1 - Creation Date    Ø3-12-9Ø Ø4:1Øp

    2 - Document Name
        Document Type

    3 - Author
        Typist

    4 - Subject

    5 - Account

    6 - Keywords

    7 - Abstract



Selection: Ø                    (Retrieve to capture; Del to remove summary)
```

Figure 4.9: Document Summary screen

- Author and Typist are for recording the author's and typist's names.

- Subject lets you enter about 3½ lines of text to describe your document. By default, if the characters *RE*: occur in the first 400 characters of the document, the text on the line following *RE*: will appear at the Subject prompt when you capture the document summary fields (you will see how to do this shortly).

- Account, which can hold up to 3 ½ lines of text, is for recording an account number or name.

- Keywords, which can also hold up to 3 ½ inches of text, lets you enter words to help identify your document.

- Abstract lets you add about 16 descriptive lines or have Word-Perfect display the first 550 characters in the document.

    Now let's see how to capture the document summary fields and display the abstract from your MEMO document in the Document Summary screen.

3. Press Shift-F10 to display the prompt:

    Capture Document Summary Fields? No (Yes)

4. Select **Yes**. The words after RE: appear in the Subject field and about the first 550 characters of the document appear in the Abstract field. The name and file type you entered will appear at the top of the screen. Hard carriage returns are shown in semicolons.

    The summary will be stored with the document when you save it. To delete the summary, display it following steps 1 and 2, then press Del to display the

    Delete Document Summary? No (Yes)

    prompt. Next, select **Yes**.

5. Press F7 to return to the document.

You won't see the summary information on the screen and it won't be printed along with the document. However, it will appear when you look at a document from the directory listing using the **File List Files** (F5) command (Figure 4.10.)

Notice the command line options at the bottom of the screen. You can use these options to display other files, display the text, print the summary, or save it as a separate disk file. If you select **Look** at text, the text of the document appears along with the usual **Next** and **Previous** options, which were explained in Lesson 9. A **Look** at Document Summary option will now be available to return to the summary screen.

You can also print the summary or save it as a file from the Summary menu. Save it as a separate file by pressing F10. The prompt

Enter filename:

will appear. Type the name for the file, then press ◄─┘.

From the Summary menu, press Shift-F7 to print the summary.

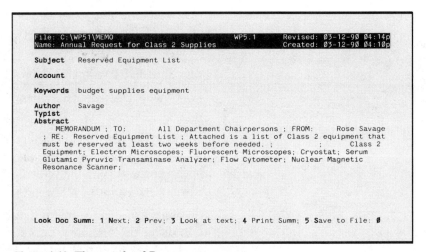

Figure 4.10: *The completed Document summary*

Comments

When you enter a document comment, first place the cursor where you want the comment to appear in the text. Comments usually relate to a specific section of text, unlike a summary, which refers to the entire document.

Follow these steps to add a comment to the text on the screen:

1. Place the cursor after the heading, just before the first paragraph.

2. Select **Edit Comment** (Ctrl-F5 C) to display the Comment menu.

3. Select **Create**, as in Figure 4.11, to display the Document Comment window. The Document Comment window is shown in Figure 4.12.

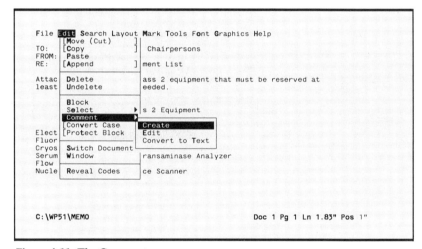

Figure 4.11: The Comment menu

You can enter up to 1,024 characters in the comment box.

4. Type

Make sure the complete list is enclosed for all departments

5. Press F7 to return to the document. The comment appears in the text, surrounded by a box, as shown in Figure 4.13.

*E*diting and Printing Comments

Although the comments appear on the screen, they will not be printed along with the document and you cannot edit them as you would edit

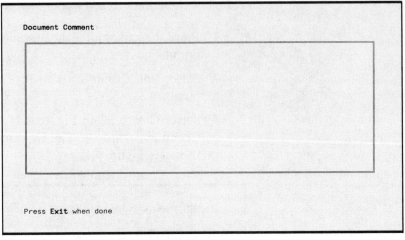

Figure 4.12: *Document Comment window*

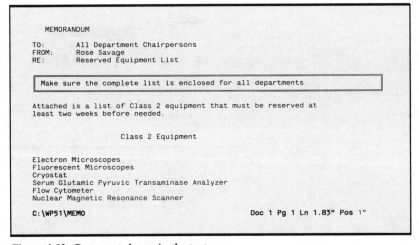

Figure 4.13: *Comment shown in the text*

normal text. To print them, you must first convert the comment to regular text. To edit them, you must redisplay the Comment screen.

Start by selecting **Edit Comment** (Ctrl-F5 C).

To edit a comment, select Edit. WordPerfect will display the first comment above the cursor position. Edit the comment and press F7.

To convert a comment to regular text, select Convert to **T**ext from the Comment menu. The box surrounding the first comment above the cursor position will disappear but the text will remain. Since it is now regular text, it will be printed along with your document. Later you'll learn how to convert regular text into a nonprinting comment.

Finally, to delete a comment, place the cursor just before it and press Del, or just following it and press Backspace. You'll see the prompt

Delete [Comment]? No (Yes)

Select **Yes** to delete the comment from the document.

Save the current document by selecting **F**ile **E**xit (FY), selecting **Y**es, typing *MEMO*, and pressing ⏎. Select **Y**es if you are not ready to continue with the next lesson. Otherwise, select **N**o to clear the screen.

This chapter covered several fundamental formatting commands. In Chapter 5 you'll learn how to format characters in order to bring attention to important points.

5

Formatting Characters for Emphasis and Variety

Featuring

Boldface and underline

Uppercase/lowercase

Superscripts and subscripts

Type styles and sizes

Viewing Documents

WordPerfect 5.1 combines a full-featured word processing program with the most practical aspects of a desktop publisher and page composition system: an unbeatable combination that enables you to produce newsletters, combine graphics with text, and create publication-quality documents.

While WordPerfect can't replace full-featured desktop publishers such as Ventura Publisher or PageMaker, it is ideal for giving that professional published look to all of your documents.

Using the ABC's approach, let's tackle the task in three steps.

Step A, formatting characters, is covered in this chapter. Here you'll learn how to use your printer's capabilities to produce text using different type styles and sizes.

Step B, arranging the text on the page, is discussed in several chapters that follow, including Chapter 12, where you'll learn how to create multicolumn documents.

Step C, adding graphics to your document, is discussed in Chapter 18. This is a complex subject, so we'll just cover the basics in this book.

Before going on, however, keep in mind that your printer may not be able to reproduce all of the features discussed in this chapter. So don't be surprised if your printouts don't look like the examples shown here. There's nothing wrong with your printer—it just doesn't have all of the capabilities discussed.

Also remember that you won't be able to see all of the features— even those that can be printed—on the screen. For instance, underlined characters may appear underlined, in reverse (highlighted), or even in a different color, depending on your computer. Monochrome monitors, for example, display normal, bold, underlined, reversed, and blinking characters. Most color systems will display the various type styles using colors instead.

*L*esson 25—How to Boldface, Underline, and Change the Appearance of Your Text

Do you want to make a particular word or phrase stand out from the rest? Is there an important point that you want to make sure is not missed by the reader? You can emphasize text by printing it boldfaced, underlined, or both.

Boldfaced text will appear darker than surrounding characters because the printer actually strikes (prints) each character twice. This results in a darker, slightly thicker image that catches the reader's eye. Underlining has the same eye-catching effect. You can boldface or underline text as you type it or afterward. Since the steps are similar for printing boldface and underlines, both are included in this one lesson.

All character formatting is performed using the Font pull down menu (or the function key commands). The Font pull down menu is shown in Figure 5.1.

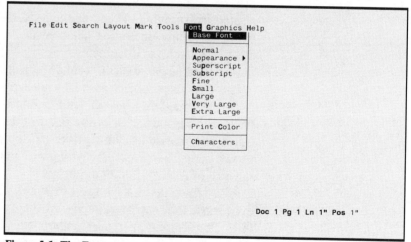

Figure 5.1: The Font menu

*B*oldfacing and Underlining As You Type

From the keyboard, just press F6, type the characters, then press F6 again to create bold-face text.

To boldface characters as you type them:

1. Select Font **A**ppearance. The Appearance submenu appears, as in Figure 5.2.

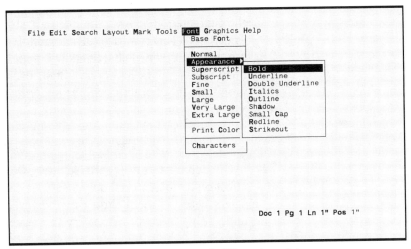

Figure 5.2: Selecting Font Appearance to boldface characters

In this section, we'll concentrate on the Bold and Underline options. The remaining appearances will be discussed shortly.

2. Select **Bold**.

3. Type the characters.

4. Press End or press → once.

If you reveal the codes, boldface on appears as [BOLD], boldface off as [bold]. When you pressed End or the → key, you moved the cursor to the right of the [bold] code so the next characters entered will be normal. You could also stop boldfacing by selecting Font Normal from the pull down menu.

When boldface is turned on, the position indicator in the status line will also appear boldfaced. If you have a color or graphics monitor, boldfaced characters will appear either as a different color or as brighter than surrounding text.

To underline characters as you type them:

From the keyboard, just press F8, type the characters, then press F8 again to underline characters.

1. Select **Font Appearance Underline**.

2. Type the characters.

3. Press End or press → once.

Underlining codes are [UND] and [und]. When underlining is on, the characters following the *Pos* indicator will appear the same way underlined characters do on the screen. If you have a color or graphics monitor, underlined characters will appear either as a different color or in reverse (dark letters on a light background). On monochrome monitors, the characters will be underlined.

Boldfacing or Underlining Existing Characters

Once characters are typed, selecting Bold or Underline will have no effect on them; it would only insert the codes in the text with no characters between them. You can, however, easily add boldfacing or underlining to existing text. Try this now:

1. Start WordPerfect and type

   This text is boldfaced.
   This text is underlined.
   This text is both.

2. Place the cursor on the letter *b* of *boldfaced*.

3. Select **Edit Block** (Alt-F4). The words *Block on* will blink in the status line. The Block function can be used to perform some powerful text manipulations, as you'll see in Chapter 10.

4. Press the → key to move the cursor to the end of the line. Notice that the characters become highlighted, or reversed, as the cursor moves over them (Figure 5.3).

5. Select **Font Appearance Bold** (F6). The highlighting disappears and the text is boldfaced.

To block text with the mouse, place the mouse pointer at one end of the text, hold down the left button, then drag the pointer to the other end of the text.

```
This text is boldfaced.
This text is underlined.
This text is both.
```

Figure 5.3: The Block function highlighting characters

6. Now underline the second sentence:

    a. Place the cursor on the *u* in *underlined*.

    b. Select **Edit B**lock (Alt-F4).

    c. Press the → key until the word is highlighted.

    d. Select **F**ont **A**ppearance Underline (F8).

7. Now underline and boldface the entire final sentence:

    a. Place the cursor at the start of the third sentence.

    b. Select **Edit B**lock (Alt-F4).

    c. Press End.

    d. Select **F**ont **A**ppearance **B**old (F6).

    e. Select **Edit B**lock (Alt-F4).

    f. Press Home ←.

    g. Select **F**ont **A**ppearance Underline (F8).

8. Make sure your printer is ready, then select **F**ile **P**rint **F**ull (Shift-F7 F) to print the three formatted lines.

Compare the printout with Figure 5.4. If your text does not appear boldfaced or underlined, make sure you have the proper printer selected.

> This text is **boldfaced.**
> This text is <u>underlined.</u>
> **This text is <u>both.</u>**

Figure 5.4: Text with underline, boldface, and both

Deleting Boldface and Underline

You can delete both styles with the codes either revealed or hidden. When codes are revealed, place the cursor on either the starting [BOLD] [UND] codes or the ending [bold] [und] codes and press Del.

When codes are not revealed, place the cursor on the first character of the formatted text. If the *Pos* indicator is not boldfaced or underlined, the cursor is actually under the code, even though it appears to be under the first character. Press Del Y to delete the code.

However, if the characters following the *Pos* indicator is boldfaced or underlined, then the cursor is on the character, not the code. Press the ← key once. The cursor will remain in the same position but the *Pos* indicator will become normal. Then press Del Y.

Underline Styles

By default, WordPerfect uses a single continuous underline, which means that both words and the spaces between words are underlined, but you can change the underline style to non-continuous. With non-continuous underlining, lines appear under words but not spaces. Lines also appear under the blank spaces that are inserted when you press Tab. Here's how:

1. Place the cursor at the location where you want to change the underline style. You can change the style for text already underlined or for new text you're about to type. To change existing underlining, place the cursor before the text. Like all codes, this affects only the text following it in the document.

2. Select Layout Other (Shift-F8 O) to reveal the Format: Other menu shown in Figure 5.5.

3. Select Underline to place the cursor on the Underline Spaces option. Select No for non-continuous underlining or Yes for continuous. The cursor moves automatically to the Underline Tabs selection. When you select non-continuous underline, the code [Undrln:] is inserted—[Undrln: Spaces] will appear if you later select continuous underlining.

4. Select Yes if you want to underline tab spaces, No if you don't. The possible codes are [Undrln: Spaces, Tabs], which underlines both tabs and spaces, or [Undrln:Tabs], which underlines just tabs.

5. Press F7 to return to the document.

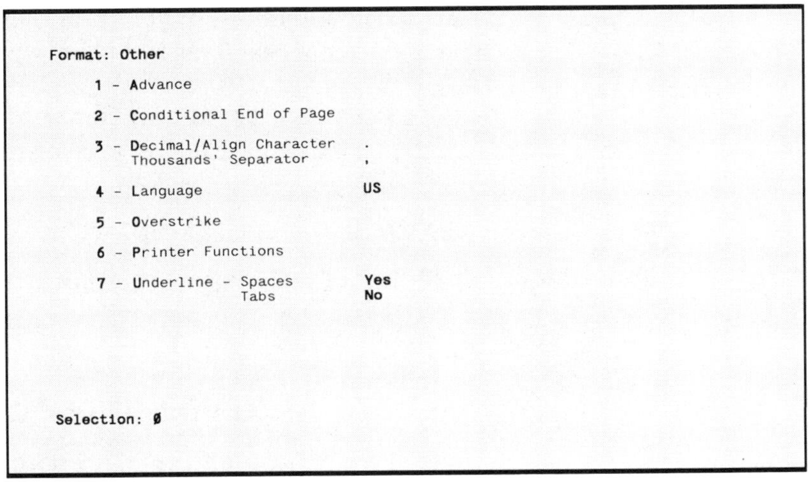

```
Format: Other

    1 - Advance

    2 - Conditional End of Page

    3 - Decimal/Align Character        .
        Thousands' Separator           ,

    4 - Language                       US

    5 - Overstrike

    6 - Printer Functions

    7 - Underline - Spaces             Yes
                    Tabs               No




    Selection: 0
```

Figure 5.5: *Format: Other menu*

6. Select **File Exit** (F7) **No No** to clear the screen without saving the text.

When you underline text, spaces inserted with the spacebar are underlined (or appear in reverse or color) on screen unless you select non-continuous style. Tab spaces will also conform to the selected style on screen, underlined or not, depending on your selection on the Format: Other menu.

Just like other format commands, the change in underline style affects all text below the cursor position. So to change styles later in the document, repeat these steps and select the type of underlining you want. If you change your mind and want to return any underlined text to the default, delete the [Underln:] code.

Other Appearance Options

While boldface and underline are the most used character formats, you can select any or all of the formats listed in the Appearance menu (see Figure 5.2). Select them just as you did Bold and Underline, either as you type or by blocking existing text.

In Chapter 19, you'll learn how to use accented characters and special symbols, and how to create mathematical formulas.

But for now, as a test of your printer, let's try using all of the possible character appearances just to see what your printer can do.

1. Select Font **A**ppearance **D**ouble Underline (Ctrl-F8 A D). The *Pos* indicator will change color or appearance depending on your computer hardware.

2. Type *Double underline.*

3. Press End or the → key. You can also select **N**ormal. Remember, the text may not appear underlined on the screen.

4. Press ←⎯.

5. Select Font **A**ppearance **I**talics (Ctrl-F8 A I).

6. Type *Italic,* press the → key once, then press ←⎯. Again, the text may change color or appear in reverse, depending on your system.

7. Select Font **A**ppearance **O**utline (Ctrl-F8 A O).

8. Type *Outline,* press → then ←⎯.

9. Select Font **A**ppearance Shadow (Ctrl-F8 A A).

10. Type *Shadow,* press → then ←⎯.

11. Select Font **A**ppearance Small **C**ap (Ctrl-F8 A C).

12. Type *Small caps,* press → then ←⎯.

13. Select Font **A**ppearance **R**edline (Ctrl-F8 A R). You use redline printing to designate text that you'd like to add to the document.

14. Type *Redline,* press → then ←⎯.

15. Select Font **A**ppearance **S**trikeout (Ctrl-F8 A S). Strikeout is for text you'd like to delete. Use these options when making tentative changes to a document, or when working with another individual.

16. Type *Strikeout,* press → then ←⎯.

17. Select **F**ile **P**rint **F**ull (Shift-F7 F) to print a copy of the test document.

Figure 5.6 shows a sample printout made with a Hewlett-Packard LaserJet printer using downloadable soft fonts.

Double underline
Italic
Outline
Shadow
SMALL CAPS
Redline
Strikeout

Figure 5.6: Sample print styles

Your own printout will show which types of appearances your printer can produce. Keep it handy when you're typing a real document.

Combining Styles

In each of the examples above, you returned the style back to normal before selecting the next. That way, each line was formatted in only one way—either italic or underlined, for example. If you didn't revert back to normal (by pressing End or the → key), the styles would be combined. Depending on your printer, some combinations may not be possible, such as italic small capitals. You'll just have to experiment with possible combinations.

Changing the Appearance of Existing Characters

If you want to change the appearance of text you've already entered, you must first block it like you did for boldface and underlining. To do this, place the cursor at the start of the text you wish to change and select **Edit B**lock (Alt-F4). Move the cursor to the end of the text and select the appearance desired.

To return formatted characters to normal, display the codes and delete the Appearance codes in the text.

Removing Redline and Strikeout

While you can remove the Redline and Strikeout codes in the same way, these serve special purposes. Remember, you strike out text to show that you'd like to delete it, and you redline text that you'd like to add. So if you really want to make these changes you can have WordPerfect do the final editing for you.

Before printing the document, follow these steps. You'll be using the Mark pull down menu, a powerful menu that's also used to create a table of contents, an index, and other reference sections. These uses, however, are beyond the scope of this book.

1. Select **Mark** (Alt-F5) to display the Mark menu, which is shown in Figure 5.7, and **G**enerate to display the Mark Text: Generate menu, which is shown in Figure 5.8.

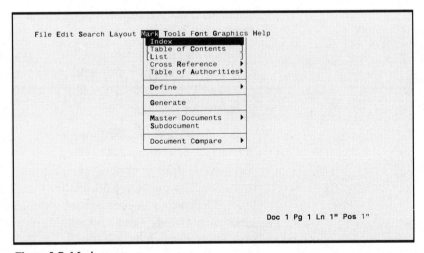

Figure 5.7: *Mark menu*

2. Select *1*. The prompt line changes to

    Delete redline markings and strikeout text? No (Yes)

3. Select **Y**es.

Any text that has been formatted as strikeout will be deleted, and the redline markings will be removed.

```
Mark Text: Generate

    1 - Remove Redline Markings and Strikeout Text from Document

    2 - Compare Screen and Disk Documents and Add Redline and Strikeout

    3 - Expand Master Document

    4 - Condense Master Document

    5 - Generate Tables, Indexes, Cross References, etc.







Selection: 0
```

Figure 5.8: Mark Text: Generate menu

Summary

Because you've learned a number of options in this lesson, let's review the basic pattern.

1. Type until you want to set the appearance of characters, or use **E**dit **B**lock (Alt-F4) to highlight existing text as a block.

2. Select the style desired from the **F**ont **A**ppearance menu (Ctrl-F8 A).

3. If you've been entering new characters rather than working with a block, press End, the → key, or select **F**ont **N**ormal (Ctrl-F8 N).

Lesson 26—How to Control the Uppercase/Lowercase Option

Have you ever accidentally pressed the Caps Lock key, then discovered several lines later that everything is in uppercase? Or have you typed titles in lowercase letters and then decided they would have greater impact in all uppercase? With the Edit Convert Case options (Figure 5.9) you can quickly change the case of a series of characters.

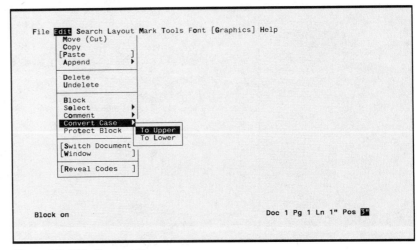

Figure 5.9: *Edit Convert Case menu*

From the keyboard, press Shift-F3.

To change all uppercase letters to lowercase, or vice versa, first highlight the text with the Edit Block command and cursor keys, then select **E**dit Convert Case to show the conversion options.

Select To **U**pper to make the highlighted block all uppercase characters, or **L**ower for lowercase. Note that Convert Case is only available when the block function is on. Otherwise, it appears in the menu as [Convert Case] but cannot be selected.

Unlike other format commands, this inserts no codes into the text. It just changes the case of the characters. To reverse your action, highlight the same text and select the opposite case.

Lesson 27—How to Change the Size and Position of Characters

In this lesson you'll take character formatting one step further into desktop publishing. You'll learn to print characters as subscripts and superscripts, and in sizes: fine, small, large, very large, and extra large (Figure 5.10). But except for superscripts and subscripts, which most printers can do, many printers will not be able to print in the different sizes and styles that we discuss here. And remember, you won't normally see any difference in the way characters appear on the screen.

H_2O
Footnote goes here[1]
Fine
Small
Normal
Large
Very Large
Extra Large

Figure 5.10: Sample character positions and font sizes

But first a little background.

A *type style* refers to the general shape of a character. Some type styles have small cross-strokes at the ends of letters—called *serifs*—and some don't—*sanserif*.

If you take all of the letters, numbers and punctuation marks of one type style in one size, you have a *font*. Fonts are measured in *points*. There are approximately 72 points to an inch, so a 12-point typeface will fit six lines of type in 1 inch of space.

A 12-point font will contain all of the characters of a type style in that size. The 12-point bold font of the same type style contains the same characters but in boldface, just as 12-point italic contains all italic characters.

With WordPerfect you can print all of the type styles and sizes that your printer allows. For some printers, this may mean only one style and one size. But many dot-matrix printers, for example, can print several sizes of characters. And laser printers can print a variety of shapes and sizes.

The main type style used is called the *base font*. This is the default character style used for normal characters. Other sizes and appearances are just variations on the base font. If your printer allows, you can change the base font to another style. That way you could have more than one style in the same document.

Let's see how to change font sizes, and test your printer at the same time. By the way, you can change font size and type style without worrying about the margins. WordPerfect will automatically adjust the margin and line spacing settings to accommodate your choice.

1. Select Font Base Font (Ctrl-F8 F) to see the possible base fonts available on your printer. The one marked with an asterisk is the default font assigned to your printer. All of the font sizes are determined from the base font. For example, Figure 5.11 shows the base fonts available for a laser printer containing *downloaded* fonts. These are type styles that are stored on a disk and loaded into the printer when needed.

```
Base Font

     Cooper Black 30pt (LS) (LF)
     Cooper Black 30pt (LS) (Outline) (LF)
     Cooper Black 30pt (LS) (Shadow) (LF)
     Coronet/Ribbon 18pt (LS) (LF)
     Courier 10 pitch (Roman-8)
     Courier Bold 10 pitch (A/C/L/Q)
     Courier Italic 10 pitch (A/C/L/Q)
     Helvetica/Swiss  6pt (US) (LF)
     Helvetica/Swiss 10pt (US) (LF)
   * Helvetica/Swiss 12pt (US) (LF)
     Helvetica/Swiss 12pt (US) Bold (LF)
     Helvetica/Swiss 12pt (US) Bold Italic (LF)
     Helvetica/Swiss 12pt (US) Italic (LF)
     Helvetica/Swiss 14pt (US) (LF)
     Helvetica/Swiss 18pt (US) (LF)
     Helvetica/Swiss 24pt (US) (LF)
     Line Draw 10 pitch
     Line Printer 16.66 pitch (Roman-8)
     Olde English 20pt (US) (LF)
     Script 20pt (US) (LF)
     Times Roman/Dutch  6pt (US) (LF)

 1 Select; N Name search: 1
```

Figure 5.11: *Base fonts for a LaserJet +*

WordPerfect uses built-in ratios for selecting font sizes based on the point-size of the base font. You can see these ratios, and change them, in the File Setup menu.

In this case, the base font is called Helvetica/Swiss 12 pt. (for *point*). The large font in this typeface would be the next size, 14 pt., the very large would be 18 pt., and the extra large, 24 pt.

However, if you changed the base font to 10 pt., everything would shift down—large would be 12 pt., very large 14 pt., and extra large 18 pt.

Look carefully at Figure 5.11. What sizes would be available if the base font were changed to Courier 10 pt.? None, because there are no other sizes in that typeface.

2. Press F7.

3. Pull down the Font menu (Ctrl-F8 S).

Don't select anything now, but when you want to change size or position, select your choice from this menu, type the characters, then press End, the → key, or select **Normal** to return the characters to normal.

4. Press F7 for now.

If you select a new size, WordPerfect will automatically compute the proper margins and line spacing for you.

Let's see what positions and sizes your printer handles. Follow these steps to enter the text shown in Figure 5.10:

1. Type *H*.

2. Select Font Subscript (Ctrl-F8 S B).

3. Type *2*.

4. Press END to return the position to normal, then type *0*.

5. Press ←, then type *Footnote goes here.*

6. Select Font Superscript (Ctrl-F8 S P).

7. Type *1*, then the → key to move the cursor beyond the Superscript code.

8. Press ←.

9. Select Font Fine (Ctrl-F8 S F).

10. Type *Fine,* press →, then ←.

11. Select Font Small (Ctrl-F8 S S).

12. Type *Small,* press → then ←.

13. Type *Normal,* then press ←.

14. Select Font Large (Ctrl-F8 S L).

15. Type *Large,* press →, then ←.

16. Select Font Very Large (Ctrl-F8 S V).

17. Type *Very large,* press → then ←.

18. Select Font Extra Large (Ctrl-F8 S E).

19. Type *Extra large,* press → then ←.

20. Select **File** **P**rint **F**ull (Shift-F7 F) to print a copy of the test document. Compare your printout with Figure 5.10. Keep in mind that my figure was printed on a LaserJet + with several downloaded fonts.

You can have more than one size on a line and you can change the appearance of various sizes, to produce large bold characters, for example. Of course, you are always limited to the capabilities of your printer.

Changing Font Families

You can have more than one type style in a document if your printer is capable. When you want to print a character other than in the base font, change to the base font containing the desired style.

To change the base font, select **F**ont **B**ase Font (Ctrl-F8 4) to display the available fonts, use the arrow keys to move the highlighting to the one you want, and press ← F7.

You can also change the default base font that WordPerfect uses every time you start the program. Here's how:

1. Select **File** **P**rint (Shift-F7).

2. Select **S**elect Printer, then **E**dit to display the Printer Selection Edit menu, just as you did in Appendix B.

3. Select **I**nitial Base **F**ont. The list of possible fonts will appear on the screen.

4. Highlight the base font using the arrow keys, press ←, then F7 three times to return to the document window. That base font will be used as the default whenever you start Word-Perfect.

Changing the Position or Size of Existing Characters

To change the position or size of text you've already entered, place the cursor at the start of the text you wish to change, then select **E**dit **B**lock. Move the cursor to the end of the text, then select the **A**ppearance.

To return reformatted characters to normal, display the codes, then delete the Size codes in the text.

Font Sizes and the Position Indicator

In Chapter 1 you learned that the *Pos* indicator in the status line shows the character position of the cursor. Using the default settings, the position indicator changes in one tenth of an inch increments as you type across the page— 1.0, 1.1, 1.2, etc. This changes when you're using font sizes that will not fit ten characters in each inch of space.

With fixed-width fonts, every character is the same size, and the *Pos* indicator changes by the same amount with each character typed. For example, using a 14-point fixed-width font, each character is approximately .12 of an inch. So allowing for rounding of fractions, the *Pos* indicator changes from 1.0, to 1.12, to 1.23, to 1.35, etc.

With proportional spaced fonts, each character takes up just the space it needs. Using Times Roman/Dutch 24-point, for example, the letter *W* requires .3 inches, while the lowercase *i* requires only .08 of an inch. The *Pos* indicator adjusts according to each individual character.

WordPerfect, however, will maintain the proper margin spacing no matter what size type you're using, and the character count will be different for each size.

In the next chapter you'll take formatting one step further by learning how to control the position of lines. You'll learn how to center text, align it with the right margin, and set and use tab stops.

Lesson 28—How to View Documents

A document appears on the screen just as it will when printed, with a few exceptions. For example, the displayed text will be one size and not justified. Page numbers, headers, footers, and footnotes (all to be discussed later) will not appear on the screen, just on the final copy. However, you may want to see exactly how formatting commands such as character size will affect the final appearance of your document.

That's when you use the View mode.

Use this command to see on screen exactly how the document will appear on paper. I view all complex documents before printing. This way I can confirm that the final copy will appear like I imagined it would when I set the formats. Viewing the document is particularly useful when using different size fonts or using WordPerfect's Graphics commands for page composition. For example, Figure 5.12 shows a page containing both text and graphics in View mode. This page also demonstrates the desktop publishing abilities of WordPerfect, and its ability to create formulas and special symbols. (These subjects are discussed in Chapters 18 and 19.)

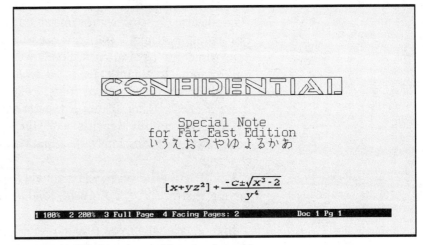

Figure 5.12: *Viewing a page with text and graphics*

How your documents appear in View mode depends on your computer hardware—the type of graphic board you have installed and the resolution of the monitor. But even without high resolution, View mode is a powerful tool.

Let's use the current document, which includes several font sizes, to see how View works.

1. Select **File Print** (Shift-F7).

2. Select **View** Document.

The screen changes to View mode with the current page displayed on the screen (Figure 5.13). You can't edit or format the text while viewing it.

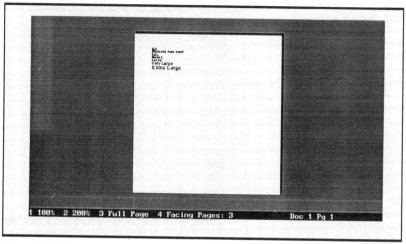

Figure 5.13: Document in View mode

The characters may not be totally legible in this mode, but you can get the general impression of how the document will look when it is printed.

The options at the bottom of the screen let you enlarge or reduce the displayed page. By default your screen shows the full page, option 3. But you can enlarge the display to show the page at its actual size (option 1—100%) or twice its size (option 2—200%). You can also see how two adjacent pages will appear. In book form, page 1 is always on top. So adjacent pages can only be displayed for facing pages such as 2 and 3, 4 and 5, etc.

3. Press *2* to display the page at 200 percent (Figure 5.14).

    Now the characters are fully readable. But the document is too large to be seen on the screen at one time.

4. Press → to scroll the screen. You can use any of the directional arrows to scroll through the displayed document. If your document is more then one page, use PgDn and PgUp to move from page to page.

5. Press F7 twice to return to the document.

94

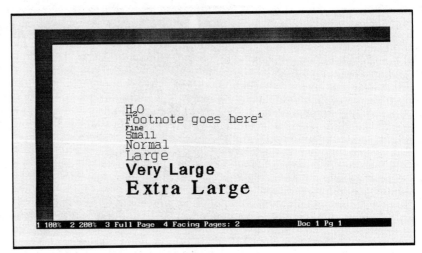

Figure 5.14: Document viewed at 200 percent

We'll be using the View mode throughout this book to see how our documents will look when printed.

6

Aligning Text and Creating Tables

Featuring

Centering text

Flush right alignment

Tabs

Creating tables

*L*esson 29—How to Center Text

You can center *single lines* of text as you type them, or as many lines of existing text as you want.

*C*entering New Text

Let's use the Center command to type a title page.

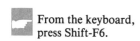
From the keyboard, press Shift-F6.

1. Start WordPerfect.

2. Press ⏎ six times.

3. Select Layout Align (Figure 6.1).

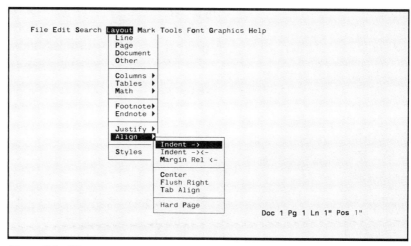

Figure 6.1: *Align menu*

In this chapter you'll learn how to use the Center and Flush Right options on the Align menu. The other selections will be discussed later.

Selecting Layout
Align **Center**
(Shift-F6) twice inserts
dot leaders.

4. Select **C**enter. The cursor moves to the center of the screen.

5. Type

   The History of the World

   Characters will alternately move to the left and right, remaining centered.

6. Press ⏎ twice.

7. In the same way, select **Layout Align Center** (Shift-F6).

8. Type

   by

9. Press ⏎ twice.

10. Select **Layout Align Center** (Shift-F6).

11. Type your name.

12. Press ⏎.

   A Begin Center code [Center] will be placed at the start of the text. If the text wraps to the next line, only the first line will be centered. Since the cursor was at the far left margin when you selected Center, the text was centered between the left and right margins. If you select Center when the cursor is not at the margin, the cursor position becomes the centering point. This is covered in detail in Lesson 31.

13. Select **File Exit** (F7) **No No** to clear the screen without saving the text.

*C*entering Existing Text

To center existing text:

1. Place the cursor anywhere in the first line.

2. Select **Edit Block** (Alt-F4).

3. Move the cursor to the end of the last line to be centered, highlighting the block.

4. Select **Layout Align Center** (Shift-F6) to see the prompt

   [Just:Center]? No **(Yes)**

5. Select **Yes**.

Each line in the highlighted block will be centered on the screen. The code [Just:Center] is inserted at the start of the text, the code [Just:Full] at the end. You'll learn more about the justification option in Chapter 7.

You can center a single line of text without blocking it first. Place the cursor at the start of the line, then select **Layout Align Center** (Shift-F6). If the line doesn't end in a carriage return, press End, then ⏎ to center the text correctly.

Let's see how block centering works.

1. Type

   The History of the World
   by
   J. Paul Samsom

   A detailed study of the history of the world from 3000 BC
   to the present time

2. Press ⏎.

3. Press Home Home ↑ to place the cursor on the first line.

4. Select **Edit Block** (Alt-F4).

5. Press Home Home ↓ to highlight the entire text.

6. Select **Layout Align Center** (Shift-F6) **Yes**. The text is centered on the screen.

7. Press Home Home ↑.

8. Select **Edit Reveal Codes** (Alt-F3) to reveal the codes. Notice the codes surrounding the text (Figure 6.2).

9. Select **Edit Reveal Codes** (Alt-F3) to remove the code display.

10. Select **File Exit** (F7) **No No** to clear the screen and remain in WordPerfect.

Uncentering Text

To uncenter the text, delete either the [Center] or [Just:Center] code. Without revealing codes, you can place the cursor at the left margin of the centered line and press Del Y.

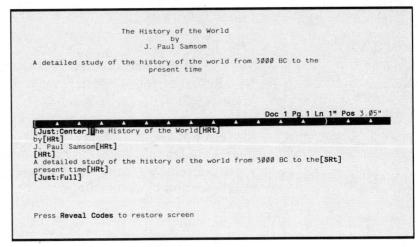

Figure 6.2: *Text centered as a block*

*L*esson 30—*How to Align Text Flush Right*

Flush right text is aligned on the right margin with an uneven margin on the left—just the opposite from regular unjustified text.

This format is most commonly used in business announcements and programs like the one below:

Introduction	Ryan Hyde
	President
Honor Awards	Jack Fanelli
	Vice President
Special Announcements	Margaret Shelby
	Treasurer
Closing Remarks	John Ryan
	Secretary

Aligning New Text on the Right

To align text on the right as you type it:

1. Select **Layout Align Flush Right** (Alt-F6). The cursor will move to the right margin.

2. Type the text. Characters entered will move to the left. If the text reaches the left margin, word-wrap will take effect and remaining lines will appear as normal.

3. Press ←.

The [Flsh Rgt] code is inserted at the start of the text.

Aligning Existing Text on the Right

To align existing text on the right:

1. Place the cursor *at the start* of the first line.

2. Select **Edit Block** (Alt-F4).

3. Drag the cursor to the end of the last line to highlight the block.

4. Select **Layout Align Flush Right** (Alt-F6) to display this prompt:

   [Just:Right]? No (Yes)

5. Select **Yes**.

Each line in the highlighted block will be aligned on the right. The code [Just:Right] is inserted at the start of the text, the code [Just:Full] at the end.

You can align a single line of text flush right without blocking it first. Place the cursor at the start of the line, then select **Layout Align Flush Right** (Alt-F6). If the line doesn't end in a carriage return, press End, then ← to align the text correctly.

Combining Left and Right Text

To format text as it is commonly used in business announcements and programs, with one column left-justified and the other column right-justified, type the text you want to appear at the left of the page, then select **F**lush Right. Just make sure the flush right text does not collide with the characters on the left.

Returning Flush Right Text to Normal

To realign the text at the left margin, delete either the [Flsh Rgt] or the [Just:Right] code. Without revealing codes, you can place the cursor at the left margin of the aligned text and press Del Y.

Lesson 31—How to Set Tabs

Tab stops are among those little things in life that can mean so much. Sometimes, like me, you might not use tabs for anything more than indenting the first line of a paragraph. But by setting tab stops, you can align columns on the page to create tables and lists, a table of contents, or forms.

A tab stop, for those of you not familiar with the old-fashioned typewriter, is a set position on the screen. When you press the Tab key, the cursor moves directly to the closest tab stop to the right. So rather than press the spacebar five times to indent the line, press the Tab key once. Press Tab again to move another five characters.

By default, WordPerfect sets tab stops every $1/2$ inch. But you can easily change these and set your own through the Line option on the Layout pull down menu (Shift-F8 L).

Column Alignment

How text aligns in columns when you press the Tab key depends on the type of tab stop you set. Text can be aligned on the left, right, or center. Columns of numbers can be aligned by the decimal point. And all tab stops can be set so a row of dots, called *dot leaders,* appears in the blank space before the text.

Left-aligned columns use regular tab stops:

William Morris
Sam Spady
Jane Pascalli

Other columns are centered, but not necessarily between the right and left margins:

William Morris
Sam Spady
Jane Pascalli

Decimal columns are aligned on the decimal point. Notice that numbers aligned on the decimal point are easier to read than left-aligned numeric columns:

345.34   345.34
.09   .09
23,456.00   23,456.00
1.12   1.12

Right-aligned columns resemble flush right text, but they are not at the far right margin.

William Morris
Sam Spady
Jane Pascalli

Finally, dot leader tabs can be of any of the above types, but periods fill the blank area preceding the text entered at the tab:

President. . . . . .William Morris
Vice President . . . . .Sam Spady
Executive Director .Jane Pascalli

Setting Tab Stops

The tab stops you set affect only the text from the cursor down. Follow these steps to enter several different types of tab stops:

1. Select **Layout Line** (Shift-F8 L).

   The Tab Set option shows the default tab stops—tabs every ¹/₂ inch starting one inch to the left of the left margin. REL means that the tabs are relative to the left margin, not the edge of the page. A tab at one inch, for example, will always be one inch from the margin. If you change the left margin, the tab will move along with it.

   You can change the tabs to absolute—measured from the left edge of the paper. In this mode, a tab set at one inch will always be one inch from the left of the page. Changing the margin will have no effect on the tab stop.

2. Select **Tab Set** to display the Tab Set form (Figure 6.3).

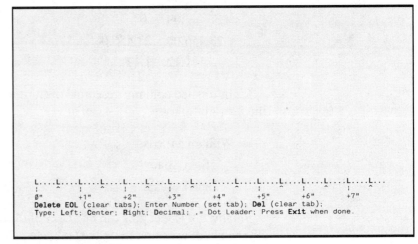

Figure 6.3: *Tab Set form*

The ruler line represents positions starting at the left margin of the page. Since tabs are set as relative, the 0" position represents the left margin, 1" is one inch from the margin, etc. If you pressed the ← key, the line would shift and the − 1" position would appear—one inch to the left of the default margin, or the edge of the page.

Half-inch positions are marked by a caret (^) and each of the default left-aligned tabs is represented by an *L*. Tabs are set up to 13" (14 inch absolute), although you can set your own up to $53^{1}/_{2}$" ($54^{1}/_{2}$" absolute).

The cursor will appear in the ruler line at the same position it was in the text. When you exit the Tab Set menu, the cursor will appear in that same position.

Below the ruler line are instructions for setting and clearing tab stops.

- To set a tab use →, ←, or the spacebar to reach the tab position you want. The line will scroll if you move the cursor past the margins. Once the cursor is at the desired position,

    - Press *L* for a left-aligned tab;

    - Press *C* for a centered tab;

    - Press *R* for a flush right tab; or

    - Press *D* for a decimal tab.

After indicating the type of tab,

    - Press the period key (.) if you want a dot leader. The letter representing the tab type will appear on the ruler line. Dot leader tabs appear in reverse.

        You can also set a left-aligned tab by just typing its position number and then pressing ←⎯. The cursor will move to that position when you press ←⎯, so to set another type of tab, type *C, E,* or *D*.

- To delete a tab, position the cursor on the tab indicator and press Del. If you delete or change tab stops, any text already entered at those positions will adjust automatically to the new, or default tab stop position.

- To delete all tabs, press Ctrl-End. This will delete all tab stops to the right of the cursor position. To delete all of the tab stops, place the cursor on position − 1 (0 if absolute).

- To set evenly spaced left-aligned tabs, type the starting position number, a comma, then the spacing and ←⎯.

For example, type *1,1* to set tabs every 1 inch, starting 1 inch from the left side of the page.

- To set evenly spaced center, right-aligned, or decimal-aligned tab stops, move the cursor to the starting position and enter the type of tab stop you want. Next, type the starting position number, a comma, then the spacing and ←⏎. The starting position must be at least at 1".

3. The cursor should be at position 0". If not, press Home ←.

4. Press Ctrl-End to delete all of the tabs.

5. Set a center tab at 1 inch.

    a. Move the cursor to the 1-inch position.

    b. Press *C*.

When you type the column, the characters will center themselves around position 2". (They will shift alternately left and right until you press ←⏎ or another tab.)

Why do the characters center themselves around the 2" position when you set the tab at the 1" position on the ruler? Remember, by default, tab stops—and thus the measurements on the tab set ruler—are relative to the left margin. But the position counter on the status line is referenced from the left edge of the page. Using the default 1" margin, the 1" position on the tab set ruler is actually the same position as the 2" measurement on the document's status line.

If you want the ruler line and position indicator to be the same, set the tab as absolute, as I'll explain at the end of this lesson.

6. Set a right-aligned dot leader tab at 5 inches:

    a. Move the cursor to the 5-inch position.

    b. Press *R*.

    c. Press . (the period key). The letter R appears reversed, signifying a dot leader tab.

When you press Tab to reach this tab stop, a series of periods will appear. Since this is a right-aligned tab, the characters will shift to the left to align evenly with position 6".

7. Set a decimal tab at 6 inches.

    a. Move the cursor to the 6-inch position.

    b. Press *D*.

    When you type at this tab stop, all characters will move to the left of position 7" until you type the decimal point. The decimal point will remain at 7" and following characters will move to the right as usual.

Figure 6.4 shows the completed tab stops.

```
.........C...............................R.........D................. ...
          ^       ^       ^       ^       ^       ^       ^
Ø"      +1"     +2"     +3"     +4"     +5"     +6"     +7"
Delete EOL (clear tabs); Enter Number (set tab); Del (clear tab);
Type; Left; Center; Right; Decimal; .= Dot Leader; Press Exit when done.
```

Figure 6.4: *Centered, right-aligned dot leader, and decimal tabs set*

8. Press F7 twice to return to the document.

9. Select **Edit** **R**eveal Codes (Alt-F3) to reveal the codes (Figure 6.5). If you delete the code you will delete all of the tab stops, returning to the default. You can only delete individual tabs through the Tab Stop menu.

10. Select **Edit** **R**eveal Codes (Alt-F3) to remove the code display.

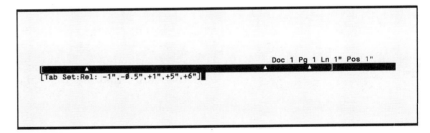

Figure 6.5: *Tab Set code*

Using Tab Stops

All of the tab stops are reached with the Tab key. Text entered will conform to the type of tab that you set. Now you will enter the table shown in Figure 6.6.

```
   Director . . . . . . . . . . . Jane Sugerman    $65,087.00
Assistant Manager. . . . . . . . . .Dean Johnson    $58,500.00
   Supervisor. . . . . . . . . John Earl Paulson    $40,500.00
      Guard. . . . . . . . . . Harvey Smithson      $32,000.00
```

Figure 6.6: A table using three tabs

1. Press Tab and type

   Director

2. Press Tab. Dot leaders will appear (Figure 6.7).

```
   Director . . . . . . . . . . . . . . . . . . . .
```

Figure 6.7: A dot leader tab

3. Type

   Jane Sugerman

   Since this is a right-aligned tab, text will move toward the left.

4. Press Tab. The prompt line shows

   Align char = .

   to let you know that the text will align on the decimal point.

5. Type

   $65,087.00

   With decimal tabs, all text entered moves to the left until the period is pressed. The decimal point will remain at the tab stop position, then following characters will move to the right as normal.

6. Press ⏎.

7. Complete the text as shown in Figure 6.6.

8. Select **F**ile **P**rint **F**ull (Shift-F7 F) to print a copy of the text.

9. Exit the document without saving and start with a new document for the next section.

Aligning Columns As You Type

If you're typing tables or long columns, set tab stops so you don't have to worry about formatting individual entries. However, for short documents, you can quickly simulate centered, right-aligned, and decimal-aligned tabs using regular left-aligned tabs as you type. This way, the default tab stops are left untouched if you need them later in the same document.

Let's see how these formats are created by entering a short inventory table, as shown in Figure 6.8.

```
        Hammers              200           3.45
      Screwdrivers            50           2.56
         Nails              1000            .02
      Socket Sets             10          15.56
```

Figure 6.8: Sample table

1. Press the spacebar or the Tab key to place the cursor at position 2".

2. Select **L**ayout **A**lign **C**enter (Shift-F6).

3. Type

    Hammers

    When you select **C**enter at a position other than the left margin, the text is centered there, rather than between the margins.

4. Press Tab four times to reach position 4".

5. Select **L**ayout **A**lign **T**ab Align (Ctrl-F6). The status line shows

    Align Char = .

and the cursor has moved to the next tab stop on the line.

Tab Align acts like a decimal tab—as you type, the characters shift to the left, instead of to the right as usual, until an Align character is entered. Characters after that move to the right as usual. The default Align character is the period, which is used to create columns of numbers aligned on the decimal point. You can use this feature to create columns that are flush right at positions other than the right margin, as you'll soon see.

6. Type

    200

Since this is a character-aligned tab, text moves toward the left.

7. Press Tab three times.

8. Select **Layout Align Tab Align** (Ctrl-F6).

9. Type

    3.45

The numbers shift left until the decimal point, which stays at the tab stop position just like a decimal-aligned tab.

10. Press ⏎.

11. Complete the text as shown in Figure 6.8. Press Tab the proper number of times to reach position 4" for the second column—three times after typing *Screwdrivers* and *Socket Sets,* four times after *Nails.*

12. Select **File Print Full** (Shift-F7 F) to print a copy of the text.

13. Select **File Exit** (F7) **No No** to exit the document without saving the text.

*C*hanging Tabs

If you change your mind about new tab stops, you can delete them individually or return quickly to the default tab stop every inch.

To delete individual tab stops:

1. Select **Edit Reveal Codes** (Alt-F3) to reveal the codes.

2. Place the cursor immediately after the [Tab Set] code.

3. Select **Edit R**eveal Codes (Alt-F3) to remove the code display.

4. Select **Layout Line Tab** Set (Shift-F8 L T).

5. Position the cursor on the tab stop and press Del.

6. Press F7 twice to return to the document.

The original Tab Set code, including the tab you just deleted, will still be in the text. But the new Tab Set code, closest to the text, will be in force.

To return to the default tab stops:

1. Select **Edit R**eveal Codes (Alt-F3) to reveal the codes.

2. Place the cursor on the [Tab Set] code.

3. Press Del.

4. Select **Edit R**eveal Codes (Alt-F3). The default tab stops are automatically returned.

The text will automatically adjust to the new, or default, tab stop position.

Setting Absolute Tabs

It's easy to set absolute tabs with WordPerfect. When the Tab Set menu is displayed, select **T**ype. The prompt line changes to:

Tab Type: **1** **A**bsolute; **2 R**elative to Margin: 0

Select **A**bsolute. (To later change to relative tabs, select **R**elative to Margin.)

The scale line will change so the 1" measurement indicates the margin position, and 0" the left edge of the paper. The ruler line measurements will now match the position indicator.

Ignoring Tab Type

No matter what type of tab you set—right, center, or decimal—you can still use them as left-aligned tabs. Press Home Tab instead of Tab by itself. The cursor moves to the tab stop position but characters will shift to the right, as if a left tab had been set. This only affects that specific use of the tab, pressing Tab by itself on another line will conform to the alignment you set.

Lesson 32—Creating Tables

In many cases you'll be using tab stops to create tables, neatly ordered rows and columns of words or numbers. Rather than manually calculate and set tabs, however, you can use the new automatic table feature added to WordPerfect 5.1.

This feature includes many advanced and sophisticated powers that are beyond the scope of an ABC's book. In this lesson, however, we'll cover the basics of creating neatly boxed tables. We'll also perform some simple spreadsheet functions.

Creating A Table

Before creating the table, plan the number of rows and columns that you'll need. You'll be able to insert and delete rows and columns as you would in a spreadsheet program, but WordPerfect will request a starting number when you begin.

Let's create the boxed table shown in Figure 6.9. Notice that this table has three columns and four rows.

1. Select **Layout Tables** (Alt-F7 T) to see the Table options (Figure 6.10).

	1989	1990
Gross Income After Taxes	1,474,186.00	1,623,983.00
Expenses	871,927.00	893,145.00
Net Income	602,259.00	730,838.00

Figure 6.9: *Sample boxed table*

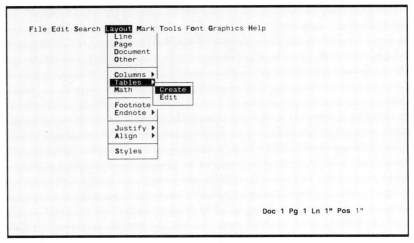

Figure 6.10: Tables menu

2. Select **C**reate. The prompt line displays:

   Number of Columns: 3

3. Press ← to accept the default number of columns. The prompt line changes to:

   Number of Rows: 1

4. Type 4, the number of rows, then press ←. The Table Edit screen appears (Figure 6.11). This menu is used to edit, or change the table structure, not the text that goes into the table.

   The blank table is on the top of the screen, with the first "cell" selected. Options for editing the table are on the bottom. Notice the new status line. In addition to the usual indicators, the line now shows the active cell, in this case cell A1.

   Columns are referenced by letters, rows by numbers. So the top left-hand cell is A1, the one to the right B1, and the one underneath A2, like this:

	A	B	C	D	E
1	A1	B1	C1	D1	E1
2	A2	B2	C2	D2	E2
3	A3	B3	C3	D3	E3
4	A4	B4	C4	D4	E4

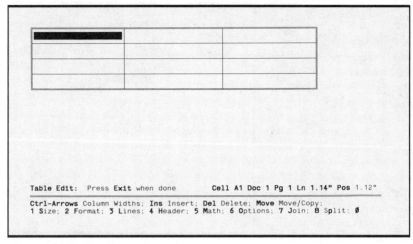

Table Edit: Press **Exit** when done   **Cell A1 Doc 1 Pg 1 Ln 1.14" Pos** 1.12"

Ctrl-Arrows Column Widths; **Ins** Insert; **Del** Delete; **Move** Move/Copy;
1 Size; **2** Format; **3** Lines; **4** Header; **5** Math; **6** Options; **7** Join; **8** Split: **Ø**

Figure 6.11: Table edit menu

5. Press the → key. The highlight moves to the cell on the right and the status line changes to B1.

6. Press the ← key to move back to cell A1.

   Using the options on the prompt line, you can edit the table structure in these ways:

1 Size	Change the number of rows or columns
2 Format	Change the font attributes of cells and columns, and the height of rows
3 Line	Change the type of lines used to draw the boxes (you can even remove the line completely)
4 Header	Designate a row or rows that will appear at the top of every page
5 Math	Perform math on row and cell contents
6 Options	Adjust spacing between text and lines, determine how negative numbers are displayed, set the position of the table on the page, or set a gray shading for the table background

| **7** Join | Combine several cells into one |
| **8** Split | Split a cell into more than one |

Above the prompt line is a list of the keys or key combinations you can use to adjust the appearance of the table:

- Ctrl and an arrow key adjusts the width of columns

- Insert adds rows or columns

- Del deletes rows or columns

- Move (Ctrl-F4) moves or copies cells, rows, or columns

7. Press F7 to accept the table as is and return to the screen. The prompt lines disappear.

Entering Text Into Tables

You are now ready to enter data into the table—the cursor is in cell A1. Notice that the cell number on the status line reads A1.

The cell height will adjust automatically to the amount of text you enter. So if you press ◄─┘ within a cell, the cell will increase by one line height. Use the ↑ and ↓ keys to move up and down within the table, and Tab, ←, and → to move across rows.

1. Press ↓ to reach cell A2.

2. Type

    Gross Income After Taxes

    The word *Taxes* word-wrapped to the next line, automatically expanding the height of the first row (Figure 6.12).

3. Press the ↓ key to reach cell A3, then type *Expenses*.

4. Press the ↓ key to reach cell A4, then type *Net Income*.

5. Use the arrow keys to reach cell B1.

6. Type *1989*. Don't worry for now how the numbers align in the cell.

Gross Income After Taxes		

***Figure 6.12:** Row height adjusts dynamically to accommodate the text.*

7. In the same way, enter *1990* in cell C1.
8. Use the arrow keys to reach cell B2.
9. Type *1,474,186.00.*
10. Complete cell C2.
    a. Press Tab.
    b. Type *1,623,983.00.*
11. Complete cell B3.
    a. Press the ↓ then ← to reach the cell.
    b. Type *871,927.00.*
12. Complete cell C3.
    a. Press Tab.
    b. Type *893,145.00.*

Figure 6.13 shows the table with text entered.

	1989	1990
Gross Income After Taxes	1,474,186.00	1,623,983.00
Expenses	871,927.00	893,145.00
Net Income		

***Figure 6.13:** Text entered in the table*

Entering Formulas and Formatting

Instead of typing entries directly in cells B4 and C4, we'll enter formulas so WordPerfect will compute the numbers for us. We'll also use the Layout Tables Edit menu to align the text properly in the cells.

1. Select **Layout Tables Edit** (Alt-F7 T E). The Table prompt lines reappear.

2. Move the highlight to cell B4, then select **Math**. The status line changes to:

   Math: **1** Calculate; **2** Formula; **3** Copy Formula; **4** +; **5** =;
   6 *: 0

   - **Calculate** recalutes the cells
   - **Formula** allows you to enter a formula within the cell
   - **Copy Formula** copies the formula from one cell to another
   - **+** inserts the subtotal of numbers above the cell
   - **=** inserts the total of numbers above the cell
   - ***** inserts the grand total of numbers above the cell

3. Select **Formula**. The prompt line changes to:

   Enter formula:

4. Type *B2-B3*, then press ←┘. The net income, the difference between cell B2 and B3, appears in cell B4 (Figure 6.14).

5. Enter the formula for net income in cell C4.
   a. Press Tab to reach cell C4.
   b. Select **Math Formula**.
   c. Type *C2-C3*.
   d. Press ←┘ to accept the formula and calculate the total.

   Now let's format the table.

6. Select **Format** to see the prompt line

   Format: **1** Cell; **2** Column, **3** Row Height: 0

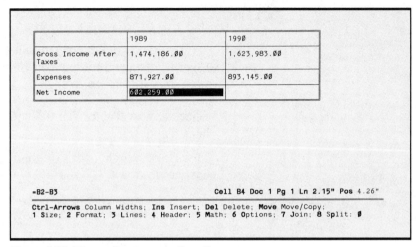

Figure 6.14: The result appears in the cell.

7. Select Col**u**mn. The prompt line changes to

    Column: **1** Width; **2** Attribute; **3** Justify; **4** # Digits: 0

8. Select **J**ustify to see the prompt

    Justification: **1** Left; **2** Center; **3** Right; **4** Full; **5** Decimal Align: 0

9. Select **D**ecimal Align. All of the numbers in column C align on the decimal, including the date (Figure 6.15). We'll take care of that shortly.

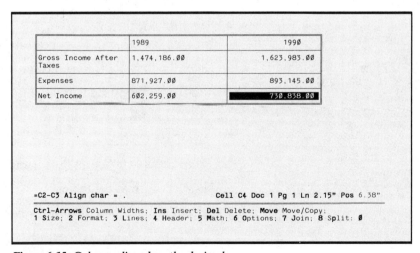

Figure 6.15: Column aligned on the decimal

10. In the same manner, align column B on the decimals.

    a. Press the ← key to reach column B.

    b. Select **Format**.

    c. Select **Column**.

    d. Select **Justify**.

    e. Select **Decimal Align**.

11. Now center the date in cell B1.

    a. Press the ↑ key until you reach cell B1.

    b. Select **Format Column Justify Center**.

12. Center the date in cell C1.

    a. Press the → key until you reach cell C1.

    b. Select **Format Column Justify Center**.

13. Press F7 to exit the Table Edit menu.

Figure 6.16 shows the completed table.

	1989	1990
Gross Income After Taxes	1,474,186.00	1,623,983.00
Expenses	871,927.00	893,145.00
Net Income	602,259.00	730,838.00

Figure 6.16: The completed table

If you change any of the numbers in the table, select **Lay-out Tables Edit**, then select **Math Calculate**.

14. Select **File Print Full** (Shift-F7 F) to print the table.

The Table feature can be used to create complete spreadsheets. If you're entering a few columns in a document, it may be easier to set and use Tab stops. But if your table is complex, requires math, or you want it surrounded by lines, this feature may be invaluable.

So far you have learned how to format characters and lines. The next chapter deals with paragraph forms.

Right and Left
Indents and Other
Paragraph Formats

Featuring

*L*esson 33—How to Indent Paragraphs

The default paragraph format used by WordPerfect is the block style. Every line, including the first one in a paragraph, starts at the left margin. If you want to indent the first line of a paragraph, just press the Tab key.

But you might want to indent a whole paragraph, like this one, from the left margin. This helps to make a specific point stand out.

You might also want to indent a paragraph from both the right and left margins. This is frequently required for long quotations.

Both styles can be created easily with WordPerfect.

*I*ndenting from the Left Margin

You can indent a paragraph by changing the left margin, but this method is cumbersome if you only want to indent one paragraph for a special effect and then switch back to the normal left margin for the remaining text.

WordPerfect's Indent commands create indented paragraphs using temporary margin changes. Word-wrap returns the cursor to the indented position, not the original margin, until you press the ⏎ key to cancel the indented margin. You can use these commands to format individual paragraphs quickly without affecting other text.

Selecting Layout Align Indent (F4) creates a temporary left margin. Each time you select Indent, the left margin moves to the next tab stop to the right and an [→Indent] code is inserted into the text. Select Indent once to indent a paragraph ½ inch (the first tab by default), twice for a 1-inch indentation, and so on.

To see how easy it is to indent paragraphs with WordPerfect, we'll create a document with several levels of indentation. Follow the steps below.

1. Start WordPerfect.

2. Select **Layout Align Center** (Shift-F6) to center the cursor.

3. Type

   Classifications of Computers

4. Press ◄┘ twice.

5. Type the following paragraph, starting at the left margin:.

   The largest computer systems are called mainframes. These are large centralized computer systems that can be accessed by a great many users at one time, performing many different tasks.

6. Press ◄┘ twice, select **Layout Align Indent** (F4) to indent the next paragraph ½ inch, and type the following text:

   The next size computers are called minicomputers. These are still centralized systems that can be used by a number of persons. However, they have less processing capability than mainframes and can accommodate fewer users.

7. Press ◄┘ twice, select **Layout Align Indent** (F4) twice to indent the next paragraph 1 inch, and type the following text:

   Supermicros are smaller than minicomputers. These are smaller computer systems, based on microcomputers, which serve a number of persons at a time. These are called multi-user, multi-tasking microcomputers.

8. Press ◄┘ twice, select **Layout Align Indent** (F4) three times, and type the following text:

   A microcomputer, also called a personal or desktop computer, can be used by only one individual at a time. Compared to the other types of computers, the microcomputer has limited processing capabilities.

9. Press ◄┘ twice, select **L**ayout **A**lign **I**ndent (F4) four times, then type the following text:

> The special purpose computer is designed to perform a very specific task. It can be large or small, but it is "dedicated" to the one job for which it was made. Special purpose computers can be found in automobiles, industrial equipment, and even home appliances.

10. Press ◄┘.

11. Select **E**dit **R**eveal Codes (Alt-F3) to reveal the codes. Move the cursor up through the document to see the [→Indent] codes in the text.

12. Select **E**dit **R**eveal Codes (Alt-F3), then select **F**ile **P**rint **F**ull (Shift-F7 F) to print the document. It should look like Figure 7.1.

13. Save the document under the name CLASSES for use in several other chapters.

The Indent -> option gives you the flexibility to vary the paragraph format quickly.

Indenting from Both the Left and Right Margins

Indent can only indent the left margin of paragraphs. If you want both margins indented, say for a long quotation, you must use the Indent -><- option on the Align menu. Each time you select this option (Shift-F4), both margins move $1/2$ inch toward the center of the screen and an [→Indent←] code is inserted.

Like Indent, Indent -><- stays in effect only until you press ◄┘. So if you want the right and left margins indented for an entire document, or even for a number of paragraphs, you should change the margins as you learned in Lesson 21.

Let's use Indent -><- (Shift-F4) to produce the document shown in Figure 7.2.

1. Start WordPerfect if you exited after the last lesson.

2. Type the paragraph below, starting at the left margin.

> The first level of classification is kingdom. This group is divided into plants and animals. It is the largest division of living things.

```
                    Classifications of Computers

The largest computer systems are called mainframes. These are large
centralized computer systems that can be accessed by a great many
users at one time, performing many different tasks.

      The next size computers are called minicomputers. These are
      still centralized systems that can be used by a number of
      persons. However, they have less processing capability than
      mainframes and can accommodate fewer users.

            Supermicros are smaller than minicomputers. These are
            smaller computer systems, based on microcomputers, which
            serve a number of persons at a time. These are called
            multi-user, multi-tasking microcomputers.

                  A microcomputer, also called a personal or desktop
                  computer, can be used by only one individual at a
                  time. Compared to the other types of computers, the
                  microcomputer has limited processing capabilities.

                        The special purpose computer is designed to
                        perform a very specific task. It can be large
                        or small, but is "dedicated" to the one job
                        for which it was made. Special purpose
                        computers can be found in automobiles,
                        industrial equipment, and even home
                        appliances.
```

Figure 7.1: Paragraphs indented on the left

```
The first level of classification is kingdom. This group is divided
into plants and animals. It is the largest division of living
things.

      The second level is phylum. A phylum is the largest
      division of a kingdom.

            The third level is class. A class is the
            largest division of a phylum.

                  The fourth level is order. The
                  members of this division possess
                  body parts and structures that are
                  very much alike.
```

Figure 7.2: Paragraphs indented on both sides

3. Press ↵ twice, select **Layout Align Indent** (Shift-F4), and type the following text:

   The second level is phylum. A phylum is the largest division of a kingdom.

4. Press ⏎ twice, select **Layout Align Indent** (Shift-F4) twice, and type the next paragraph.

> The third level is class. A class is the largest division of a phylum.

5. Press ⏎ twice, select **Layout Align Indent** (Shift-F4) three times, and type the final paragraph.

> The fourth level is order. The members of this division possess body parts and structures that are very much alike.

6. Select **File Print Full** (Shift-F7 F) to print the document. If WordPerfect is set for justified printing, each paragraph will appear neatly centered below the one above.

7. Select **Edit Reveal Codes** (Alt-F3) to reveal the codes. Even though the paragraphs are indented on both sides, the [->Indent<-] codes are only at the start of each.

8. Select **Edit Reveal Codes** (Alt-F3), select **File Exit** (F7) **No No** to clear the screen.

The Indent codes can be deleted or inserted to modify the appearance of the text at any time. It is always easier to delete codes when they are revealed on the screen. Just place the cursor on the code and press Del. The text both below and above the scale line will adjust.

If the codes aren't revealed, place the cursor at the far left edge of the screen on the first line and press Del. In the next lesson, you'll use Indent to create another type of indented paragraph—the hanging indentation.

Lesson 34—How to Create Hanging Indentations

Standard paragraphs have only the first line indented with remaining text flush on the left. *Hanging indentations* are just the opposite; the first line starts to the left of the rest of the paragraph. Use hanging indentations when you want paragraphs to stand out from each other, as with numbered paragraphs and outlines.

1. These lines are an example of a numbered paragraph with a hanging indentation. The main text is indented to the right of

the level number. In this case the level number *(1.)* is at the far left margin. Because the level number stands out from the text, it is easy to see and can be differentiated from other paragraphs and levels.

By moving the left margin and indentation positions, you can create several levels of hanging indentations to make an outline.

Numbered Paragraphs

WordPerfect provides an automatic outlining feature for larger documents, but for shorter ones, you can use the Indent option and Tab keys. As an example, we'll create the portion of a topical outline shown in Figure 7.3.

```
1.    The choice of media used for data communications depends upon
      the speed of the transmission and the distance it must travel.
      There are three general classifications of media.
      a.    Wire media include open copper wire, twisted pair, and
            coaxial cable.
      b.    Airborne   media   include   broadcast   and   microwave
            transmission.
      c.    New technology includes fiber optics and laser beam
            transmission.
```

Figure 7.3: *An outline using hanging indentation*

1. Type *1.* to begin the outline. It is not necessary to type any spaces after the level number, since these will be added automatically when you select **Indent (F4)** in the next step.

2. Select **Layout Align Indent (F4)**, then type

   The choice of media used for data communications depends upon the speed of the transmission and the distance it must travel. There are three general classifications of media.

3. Press ←⏎. The text indents to the first tab position while the level number "hangs" at the left margin.

4. Press Tab, then type *a.*

5. Select **L**ayout **A**lign **I**ndent (F4), then type

> Wire media include open copper wire, twisted pair, and coaxial cable.

6. Press ◄──┘.

The Indent option creates a temporary left margin at the next tab stop position from where it was pressed. You used the Tab key to reach the position for the hanging letter, then the Indent option to create the indentation.

7. Press Tab, then type *b*.

8. Select **L**ayout **A**lign **I**ndent (F4), then type

> Airborne media include broadcast and microwave transmission.

9. Press ◄──┘.

10. Press Tab, then type *c*.

11. Select **L**ayout **A**lign **I**ndent (F4), then type

> New technology includes fiber optics and laser beam transmission.

12. Select **F**ile **P**rint **F**ull (Shift-F7 F) to print the text.

13. Save the document under the name MEDIA for use later, then clear the screen.

Changing the Format of Existing Text

If you've already typed some text using one paragraph style, you can easily change it to another. To change the format:

1. Select **E**dit **R**eveal Codes (Alt-F3) to reveal the codes.

2. Delete the codes for the format you want to change.

3. Select **E**dit **R**eveal Codes (Alt-F3) to return to the document.

4. Finally, place the cursor where you want the new format to start and select the appropriate format. The existing text will adjust to the new format.

*L*esson 35—How to Set Justification

Justified text has even margins on both the left and the right. For example, the text in this book is justified. Although WordPerfect does not display the text justified on the screen, it will print it justified by default and it will appear justified in the View mode.

During printing, extra spaces are inserted between words to spread out the line to the right margin. Only lines that end in the [SRt] codes from word-wrap are affected. These extra spaces often leave large gaps. If you find these gaps unsightly and do not want to hyphenate, turn off justification. Here's how:

1. Place the cursor at the start of the text you want to justify.

2. Select **L**ayout **J**ustify (Shift-F8 L J) to see the available options (Figure 7.4).

   • **L**eft aligns text only on the left margin

   • **C**enter centers text between the margins

   • **R**ight aligns text only on the right margin

   • **F**ull aligns text on both the left and right margins

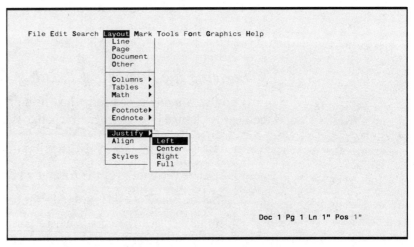

Figure 7.4: Layout Justify menu

3. Select the type of justification you want. Left turns off the default full justification setting. (If you used Shift-F8 L J, press F7 to return to the document.) A [Just:type] code is inserted into the text. All text between the code and the next [Just:] setting will automatically conform to the new justification style.

If you change your mind, select Edit **R**eveal Codes (Alt-F3) to display the codes, place the cursor on the [Just:type] code, then press Del.

As you now know, there are two ways to center and right-justify text—by using Layout Justify or by blocking text and using Layout Align.

Use Layout Align for formatting single lines or blocks of text you've already typed. Since it places a [Just:Full] code at the end of the block, paragraphs you don't block will not be affected.

Use Layout Justify to set the format of an entire document. If you use it for a section of text already typed, you'll have to manually insert a [Just:Full] code where you want the default justification to continue. Layout Justify, by the way, is not available when text is blocked.

Lesson 36—How to Hyphenate Text

Word-wrap lets you type without pressing ◄─┘ at the end of each line. But at times, such as when long words are carried to the next line, a justified paragraph can have too many extra spaces between words. Hyphenation is particularly useful when you're typing justified columns, as you will do in Chapter 12. For example, the following text, without hyphenation, has many noticeable gaps:

Word-wrap

automatically

returns   the

carriage   to

the left.

To avoid such problems, the text should be hyphenated. There are two methods of hyphenation in WordPerfect: entering hyphens yourself without help from WordPerfect or having WordPerfect enter them for you automatically.

Entering Hyphens Yourself

As you type, you can hyphenate words at the end of a line yourself. But what happens if you later add or delete text, and the hyphenated word moves to another line; bringing the hyphen with it? WordPerfect needs some way to distinguish those hyphens from symbols that belong in the text wherever it is placed, such as dashes and minus signs. So there are three different ways to enter a hyphen:

- Press the hyphen key (-) by itself in words that require hyphens, such as mother-in-law and son-in-law. If the paragraph is later reformatted, the hyphen could be used by word-wrap to divide the word between lines. A [-] code is inserted into the text.

- Press Home - (the Home key and the - key together) to insert a minus sign for formulas, such as N = G-E. Word-wrap will never break a formula at the minus. To enter a dash, first press Home followed by - then - by itself.

- Press Ctrl- (the Ctrl key and the - key together) to enter a "soft" hyphen when you want hyphenation to limit extra spaces. No hyphen will appear on the screen until word-wrap uses it to hyphenate the word between lines. The hyphen will be displayed if you reveal codes. Use this when typing long words that are close to the end of a line but not yet affected by word-wrap. If later editing forces the word to be wrapped, it will be hyphenated instead, resulting in fewer extra spaces.

- Press Home ⏎ to insert an *invisible soft hyphen*, the [ISRt] code. WordPerfect will use that position to divide the word if later editing requires the word to be divided at the end of a line, but no hyphen will appear.

If you find it troublesome to add hyphenation manually, you can have WordPerfect help you or even hyphenate automatically.

Let's see how.

*A*utomatic Hyphenation

Ordinary manual hyphenation slows down your typing by making you pause at the end of lines to make hyphenation decisions. You can activate automatic hyphenation, however, and have WordPerfect divide words for you automatically and add the hyphens. Before typing or editing, follow these steps to turn on automatic hyphenation:

1. Select **Layout Line Hyphenation** (Shift-F8 L Y). The hyphenation option appears as:

   1 - Hyphenation   No (Yes)

2. Select **Y**es to turn on automatic hyphenation. (If you later want to turn the feature off, select **No**.)

3. Press F7 to return to the document. The [Hyph On] code will be inserted.

In most cases, as you type, WordPerfect will automatically insert a soft hyphen where appropriate, without stopping for you to position the cursor. However, if WordPerfect's rules of hyphenation don't apply, the message

Position Hyphen; Press ESC

will appear, followed by the word and a suggested hyphenation site.

Use the → and ← keys to move the hyphen to an appropriate place, then press Esc to insert a soft hyphen into the text.

To delete or change the hyphen, delete the - character and edit accordingly.

If you're typing a long word that you do not want WordPerfect to hyphenate, press Home / before the word. A [/] code is inserted. This code prevents automatic hyphenation from taking place for that word only. You can also enter a [/] code to cancel a hyphen you already inserted. Place the cursor on the first character of the word, press Home /, then delete the hyphen. The word will wrap to the next line.

By now you should see WordPerfect's great potential. So now let's work on even more formatting skills.

Page Formatting
for a Professional Look

Featuring

Lesson 37—How to Set Top and Bottom Margins

The top and bottom margins, along with the font size, determine the number of lines you'll be able to fit on each page. Using the default font that prints six lines of typing per inch, the standard 8½" by 11" page is 66 lines long. So if you subtract the default 1-inch top and bottom margins, you'll have 54 actual lines of typing per page.

When you change the size of the top or bottom margin, Word-Perfect automatically computes the number of lines per page, so the soft page break line will appear at the proper place.

Before changing margins, place the cursor at the start of the document if you want every page formatted the same way. To format a specific page, place the cursor at the start of that page.

Let's see how this is done by changing the top and bottom margins to 1½ inches.

1. Start WordPerfect.

2. Select **Layout P**age (Shift-F8 P) to display the Format Page menu (Figure 8.1).
   These options control the arrangement of text and other elements on the page. You'll learn about most of these settings in other chapters. For now, notice that option 5 sets top and bottom margins.

3. Select **M**argins to move the cursor to the top margin setting.

4. Type *1.5,* the size of the top margin in inches, then press ←. WordPerfect adds the inches sign (") for you. If you only wanted to change the bottom margin, you would just press ← at this prompt.

```
Format: Page

        1 - Center Page (top to bottom)    No

        2 - Force Odd/Even Page

        3 - Headers

        4 - Footers

        5 - Margins - Top                   1"
                      Bottom                1"

        6 - Page Numbering

        7 - Paper Size                      8.5" x 11"
                      Type                  Standard

        8 - Suppress (this page only)




    Selection: 0
```

Figure 8.1: *Format: Page menu*

5. Type *1.5*, the size of the bottom margin, then press ←┘. If you just wanted to set the top margin and accept the default bottom, you would press ←┘ instead.

6. Press F7 to return to the document. The [T/B Mar:1.5", 1.5"] code is inserted in the text.

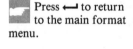 Press ←┘ to return to the main format menu.

As you type, WordPerfect will end each page at the appropriate place. So with 1 ½-inch top and bottom margins you'll get only 48 lines before the page break is inserted.

To return to the original default margins, select **Edit Reveal Codes** (Alt-F3) to display the codes and delete the Top and Bottom Margin code.

Changing margins, however, does not affect the overall size of the page. So it's time to look at a special WordPerfect feature—forms.

*L*esson 38—How to Set Page Size and Shape with Forms

You determine the length and width of the page by selecting a *form*.

A form represents the size and type of material you'll be printing on. The most common size is 8½ by 11 inches (called *Standard*). However, you might have several types of material in that size—plain paper, letterhead, large envelopes, label stock, etc. So in selecting a form you have to specify both the size and the type.

The default page size is 8½ by 11 inches and the type is Standard. While there are nine preset form sizes (you can always set your own), some printers only have the standard size and type *defined,* or ready to use. Most printers also have a form called All Others.

So to use another form size and type, you must first add it to the list of those available to your printer. Once you add the form to the list it will be available whenever you use WordPerfect. This way, you can use that form anytime without defining it again.

This may all seem very complicated. And it *can* be, depending on how many special form characteristics you want to add. But let's start by seeing what forms are available for your printer and, if necessary, adding a legal size form—8 by 14 inches—to your printer's list. Because a legal size form is longer than the standard 11 inches, you must make sure it is defined before using it.

Here's how to change your paper size to legal:

1. Select **L**ayout **P**age Paper **S**ize (Shift-F8 P S) to display a list of defined forms for your printer (Figure 8.2).

   You'll learn what the options mean shortly. For now, is there a listing for a legal size form on your display? It would look

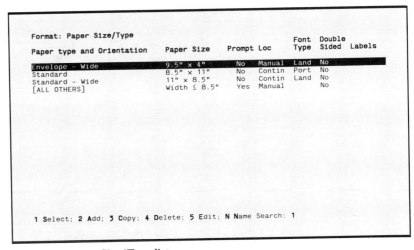

Figure 8.2: *Paper Size/Type list*

someting like this:

Legal 8.5″ × 14″

If you have a legal form defined, then you don't have to continue with steps 4 through 10—just press F7 twice. But review the steps anyway in case you want to define some other custom form size later on.

2. Select **A**dd to see the list below.

Format: Paper Type

1 - Standard
2 - Bond
3 - Letterhead
4 - Labels
5 - Envelope
6 - Transparency
7 - Cardstock
8 - [ALL OTHERS]
9 - Other

3. Select **S**tandard (normally used for plain paper). The Format: Edit Paper Definition menu is displayed (Figure 8.3).

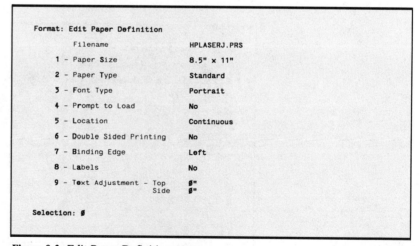

Figure 8.3: Edit Paper Definition menu

4. Select Paper **Size** to set the form size. You'll see the Format: Paper Size menu (Figure 8.4).

5. Select **Legal**. The Edit Paper Definition menu will be redisplayed.

6. Look at the **Location** option. If it says Continuous, then WordPerfect assumes you're using continuous feed paper and it won't stop to let you insert individual sheets into the printer. For this to happen, the **Location** option would have to say Manual. If the location is correct, then skip to step 12. Otherwise continue here.

7. Select **Location** for the prompt line:

   Location: **1** Continuous; **2 B**in Number; **3** Manual: 0

8. Select the option corresponding to the paper source. If you select **B**in Number, you'll see the prompt

   Bin number:

   Enter the letter or number of the paper tray or bin containing the paper you'll be using.

9. Now look at the **Prompt to Load** option. A **No** at this option means that the form is available for use and WordPerfect will

```
Format: Paper Size              Width  Height

    1 - Standard               (8.5" x 11")

    2 - Standard Landscape     (11" x 8.5")

    3 - Legal                  (8.5" x 14")

    4 - Legal Landscape        (14" x 8.5")

    5 - Envelope               (9.5" x 4")

    6 - Half Sheet             (5.5" x 8.5")

    7 - US Government          (8" x 11")

    8 - A4                     (210mm x 297mm)

    9 - A4 Landscape           (297mm x 210mm)

    o - Other

Selection: 0
```

Figure 8.4: Format: Paper Size menu

not stop and prompt you to insert the proper size paper. If you want to change this option, select **P**rompt, then **Y**es. The other options on the last menu are used infrequently.

- **F**ont Type is used primarily with laser printers. With this option you can select *Portrait* orientation (the normal method, with the characters printed across the width), or *landscape* orientation (with the characters printed down the length of the page).

- **D**ouble Sided Printing is used for laser printers that print on both sides of the page. Options are Yes and No.

- **B**inding edge is for choosing paper sides for binding. The options are top and left.

- **L**abels is used to create a form for printing labels.

- **T**ext Adjustment sets any additional margin space at the top or left of the form. For example, multi-part 8½" by 11" forms often have a narrow area before the perforation at the top margin. The total form length is actually 8½ by 11½ inches. A top page offset of ½ inch and a top margin of 1 inch would advance the form 1½ inches before printing. Left offsets can be used with continuous form paper to accommodate the tractor holes.

10. Press F7 three times to return to the typing window.

The form definition you just made is now added to those available. It can be easily selected when you want to print on legal paper. Here's how:

1. Make sure the cursor is at the start of the document, then select **L**ayout **P**age Paper **S**ize (Shift-F8 P S) to display the list of available forms.

2. Use the ↓ key to highlight the form sized 8.5" × 14", then press ↵. The Format: Page menu appears with that size page at the Paper Size prompt.

3. Press F7 to return to the document.

    The code [Paper Sz/Typ: 8.5" × 14", Standard] is inserted into the text. Because the form is now 14 inches (84 lines) long, you'll be able to enter 72 lines between the top and bottom margins.

Creating Custom Forms

Use the techniques below to print on pages of any size, such as 3 by 5 inch index cards.

1. Select **Layout P**age Paper Size **A**dd (Shift-F8 P S A) to display the Paper Type menu.

2. Select **O**ther to see the prompt:

   Other form type:

3. Type *Index*, then press ◄─┘. The Edit Paper Definition menu (see Figure 8.3) appears.

4. Select Paper **S**ize to display the size option.

5. Select **O**ther for the prompt:

   Width: 0″   Height:

6. Type *5*, then press ◄─┘.

7. Type *3*, then press ◄─┘.

8. Set the **L**ocation and P**r**ompt to Load options to match your hardware.

9. Press F7. The Paper Size/Type list appears with the Index -Wide form highlighted.

10. Press ◄─┘ to select the form, then F7 to return to the typing window.

    Now let's confirm that the 3" by 5" form size is being used.

11. Type the numbers from 1 through 7 down the side of the screen, like so:

    ```
    1
    2
    3
    4
    5
    6
    7
    ```

The page break line appeared after the sixth line. Isn't that after just 1 inch of typing? Well, keep in mind that changing the page size does not change the top and bottom margins. So with the default 1-inch margin still in force, you only have 1 inch, or 6 lines, of typing per page. To fit more on the page, change the top and bottom margins as you learned in Lesson 37. Figure 8.5 shows the index card in View mode.

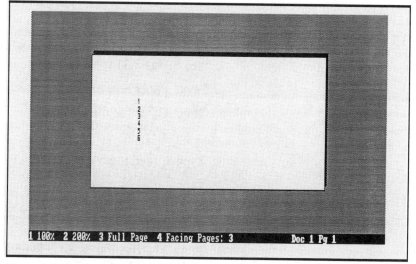

Figure 8.5: Index card in View mode

*F*orms and Page Feed

As you saw, you set the paper feed to manual, continuous, or sheet feeder when you define the location of the form. So, for example, you can feed envelopes manually into the printer or use continuous feed for tractor paper—sheets of paper connected with perforations.

But let's consider some special situations.

If you have a laser printer, use continuous feed for paper that's loaded in the tray. Even though they are individual sheets of paper, laser printers treat them as continuous feed.

What about printers that handle both single sheets and continuous paper? You might use plain continuous paper for some jobs but change to single sheets for letterhead or special paper. Each defined form can have only one location. Yet the solution is simple: define two forms. Define and use the standard size and standard type as continuous paper. But also define a standard size and letterhead or bond type as manual. When you're ready to print, place the cursor at the top of the document and select the form type desired. The standard form type will use continuous paper, the letterhead or bond type will use manual.

Changing Paper Feed

To change the feed from the default—such as from manual to continuous—select **Layout Page Paper Size**, highlight the form you want to change, then select **Edit**. Set the **Location** option, then press F7 until the document appears.

Lesson 39—How to Eliminate Orphan and Widow Lines

The page settings determine how many text lines will be printed on a page. But because pagination simply counts lines before breaking pages without considering how the page looks, some paragraphs may be divided inappropriately.

An *orphan* is the last line of a paragraph that is printed by itself on the top of a page. A *widow* is the first line of a paragraph appearing by itself on the bottom of a page. Both can be avoided using the Page Format menu.

1. Press Home Home ↑ to place the cursor at the start of the document.

2. Select **Layout Line** (Shift-F8 L) for the Format Line menu.

3. Select **Widow/Orphan Protection**.

4. Select **Yes**.

5. Press F7 to return to the document. The [W/O On] code is inserted into the text.

6. Select **File Exit** (F7) **No No** to clear the screen.

When changing pages, WordPerfect will now shift lines up or down, sometimes printing fewer than the set number of lines per page, to avoid widow and orphan lines.

Lesson 40—How to Create Title Pages

Title pages usually contain several lines of text centered both horizontally and vertically on the page. To get this effect and place your text in the very center of the page, you can use the Center Page Top to Bottom option on the Page Format menu. You will also have to select Layout Align Center (Shift-F6) to center text between the right and left margins. Follow these steps to create a title page:

1. Press Home Home ↑ to place the cursor at the left margin of line 1.

2. Select **Layout Page** (Shift-F8 P) for the Format Page menu.

3. Select **Center Page** (top to bottom).

4. Select **Yes**.

5. Press F7 to return to the document. The [Center Pg] code is inserted into the text.

6. Select **Layout Align Center** (Shift-F6) and type

   Tae Kwon Do in the Martial Arts

7. Press ◄┘ twice, select **Layout Align Center** (Shift-F6), then type

   by

8. Press ◄┘ twice, select **Layout Align Center** (Shift-F6), then type

   Liz Bressi-Stoppe

9. Press Ctrl-◄┘ to insert a page break.

10. Press Home Home ↑ to reach the top page, then select **E**dit **R**eveal Codes (Alt-F3) to reveal the codes (Figure 8.6).

    The [Center Pg] code will automatically add the necessary blank lines to center the text between the top and bottom margins.

    If you want the text slightly higher than center, just add a few blank lines with the ◀━ key after typing the text. To print it slightly lower than center, add the lines above the text, but after the [Center Pg] code.

11. Select **E**dit **R**eveal Codes (Alt-F3) to return to the typing area.

12. Select **F**ile **P**rint **V**iew Document (Shift-F7 V) to see how the page will appear when printed (Figure 8.7). Press F7 when you have finished looking at the preview.

13. Save the title page under the name TITLE for use in an upcoming chapter.

If you later add or delete lines on the title page, WordPerfect will automatically adjust the page when printing. To return the page to normal, delete the [Center Pg] code. Changing the setting in the menu has no effect.

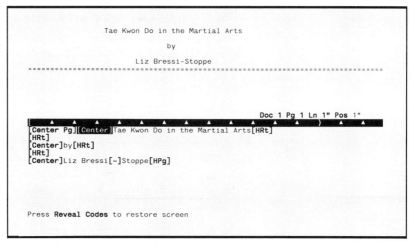

Figure 8.6: *Title page with codes revealed*

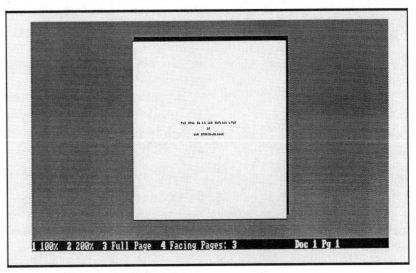

Figure 8.7: *Title page in View mode*

*L*esson 41—How to Print Envelopes

So far you've printed everything on either business or legal sized paper. Wouldn't it be nice if life were always so simple?

Well, it's not. Take envelopes for example.

Some people believe that if you don't print envelopes often, you may find it easier to revert back to the typewriter for these. If you have a laser printer, this might be particularly true because of special formatting problems. But in reality, envelopes are just another page of a different size.

Printing envelopes is a very useful skill, particularly if you do it a lot. By combining the formatting skills you'll learn in this lesson with form letter techniques you'll learn later on, you can print envelopes for an entire mailing list easily and quickly.

If your printer already has an envelope form defined, then you can just select it as explained in the section below called "Selecting the Envelope Form." Using a laser printer will be discussed in a separate section.

Otherwise, let's create the envelope form right now and print a sample envelope. Using WordPerfect's Forms feature, you'll have to do this in three steps. First, you'll define the envelope form for a standard business envelope, $9\frac{1}{2}$ by 4 inches. Then, you'll select the form from the Paper Size/Type menu. Finally, you will have to adjust the margins to print the address in the correct location.

Defining the Envelope Form

1. Select **Layout P**age Paper Size **A**dd (Shift-F8 P S A) to display the Paper Type menu.

2. Select Envelope. The Edit Paper Definition menu appears (see Figure 8.3).

3. Select Paper Size to display the size option.

4. Select Envelope. The Edit menu reappears.

5. Set the Location and Prompt to Load options to match your hardware.

6. Press F7. The Paper Size/Type list appears with the Envelope -Wide form now included.

7. Press F7 twice to return to the typing window.

Selecting the Envelope Form

When you're ready to address and print an envelope, follow these steps:

1. Select **Layout P**age Page Size (Shift-F8 P S).

2. Highlight the Envelope form on the list.

3. Press ←┘, then F7.

Setting Envelope Margins

If you're in business, you probably have your return address already printed in the left corner of your envelopes. So you should set the margins to quickly print the recipient's address in the correct location. Let's do this first. Then I'll show you how to set the margins if you're using blank envelopes.

Business Envelopes

When you're ready to format and print an envelope, first select the form as you did above. Then set all of the margins— top, bottom, left, and right—in order to streamline envelope printing.

1. Select **Layout Page Margins** (Shift-F8 P M) to set the top and bottom margins.

2. Type *2* for a 2-inch top margin, then press ←┘.

3. Type *.5* for the bottom margin, then press ←┘. This will give you nine lines for the address.

4. Press ←┘ to display the Format menu.

5. Select **Line** for the Format Line menu.

6. Select **Margins** to set the margins.

7. Type *4* for the left margin.

8. Press ←┘ twice, then F7 to accept the default 1-inch right margin and return to the document.

With the margins set this way, you can type the address without worrying about formatting. Just type the address starting at the first line.

1. Type

   Barbara E. Cohen
   9642 Friendship Street
   Philadelphia, PA 19111

2. Insert an envelope into the printer. Line it up vertically so the top edge of the envelope is aligned with the print head, just where you'd start a regular piece of paper.

3. Select **File Print Full** (Shift F7 F) to print the envelope. If your printer is set for manual feed, select **File Print Control Printer Go** (Shift-F7 C G) to issue the Go command. Figure 8.8 shows the envelope in View mode.

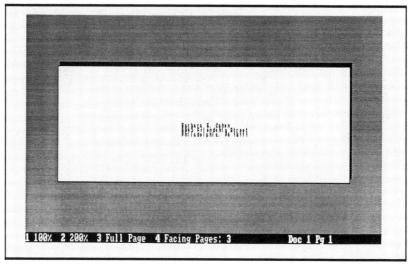

Figure 8.8: *Completed envelope in View mode*

The envelope will move up past the 2-inch top margin and the address will start printing 4 inches from the left.

Blank Envelopes

If you want to print your return address on the left corner, set the top, bottom, and left margins at $\frac{1}{2}$ inch. Then type your address starting at the top of the screen.

Press ⏎ to reach line 18, and tab to position 40. Enter the recipient's address at this location and print the envelope as explained above.

Printing Envelopes on Laser Printers

There is already an envelope size predefined when you're using a laser printer. However, because of the way different laser printers handle manual-fed envelopes, follow these suggestions:

- Use or create a *standard wide* form—11 by $8\frac{1}{2}$ inches with a landscape font type.

- Either set the location as manual, or use the printer's control panel to select manual feed.

- With printers such as the LaserJet II, IID, and IIP, set the top and left margins at 4.5 inches. With older model LaserJet printers, set the top margin at 6.5, the left at 4.5. These settings are for printing the address. You might have to adjust these settings to suit your own envelopes and spacing requirements.

- To print your own return address in the corner, set the top margin at 4.5 and the left margin at 2. Test these settings on a sample envelope.

You have now learned all of the fundamental ways to format your documents. In the next chapter you'll learn about headers, footers, and page numbers.

9

Adding Headers, Footers, and Page Numbers

Featuring

Creating and editing headers and footers

Printing page numbers

Suppressing headers and footers

New page numbers

*L*esson 42—How to Create Headers and Footers

A *header* prints specified lines of text at the top of every page. *Footers* do the same at the bottom.

The most useful headers are those that identify the document to which the page belongs. That way, if individual pages get separated from the document, the reader will have little trouble locating their source.

In most cases, footers contain a page number and perhaps a continuation message, such as *(Continued on the next page)* or *(Please turn the page).* Page numbers can be printed in headers or footers, or by themselves, as explained in Lesson 43.

Before computers, the problem with typing headers was to remember to type them on the page; with footers it was to leave enough room for them at the bottom of the page. WordPerfect's automatic Header/ Footer function overcomes these problems.

Using this option, you first decide where to place the header or footer. Do you want it to appear on every page including the first, only on odd-numbered pages, or only on even ones? Do you want the same headers and footers throughout the entire document, or different ones on specific pages? All of these options are available in WordPerfect.

After you've decided where to place them, you enter and save the text in a special typing area. Headers and footers will not appear on the screen when you are typing, but they will be added automatically to the printed text.

The header starts printing at the first line of text (not in the margin) with an extra blank line between it and the text. Footers begin printing on the last text line (54 by default) and may extend into the bottom margin. An extra blank line is inserted before the first footer line.

Because of their placement, headers and footers reduce the number of text lines on the page. A one-line header, for example, takes up two text lines, one for the header itself and one for the blank line following it. This leaves only 52 text lines. If you add a one-line footer, only 50 lines of text will be printed on the page. So avoid cluttering documents with unnecessary headers or footers.

Let's create a document in which every page has a one-line header and a one-line footer containing the page number.

1. Start WordPerfect.

2. Select **Layout Page** (Shift-F8 P) to display the Format Page menu.

3. Select **Headers**. The prompt line changes to

   1 Header **A**; **2** Header **B**: 0

   At any time you can have two different headers and two different footers, known as *A* and *B*. You can have all four types of headers and footers in the same document, even more than one of each type if they are on different pages. Both headers A and B can appear on every page, on odd or even pages only, or just on specified pages. You can put both A and B on the same page. The same is true for footers.

4. Select **A** to create header A. The status line changes to

   1 Discontinue; **2** Every page; **3** Odd pages; **4** Even pages; **5** Edit:0

1 Discontinue	Stops printing the header or footer beginning on the page where the command is issued. To place a header or footer on just one page, create it on the desired page and then select the Discontinue option on the following page.
2 Every **page**	Prints the text on each page of the document, unless discontinued.
3 Odd pages	Prints the text only on odd-numbered pages.

4 Even pages	Prints the text only on even-numbered pages.
5 Edit	Allows you to edit the text of the selected header or footer.

5. Select Every **P**age. The screen clears to display the Header/ Footer Creation window, which is blank except for the status line:

Header A: Press Exit when done   Ln 1″ Pos 1″

Here is where you type the text of the header or footer. You can use all of the normal editing and cursor movement keys, and you can boldface, underline, or otherwise format the text.

6. Type the following header, but do not press ↵ when you are done:

1988 Computer Seminar

If you had pressed ↵, an extra blank line would have been included in the header, in addition to the blank line inserted to separate the header from the text.

7. Press F7 to save the header and redisplay the Format: Page menu. The header is saved within the document, not as a separate file.

8. Select **F**ooters **A** Every **P**age to create Footer A on every page.

9. Select **L**ayout **A**lign **C**enter (Shift-F6) to center the cursor.

10. Type *Page.*

11. Press the spacebar.

12. Press Ctrl-B. The ^B code, which stands for the page number, will be displayed (Figure 9.1).

WordPerfect will display the current page number at the location of the ^B code in the text, in this case next to the word *Page.* The ^B code can be in either the header or the footer.

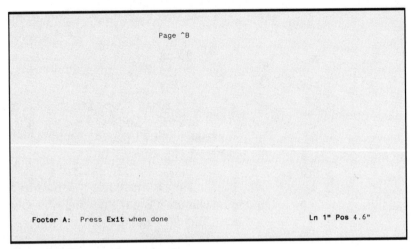

Figure 9.1: *Footer with page number*

In Lessons 43 and 45 you'll learn how to change the printed page number and how to include a page number without entering a header or footer.

13. Press F7 to accept the footer. The Format: Page menu appears, showing the selected position of the header and footer you just set.

14. Press F7 twice to return to the typing window.

15. Select **Edit R**eveal Codes (Alt-F3) to reveal the codes. The first 50 characters of each header or footer will be displayed along with the codes (Figure 9.2).

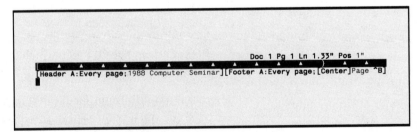

Figure 9.2: *Header and Footer codes*

16. Select **Edit R**eveal Codes (Alt-F3) to return to the document, then type

   To All Seminar Participants:

   The enclosed materials will be discussed during the seminar. Please bring them with you to every session.

17. Select **File P**rint **V**iew (Shift-F7 V) to view the document as it will appear when printed (Figure 9.3).

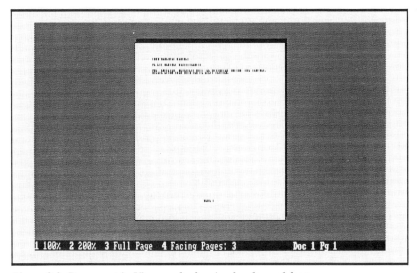

Figure 9.3: Document in View mode showing header and footer

18. Press F7 to return to the document.

Leave the text on the screen for use in the next section.

Header/Footer Suggestions

The header should always be created at the top of a page. If the Header code follows text on a page, the header will not start printing until the next page. This can be used to your advantage in suppressing the header on an initial title page.

Headers and footers A and B should be coordinated carefully. The main advantage of having two headers or footers is to print them on alternating pages. One can print on the left side of even-numbered pages, the other on the right side of odd pages. You can also create both A and B at the start of the document and switch back and forth when needed.

But if you set their occurrences the same so they print on the same page, both headers or both footers may print on the same line, destroying the line format used to create them. One alternative is to enter header A on the left side of the first header line, and header B flush right. Then they will not interfere with each other. Otherwise, enter the headers on different lines, such as header A on line 1 and header B on line 2.

Editing Headers and Footers

To change the text of a header or footer, select **Layout Page** (Shift-F8 P), then either **Headers** or **Footers**. Select **A** or **B**, then **Edit**.

WordPerfect searches back through the document to the most recent header or footer of the type selected, then displays it in the editing window. Make the changes you want and press F7.

Delete a header by deleting its code, or just discontinue it with the Discontinue option.

In the next lesson you will learn a quick way to print page numbers without including them in a header or footer. So delete the footer in the current document by following these steps:

1. Press Home Home ↑ to go to the beginning of the document.

2. Select **Edit Reveal Codes** (Alt-F3) to reveal the codes. The cursor is to the right of the Header and Footer codes.

3. Press Backspace to delete the Footer code.

4. Select **Edit Reveal Codes** (Alt-F3).

5. If you are not ready to continue with Lesson 43, save the text under the name ENCL for use later on.

Lesson 43—How to Insert Page Numbers

A page number can be printed by itself on every page even without including a ^B code in a header or footer. You can select the position of the number, include text such as *Page 30,* and even change the number that will be printed. Like headers and footers, the page number will not appear on the screen (unless previewed in View mode), but it will be printed.

In this lesson, you will add page numbers to the text you created in Lesson 42 and you will merge it with the CLASSES document you entered in Chapter 7. If you exited WordPerfect after the last lesson, start the program and recall the ENCL document. Then continue with the steps below.

1. Press Home Home ↓ to reach the end of the document.

2. Press Ctrl-◄┘ to insert a page break. Now recall the CLASSES document.

3. Select **File Retrieve** (Shift-F10), type *CLASSES,* then press ◄┘ to recall the document, adding it to the end of the text already on the screen.

4. Press Home Home ↑ to make sure the cursor is at the top of the document. Now let's add a page number at the bottom right of the page. While this will number your pages consecutively starting from page 1, you'll learn how to handle title pages in Lesson 44.

5. Select **Layout Page** (Shift-F8 P) to display the Format Page menu.

6. Select Page **N**umbering to display the Format: Page Numbering menu (Figure 9.4).

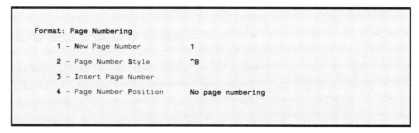

Figure 9.4: Format: Page Numbering menu

The Page Number Style option is used to specify any text you want to appear along with the number. The code ^B means that by default only the number itself will print. (By the way, the Insert Page Number option on the menu simply places the page number at the position of the cursor in the text—the same result as entering ^B (Ctrl-B) while typing. It does not turn on page numbering, but prints the page number on that page only.)

7. Select Page Number **S**tyle, type *Page*, press the spacebar, then ←.

   WordPerfect added the ^B code for you to insure that the page number appears after your text.

Now let's select the position of the page number.

8. Select Page Number **P**osition to display the Page Number Position menu (Figure 9.5).

   Selecting a number from 1 to 8 will cause the page number to print at the position indicated on the menu. Number 9 turns off page numbering.

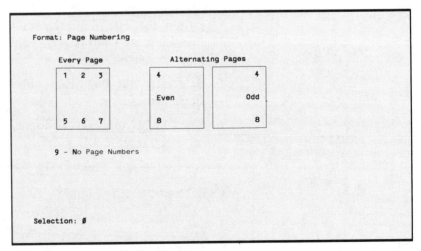

Figure 9.5: Page Number Position menu

9. Press *7* to print the page number at the bottom right of every page. The Format: Page Numbering menu will reappear.

10. Press F7 to return to the document. The codes [Pg Num Style: Page ^B] and [Pg Numbering:Bottom Right] have been added.

11. Select **F**ile **P**rint **V**iew Document (Shift-F7 V) to view the first page of the document as it will appear when printed (Figure 9.6). The page number, along with the word *Page*, is in the lower-right corner.

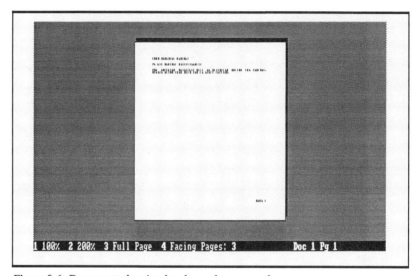

Figure 9.6: *Document showing header and page number*

12. Press F7 to return to the document.

Leave the document on the screen for use in the upcoming lessons. The document now contains two pages, a short cover page and one listing the various classes of computers. The header will be printed on the top of both pages, and each will be numbered at the bottom right.

Lesson 44—How to Suppress Headers, Footers, and Page Numbers

If page numbering or headers and footers are selected, they are printed on every page. But in the case of the text now on the screen, the first page is just a cover letter; it is not really part of the document, and should not contain the header or be numbered. So let's keep the header and page number from appearing on the cover letter.

1. Select **L**ayout **P**age (Shift-F8 P) to display the Format Page menu.

2. Select Suppress (this page only) to reveal the menu shown in (Figure 9.7).

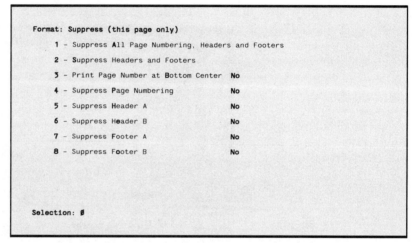

Format: Suppress (this page only)

    1 - Suppress **A**ll Page Numbering, Headers and Footers

    2 - **S**uppress Headers and Footers

    3 - Print Page Number at Bottom Center   **No**

    4 - Suppress Page Numbering   **No**

    5 - Suppress Header A   **No**

    6 - Suppress Header B   **No**

    7 - Suppress Footer A   **No**

    8 - Suppress Footer B   **No**

Selection: **0**

Figure 9.7: Format: Suppress (this page only) menu

Through this menu, you can temporarily suspend any headers, footers, or page numbers from printing on the current page. Other pages are not affected.

You can individually suppress headers, footers, or page numbering by selecting options 4 to 8. If you select option 2, all headers and footers are suppressed, and options 5 through 8 change to Yes. Option 1 also suppresses headers and footers, as well as any page numbering you set with the Page Number Position option. Prompts 4 to 8 change to Yes. Option 3 is used to print just a page number at the bottom center even if headers, footers, and other page numbering have been suppressed.

3. Press *1* to suppress the header and page number.

4. Press F7 to return to the document. The [Suppress:PgNum, HA, HB, FA, FB] code is inserted into the text.

Lesson 45—How to Set New Page Numbers

Now only one problem remains. While a page number will not appear on the first page, it is still counted as page 1 as far as numbering is concerned. So what we want to count as the first page of the text, the classifications of computers, will be numbered as page 2. The New Page Number option will solve this problem.

1. Press PgDn to place the cursor at the top of the second page.

2. Select **Layout P**age Page **N**umbering (Shift-F8 P N) to display the Page Numbering menu (see Figure 9.4).

3. Select **New Page Number**. The cursor moves to that prompt on the menu.

4. Type *1*, press ⏎, then F7 to return to the document.

    Page numbering will now begin with the number you selected with this option for the current page. Following page numbers will continue from there, unless you enter a new page number on another page.

    Look at the page indicator in the status line. Even though you are in the second page of the text on the screen, it is marked as *Pg 1*. Press PgUp to reach the first page. It too is marked as *Pg 1* in the status line.

    If you want to number pages in Roman numerals, enter a new page number such as *i* or *I*, depending on whether you want to print with upper- or lowercase Roman numerals. The page indicator on the status line will show Arabic numbers, but Roman numerals will appear when the document is printed.

5. Select **File P**rint **F**ull (Shift-F7 F) to print a copy of the document.

6. Save the document and exit WordPerfect.

Use the New Page Number option, as you did here, to start a document as page 1 even if it is preceded by a title page or cover letter. This option is also practical when you're composing and printing long documents in sections. Say you have typed, saved, and printed the first section of a long report, numbered 1 through 10. You then decide to add another section and type the next ten pages as a separate document. Before printing, place the cursor at the start of this second section and use the New Page Number option to start numbering at 11.

The next chapter revisits an old subject—blocks. You'll learn how to make major changes to your documents in just a few keystrokes.

Editing
Entire Blocks

Featuring

Deleting, moving, and copying blocks

Printing, saving, and appending blocks

Lesson 46—How to Delete, Move, and Copy Blocks

You've already learned how to boldface, underline, and otherwise format existing characters: select Edit Block (Alt-F4) and move the cursor until the text is highlighted, then select the appropriate format. This is called a *Block* command because it affects an entire section, or block of text.

Using similar techniques, you can delete a section of text, make a copy of it at another location, or even move it from one location or document to another. Let's say that you just completed a letter and noticed that one paragraph should be moved elsewhere. Rather than delete and retype it, use the Block command to move it.

Now let's use these commands. Imagine that after a document was completed you realized that the text needed to be rearranged. Rather than start from scratch, you'll use the Block commands to rearrange the text, making major changes with just a few keystrokes. Follow these steps:

1. Start WordPerfect.

2. Type the following:

   There are a number of programming languages in use today. Here are the most common in order of popularity:

   FORTRAN stands for Formula Translator and was the first natural language compiler.

   COBOL comes from Common Business Oriented Language and is designed for large business and commercial applications.

BASIC stands for Beginners All-purpose Symbolic Instruction Code. This language was initially developed for non–computer science majors but has grown in popularity with the use of microcomputers.

PASCAL was named for Blaise Pascal. It was created primarily as a tool for teaching programming and algorithms.

To update this review of computer languages, you want to delete the paragraph about FORTRAN and place the paragraph about BASIC before COBOL.

First perform a block deletion.

3. Place the cursor on the letter *F* in *FORTRAN*.

4. Select **Edit B**lock (Alt-F4), then move the cursor to the letter *C* in *COBOL* to highlight the paragraph you want to delete. If you move it too far, just move the cursor back again (Figure 10.1).

5. Select **Edit D**elete (Del) to display the prompt

Delete Block? No (Yes)

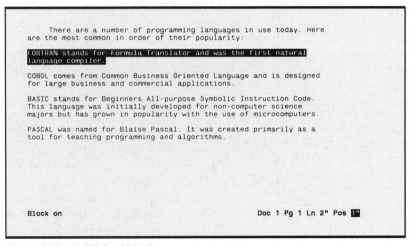

Figure 10.1: Highlighted block

6. Select **Yes** to delete the block.

Placing the cursor under the letter *C* in COBOL also caused the [HRt] codes between the sentences to be deleted, so the remaining text moved up to replace the deleted paragraph.

Now let's move a block from one location to another.

7. Place the cursor on the letter *B* in *BASIC*.

8. Select **Edit B**lock (Alt-F4).

9. Move the cursor to the letter *P* in *PASCAL* (Figure 10.2).

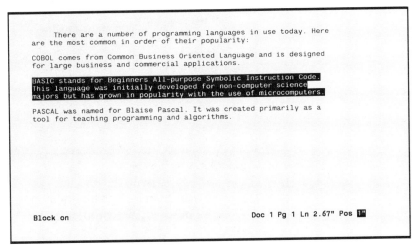

There are a number of programming languages in use today. Here are the most common in order of their popularity:

COBOL comes from Common Business Oriented Language and is designed for large business and commercial applications.

BASIC stands for Beginners All-purpose Symbolic Instruction Code. This language was initially developed for non-computer science majors but has grown in popularity with the use of microcomputers.

PASCAL was named for Blaise Pascal. It was created primarily as a tool for teaching programming and algorithms.

Block on   Doc 1 Pg 1 Ln 2.67" Pos

Figure 10.2: Highlighted block ready to be moved

10. Select **Edit M**ove (Ctrl-F4 B M) to select Block Move. The text disappears from the screen and the status line changes to

Move cursor; press Enter to retrieve

11. Place the cursor on the letter *C* in *COBOL*.

12. Press ◄─┘ to reinsert the cut text from the retrieval area.

Finally, let's copy a block from one location to another. This time, however, you will perform a "speed block" function. If you want to cut or copy just one sentence, paragraph, or page, you do not have to highlight it first as a block.

13. Place the cursor anywhere in the second sentence of the last paragraph.

14. Select **Edit Select** (Ctrl-F4) to display the Select options (Figure 10.3).

    From this menu, you can quickly select the sentence, paragraph, or page in which the cursor is located.

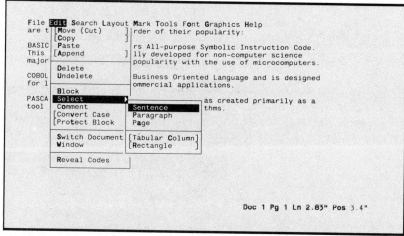

Figure 10.3: *Select options*

15. Select **Sentence**. The document appears with the sentence highlighted. The prompt line is:

    1 Move; 2 Copy; 3 Delete; 4 Append: 0

16. Select **Copy** to display the same prompt line seen in step 10. Notice that the block is not erased from its original position. The Move command removes the highlighted text; Copy makes a duplicate of it.

17. Now place the cursor at the end of the paragraph describing BASIC.

18. Press the spacebar to insert a space.

19. Press ◄─┘ to retrieve the copy of the block and insert it into the text at this new location (Figure 10.4).

20. Save the document under the name LANGUAGE.

```
        There are a number of programming languages in use today. Here
    are the most common in order of their popularity:

    BASIC stands for Beginners All-purpose Symbolic Instruction Code.
    This language was initially developed for non-computer science
    majors but has grown in popularity with the use of microcomputers.
    It was created primarily as a tool for teaching programming and
    algorithms.

    COBOL comes from Common Business Oriented Language and is designed
    for large business and commercial applications.

    PASCAL was named for Blaise Pascal. It was created primarily as a
    tool for teaching programming and algorithms.




                                              Doc 1 Pg 1 Ln 2" Pos 1"
```

Figure 10.4: Completed document

You can also move or copy text without inserting it immediately at its new location. Just press F1 when you see the prompt

Move cursor; press Enter to retrieve

The prompt will disappear. Now when you want to insert the text, select **Edit P**aste (Ctrl-F4 R) to see the prompt line

Retrieve: **1 B**lock; **2 T**abular Column; **3 R**ectangle: 0

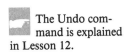 The Undo command is explained in Lesson 12.

Select **B**lock. Unlike the Undo command, which can remember three deletions, you can only store one copied or moved block of text in the Retrieve area. But as long as it is in the Retrieve area, you can insert it as many times as you want by selecting **Edit P**aste **B**lock (Ctrl-F4 R B).

Converting Text into a Comment

You can also use block techniques to convert regular text into a comment. But because comments will not be printed along with the document, this has the effect of cutting it from the text.

To convert text, highlight it as a block using **Edit Block**, then select **Edit Comment Create**. The prompt changes to

Create a comment? No (Yes)

Select **Yes** to place a comment box around the blocked text.

Lesson 47—How to Move Text between Documents

Cut or copied text remains in the retrieval area until you either exit WordPerfect or cut or copy another block. Saving a document, or switching to another, will not affect the stored text.

You can take advantage of this fact to move text between two or more documents. For instance, I have several research papers that contain paragraphs I can use in other documents. Rather than retype the paragraphs, I copy them from one document to the other. Keep in mind that there are two basic ways to store text for moving. Besides using the Move and Copy commands, you can delete highlighted text by pressing Del Y.

- Using Edit Delete with blocked text (or the Del key), the text is stored in an "undelete" area that can hold the last three deletions. Deleted text is recalled by selecting Undelete (F1).

- Text moved or copied using Edit Move or Copy (Ctrl-F4) is stored in a separate retrieval area, which can only hold one piece of block-cut text. Block-cut text is recalled by selecting Edit Paste (Ctrl-F4 R B).

Since the two storage areas are independent, you can have four deleted blocks safely stored away for retrieval. Three will be in the Undelete area (F1), the other in the block retrieval area recalled with Edit Paste (Ctrl-F4 R B).

Let's review the basic procedures for both methods and for moving text between documents.

Multiple Documents

Let's say you have text in both the Doc 1 and Doc 2 windows. You see a line, a paragraph, or other text in one document that you can use in the other. Here's how to move it between typing windows:

1. Switch to the window that has the text you want to move.

2. Move the text into the retrieval area.

   a. Highlight the text with the **Edit B**lock (Alt-F4) and cursor keys.

   b. Select **Edit M**ove (Ctrl-F4 B M) to move the block, or **Edit C**opy (Ctrl-F4 B C) to copy it.

3. Select **Edit S**witch Document (Shift-F3) to switch to the other document.

4. Place the cursor where you want to insert the text.

5. Press ⏎ to insert the text.

6. Save the document.

After Exiting a Document

In this case, you are only working with one document at a time. You want to save, or just exit the current document and insert some text from it into another. Here's how:

1. Move the desired text into the retrieval area.

   a. Highlight the text with the **Edit B**lock (Alt-F4) and cursor keys.

   b. Select **Edit M**ove (Ctrl-F4 B M) to move the block, or **Edit C**opy (Ctrl-F4 B C) to copy it.

2. Clear the current document from the screen. If you do not want to save it, select **File E**xit (F7) **No No**.

3. Recall the other document, the one in which you want to insert the text, to the screen.

4. Place the cursor where you want to insert the text.

5. Press ◄━┘ to insert the text.

6. Save the document.

Using these techniques, you can copy the same block to as many documents as you wish.

*L*esson 48—How to Print Blocks

Another reason to highlight a block is to print a selected portion of the text. You might want a quick printed record of a certain list of names or a particular paragraph without printing the entire document. Here's how:

1. Place the cursor at one end of the block you want to print.

2. Select **Edit B**lock (Alt-F4).

3. Move the cursor to the other end of the block you want to print.

4. Select **File P**rint (Shift-F7) to show the prompt

   Print Block? **No (Yes)**

5. Select **Y**es to print just the highlighted block.

6. Select **Edit B**lock (Alt-F4) to turn off the Block function.

The block will be printed with any headers, footers, page numbers, or other formatting marked in the document—even if the format codes are not in the highlighted section. If the block spans a page boundary, the text will appear on two pages. If you don't want to include the formatting codes from outside the section, use the method described in the next lesson to save the block, then print the text.

*L*esson 49—How to Save and Append Blocks

Yet another reason for blocking text is to save smaller portions of a larger document. Once text is marked as a block it can either be saved or appended.

Saving Blocks

Sometimes as you write you create a phrase or paragraph that you know you can use somewhere else. Rather than leave it lost in the current document, you can save just that text as a separate file on the disk. The saved block should be stored with a new name. If you give it the name of an existing document, the original will be replaced.

Here are the general procedures:

1. Place the cursor at one end of the block.

2. Select **Edit B**lock (Alt-F4).

3. Move the cursor to the other end of the block.

4. Select **File S**ave (F10) to show the prompt

   Block Name:

5. Type the name you wish to save the highlighted block under.

6. Press ◄─┘. The text will be saved on the disk. If there already is a document with that name, you will be prompted with

   Replace (document-name)? No (Yes)

   Select **Yes** to erase the existing document, or **No** to enter another name. Press F1 if you change your mind about saving the block.

7. Select **Edit B**lock (Alt-F4) to turn off the Block function.

Unlike when you print blocks, when you save a block only the text and codes within the highlighted block are saved. The formatting codes outside of the block, even those that would affect it when printed, are not included in the saved document.

Now that the block is saved, you treat it as any document. You can edit it, print it, or even add it to another document— just place the cursor where you want to insert it in the text and recall the block from the disk.

However, if you just want to add the block to the end of another document, read on.

*A*ppending Blocks

An *appended* block is added to the end of an existing document. This might be a collection of commonly used paragraphs, or an addition to a document that you are editing separately. It might be a small section of a long document that you want to work on without worrying about accidentally changing existing text; in this case, you can work on new sections individually and append them to the "master" document when they are edited and complete. Appending a block is easy because you don't have to recall and resave the other document.

When you append a block, the document to which it will be added must already exist on the disk. Follow these steps:

1. Place the cursor at one end of the block.

2. Select **Edit Block** (Alt-F4).

3. Move the cursor to the other end of the block.

With the keyboard, press Ctrl-F4 B A, type the file name, then press ◄─┘.

4. Select **Edit Append** to see the append options (Figure 10.5). The To Clipboard option is for use with WordPerfect's Shell environment.

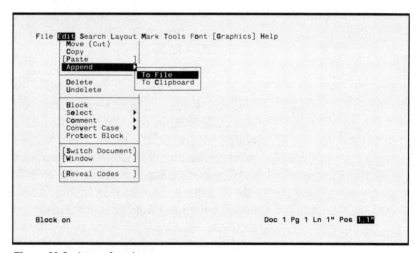

Figure 10.5: *Append options*

5. Select **To File** to see the prompt

Append to:

6. Type the name of the document you wish to add the high-lighted text to.

7. Press ↵. The text will be added to the end of that document. If there is no document with that name, the message

   ERROR: file not found

   will appear for a moment.

8. Repeat the process or select **E**dit **B**lock (Alt-F4) to turn off the Block function.

Block commands provide fast and convenient ways to manipulate sections of text. In the next chapter you'll learn ways to delete or change words or phrases throughout the entire document.

*Streamlining
Your Editing with
Search and Replace*

Featuring

Forward search

Backward search

Search and replace

Lesson 50—How to Search for Text

Much of your time editing a document is spent scrolling through it to locate a particular reference or passage of text. Often you are looking for a specific word or phrase. You're sure it is somewhere in the document, but you don't know the exact page number. You can save time with WordPerfect's Search command. Just type the text you are looking for and WordPerfect will search for it, either backward or forward through the document, and place the cursor directly on the specific word or phrase.

- A forward search locates the first occurrence of the search characters from the position of the cursor toward the end of the document. To search the entire text, begin with the cursor at the start of the document.

- A backward search locates the first occurrence of the search characters from the position of the cursor toward the beginning of the document. To search the entire text, begin with the cursor at the end of the document.

The text to be searched for can be from 1 to 58 characters, including letters, numbers, spaces, punctuation marks, and even codes, such as a hard return or a format change.

Now let's see how the Search feature works. You will recall the LANGUAGE document and use the Search command to locate specific text.

1. Start WordPerfect.

2. Recall the LANGUAGE document. With the document now on the screen, let's first search for the word *language*.

3. Select Search (F2) to display the Search menu (Figure 11.1).

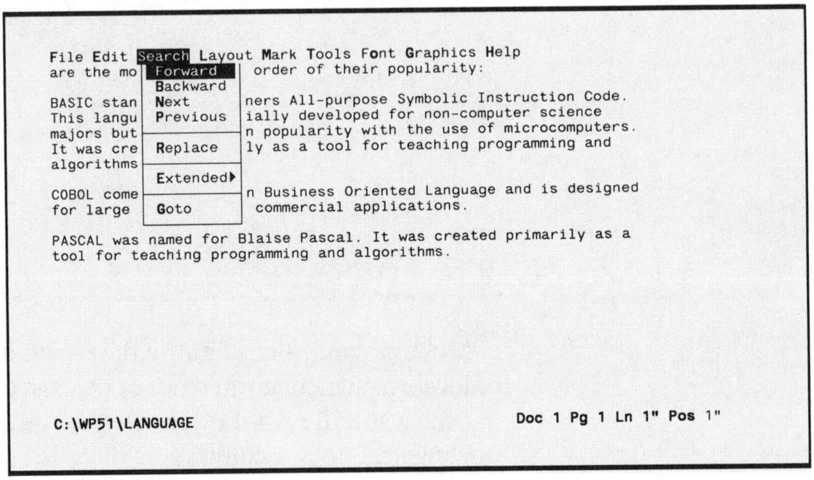

```
File Edit Search Layout Mark Tools Font Graphics Help
are the mo  Forward  | order of their popularity:
            Backward
BASIC stan  Next     ners All-purpose Symbolic Instruction Code.
This langu  Previous  ially developed for non-computer science
majors but           n popularity with the use of microcomputers.
It was cre  Replace  ly as a tool for teaching programming and
algorithms
            Extended▶
COBOL come           n Business Oriented Language and is designed
for large   Goto      commercial applications.

PASCAL was named for Blaise Pascal. It was created primarily as a
tool for teaching programming and algorithms.




C:\WP51\LANGUAGE                              Doc 1 Pg 1 Ln 1" Pos 1"
```

Figure 11.1: *Search menu*

4. Select Forward to see the prompt

   — > Srch:

   The forward-pointing "arrow" (—>) indicates a forward search.

5. Type

   language

   Do not press ↵ after typing the word. If you did, you'd see

   language[HRt]

   on the screen, and WordPerfect would search only for the word *language* followed by a Hard Return code.

6. Press F2 to begin the search.

   The cursor will move to the word *languages* in the first paragraph. Why did the cursor stop there, and not at the first occurrence of the singular *language*? Actually, WordPerfect is not searching for a word at all. Instead, it is looking for the first occurrence of the characters *l a n g u a g e* in the text, even if they are part of another word. (So a search for *the* would place the cursor on words such as *their* and *other*.)

   Now let's find the next occurrence of the same word.

7. Select Search Next (F2 twice) to locate the next occurrence. If you select Search **Previous**, WordPerfect will move toward the start of the text and look for the word there.

8. Select Search Next (F2 twice) again. The search will repeat and the cursor will be placed on the word *Language*. Now let's search for another word.

9. Select Search Forward (F2), type *PASCAL* (all uppercase), then press F2. The cursor finds the word in the last paragraph.

10. Select Search Next (F2 twice). The prompt displays *∗Not Found∗* in the status line for a few seconds, even though *Pascal* appears later in the same paragraph. The cursor remains at the current location when the search characters are not found.

    Lowercase letters entered at the Search prompt will be matched with either lowercase or uppercase characters in the document. So a search for *language* found *Language*. Uppercase letters entered in the Search prompt will match only uppercase letters in the text. So *PASCAL* will not locate *Pascal*, and *Language* would not be matched with *language*.

11. Select Search **Backward** (Shift-F2) for a backward search. The prompt shows

    <— Srch:PASCAL

    The backward-pointing "arrow" (<—) indicates a backward search.

12. Type the text you want to search for next:

    teach

13. Press F2 to begin the search. The cursor moves backward through the document, from the cursor position toward the start of the text, and lands on the word *teaching* in the second paragraph. Remember that if you want to search the entire document you must first move the cursor to either end by pressing Home Home ↑ or Home Home ↓.

    Now let's search for a code, in this case [Tab].

14. Select Search **Backward**.

15. Press the Tab key. Notice that the [Tab] code is entered in place of the text in the Search prompt.

16. Press F2. The cursor moves to the start of the first sentence, where the Tab key was used.

17. Leave the text on the screen for use with the next lesson.

The Search command only "looks" at the parts of the document that you see on the screen—not for matching text in headers, footers, endnotes, footnotes, graphic box captions or text boxes. If you want these areas searched as well, select Search Extended (Home F2), as in Figure 11.2.

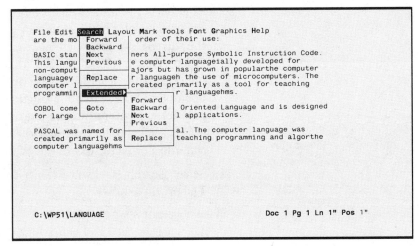

Figure 11.2: Search Extended menu

*S*earching for Codes

To search for codes that are inserted with single keystrokes, such as tab and ↩, just press the same keystroke at the Search prompt.

However, to search for codes that require using the pull down menus (such as bold or underline), you must use the WordPerfect function keys instead.

For example, to search for the [Bold] code, select Search **Forward** or **Backward**, then press F6, the function key equivalent to selecting **F**ont **A**ppearance **B**old.

If the code requires more than one keystroke, start with the first keystroke. A second prompt line will appear. Make your selection and press F2.

For instance, to search for large type size, select **Search Forward** or **B**ackward, then press Ctrl-F8. The prompt changes to

1 Size; **2** Appearance; **3** Normal; **4** Base Font; **5** Print Color: 0

Select **Size** to display the prompt

1 Suprscpt; **2** Subscpt; **3** Fine; **4** Small; **5** Large; **6** Vry Large; **7** Ext Large: 0

Select **Large**. The Search prompt will appear:

—> Srch: [LARGE]

Press F2 to start the search.

The Search function is an invaluable aid for editing. Rather than scan an entire document for a specific reference, just search for it.

I also use the Search function to move quickly to specific locations in a document. I'll insert a placeholder at appropriate reference points in the document. The placeholder is usually something like *xxxx*—text that I know won't be appearing anywhere else. When I have to refer back to that section of text, I search for the placeholder.

Lesson 51—How to Replace Text

Have you ever misspelled the same word several times in one document or realized that you entered the wrong information in several places? Or do you have a certain document that could easily be modified for another use if the same word were changed several times—for example, a letter that could be used another time if you just changed "he" to "she"?

Using the Replace command, you can automatically locate any text and replace it with something else, no matter how many times it appears. Repeated mistakes can be corrected in a few keystrokes.

To see how Replace works, let's make some changes to the LANGUAGE document.

In that document, you used the word *popularity* twice. Let's use the Replace function to change the first of these occurrences to the word *use*. Recall the document if it is not still on the screen from Lesson 50.

1. Press Home Home ↑ to place the cursor at the start of the document. Like a forward search, Replace works from the position of the cursor to the end of the document. So to replace every occurrence of the text, place the cursor at the start of the document.

2. Select Search **R**eplace (Alt-F2) to start the Replace procedure. The prompt changes to

   w/Confirm? No (Yes)

   If you select **Y**es, you will be given the opportunity to confirm each possible replacement. If you select **N**o, the replacements will occur automatically. The Confirm option is useful if you are unsure whether you want to replace all occurrences of the text.

3. Select **Y**es for a confirmed replacement. The — > Srch prompt appears, followed by the last search phrase you used, if any.

4. Type the term you want to replace:

   popularity

   Any search phrase or code already at the prompt is deleted as soon as you type another.

5. Press F2. The prompt changes to

   Replace with:

6. Type the word you want to insert:

   use

7. Press F2 to begin the replacement.
   WordPerfect first does a forward search for the word *popularity*, using the same uppercase-lowercase rules as a regular search.

Since this is a confirmed search (because you selected **Yes** in Step 3), the cursor stops at the first occurrence of the word and the prompt changes to

Confirm? No (Yes)

8. Select **Yes** to replace the word *popularity* with the word *use*. The search will continue until it finds the next occurrence of the word.

9. Press F7 to stop the function since you only wanted to replace that one occurrence.

   Now let's try an automatic replacement.

10. Press Home Home ↑.

11. Select **S**earch **R**eplace **N**o (Alt-F2 N) for an automatic (non-confirmed) search.

12. Type *teaching* (the word you want to replace), then press F2.

13. Type *learning* and press F2. The word *teaching* will be replaced with *learning* in the two instances where it was used.

   If you type the search and replace words in all lowercase letters and the original word in the text is capitalized, the replacement will be capitalized. For example, say the text contains the words *Computer* and *computer*. If you enter *computer* as the search phrase and *machine* as its replacement, both occurrences will be replaced, by *Machine* and *machine* respectively.

   However, if you enter *Computer* as the search phrase and *machine* as its replacement, only the capitalized *Computer* will be replaced—by *machine* in all lowercase letters.

   Type the search phrase in all lowercase letters if you want to replace every occurrence of the word while maintaining the same capitalization as the original.

   When the replacement is complete, the cursor remains at the last location where a replacement was made.

   Automatic replacement is a powerful tool when editing documents. But because it changes the text, it can also result in unexpected and unwanted results. As an example, two sentences in the LANGUAGE document use the word *It* to refer to a computer language. So let's automatically replace the word *it* with *the computer language*.

14. Press Home Home ↑.

15. Select Search **R**eplace **N**o (Alt-F2 N) for an automatic search.

16. Type *it* and press F2.

17. Type *the computer language* and press F2. The two sentences that began *It was* now read *The computer language was*—just as we wanted.

    But look at the second paragraph. The *it* in *initially* was also replaced, resulting in *This language was inthe computer language ially developed.* The same problem occurs at other places in the text where the characters *it* were replaced.

    Use automatic replacement carefully.

18. Select **F**ile E**x**it (F7) **N**o **Y**es to exit WordPerfect without saving the changed document.

Like searching, the Replace command only works on the parts of the document that you see on the screen. If you want other areas searched for replacement as well, select Search Extended **R**eplace (Alt-F2 for extended replace).

As you've seen, WordPerfect is a comprehensive yet easy-to- learn word processing program. In the first eleven chapters, you learned how to edit, format, and print text. Beginning with Chapter 12 you'll learn some special "power-user" features of WordPerfect.

12

Creating
Multicolumn Layouts

Featuring

Newspaper columns

Parallel columns

Lesson 52—How to Create Newspaper Columns

Desktop publishing seems to be a magic phrase these days. If you're responsible for producing a newsletter or other multicolumn document, you can take advantage of WordPerfect's built-in Newspaper Column feature.

Newspaper columns (Figure 12.1) automatically run from one column to the next on the page, from left to right. When the far right column is filled, text moves to the left column on the next page.

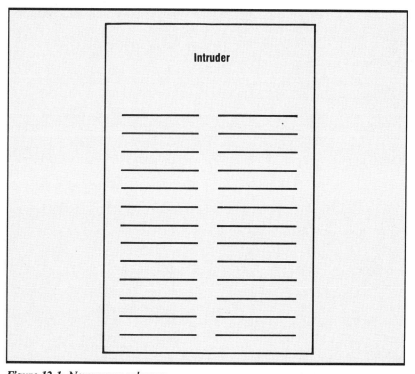

Figure 12.1: Newspaper columns

Since there can be so much variation in the number and size of columns, you must first *define* the format of the page; that is, you must set the number and spacing of columns on the page.

In this lesson you will create a two-column newsletter with a title across the top of the page.

Defining Column Layouts

You must first define the number of columns and their spacing on the page. While it is possible to have columns of different sizes on the same page, equal width is more common. If you want equal-sized columns, WordPerfect will calculate the spacing for you.

Once you define a column layout it stays in effect throughout the document. You do not have to define it again, unless you want a different number or size of columns. Just turn on the Column mode when you want to type columns and turn it off for regular typing.

You can define up to 24 text columns on a page. Right now let's define a format for two even-sized columns, five spaces apart.

1. Start WordPerfect.

2. Select **Layout Columns** (Alt-F7 C) to see the column options (Figure 12.2).

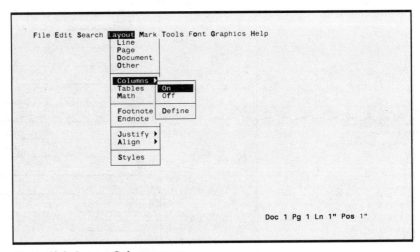

Figure 12.2: Layout Columns menu

3. Select **D**efine to see the Text Column Definition menu (Figure 12.3).

```
Text Column Definition

    1 - Type                              Newspaper

    2 - Number of Columns                 2

    3 - Distance Between Columns

    4 - Margins

    Column    Left      Right     Column    Left      Right
      1:      1"        4"          13:
      2:      4.5"      7.5"        14:
      3:                            15:
      4:                            16:
      5:                            17:
      6:                            18:
      7:                            19:
      8:                            20:
      9:                            21:
     10:                            22:
     11:                            23:
     12:                            24:

Selection: 0
```

Figure 12.3: *Text Column Definition menu*

The default column style is two newspaper columns spaced $1/2$ inch apart. Each column is 3 inches wide, and the first column begins at the left margin.

If you wanted to change the number of columns or the spacing, you would select the appropriate option. For instance, for three columns, select Number of Columns, type *3*, then ◄─┘. The measurements would automatically appear. Change intercolumn spacing by entering the measurement at option 3, Distance Between Columns. Change column width by selecting option 4, Margins.

4. Press ◄─┘ to accept all of the default settings. You'll see the prompt:

Columns: **1** On; **2** Off; **3** Define: 0

5. For now, press ◄─┘ to clear the Columns prompt line.

With the column definition code now inserted into the document, you can turn columns on and off whenever you want to.

Typing Columns

Once the layout has been defined, it is easier if you turn Columns on before typing the columns themselves. This way you'll see how the columns will appear as you type them. You will first type any desired single-column text, such as a title or introductory paragraph, then turn on Columns and type the rest of the text. Follow these steps to create a newsletter:

1. Select **Layout Align Center** (Shift-F6).

2. Type the title of our newsletter:

   Faculty Research Projects

3. Press ◄─┘ three times to add space between the title and the text of the newsletter.

4. Select **Layout Justify Left** (Shift-F8 L J L F7) to turn off justification. Because of the short line length, too many extra spaces would be inserted in justified columns.

5. Now turn on the Column mode by selecting **Layout Columns On** (Alt-F7 C O). You must have a column layout defined before turning Columns on.

   With the Column mode now on, the word *Col* appears on the status line followed by the column number in which the cursor is placed.

6. Type the following, noticing how the text conforms to the two-column layout:

   Factors Involved in French Language Word Processing Utilizing The Standard English Language Keyboard, Dr. Renee Voltaire, French Department

   Dr. Voltaire analyzed several popular word processing programs for their capacity to display and print French language characters. Dr. Voltaire then studied the difficulties encountered in typing French documents using the standard QWERTY keyboard.

   The Possible Contributions of Computers to the Creative Writing Process, Dr. Leslie Van Mot, English Department

Dr. Van Mot tested the effects of using word processing programs on the creative output of students. The writing of student volunteers was measured using several criteria. These included sentence complexity, character development, and grammatical accuracy. The students were divided into test and control groups. The test group was trained in using a word processing program, while the control group was given standard writing practice exercises. This report studies the results of the training.

The Economic Impact of Computer Technology on the Gross National Product, Dr. William Duke, Economics Department

Dr. Duke abstracted data from the past ten years supplied by the National Economics Institute. He concludes that starting in 1984 there has been a direct relationship between the GNP and the fortunes of the computer industry.

Art Education and the Computer, Dr. Wilma Stephens, Art Department

Dr. Stephens has been researching the use of computer technology in the design process. Her primary interest is in the use of simulated graphics to project light patterns on angular objects and the effects of the projections on color density as observed by the human eye.

7. Select **Layout Columns Off** (Alt-F7 C F) to exit Columns mode.

8. Select **File Print Full** (Shift-F7 F) to print the newsletter (Figure 12.4).

9. Save the document under the name NEWS, and stay in Word-Perfect for the next lesson.

No matter how long the document, text will flow from column to column and from page to page. To type single-column text again, press Ctrl-◄━ to end the last column, then select **Layout Columns Off** (Alt-F7 C F) to turn off the Column mode.

```
                    Faculty Research Projects

Factors Involved in French          been a direct relationship
Language Word Processing            between the GNP and the
Utilizing The Standard English      fortunes of the computer
Languages Keyboard, Dr. Renee       industry.
Voltaire, French Department
                                    Art Education and the
Dr. Voltaire analyzed several       Computer, Dr. Wilma Stephens,
popular word processing             Art Department.
programs for their abilities
to display and print French         Dr.Stephens has been
language characters. Dr.            researching the use of
Voltaire then studied the           computer technology in the
difficulties encountered in         design process. Her primary
typing French documents using       interest is in the use of
the standard QWERTY keyboard.       simulated graphics to project
                                    light patterns on angular
The Possible Contributions of       objects and their effects on
Computers to the Creating           color density as observed by
Writing Process, Dr. Leslie         the human eye.
Van Mot, English Department.

Dr. Van Mot tested the effects
of using word processing
programs on the creative
output of students. The
writing of student volunteers
was measured using several
measurements. These included
sentence complexity, character
development, and grammatical
accuracy. The students were
divided into a test and
control group. The test group
was trained in using a word
processing program, the
control group given standard
writing practice exercises.
The report studies the results
of writing after the training.

The Economic Impact of
Computer Technology on the
Gross National Product, Dr.
William Duke, Economics
Department.

Dr. Duke abstracted data from
the past 10 years supplied by
the National Economics
Institute. He concludes that
starting in 1984 there has
```

Figure 12.4: Sample newsletter

When editing, you can move from column to column with the Ctrl-Home (GoTo) command. Press Ctrl-Home → to move to the column on the right, Ctrl-Home ← to the column on the left.

Lesson 53—How to Create Parallel Columns

In some cases you don't want text to flow freely from column to column because text on the left refers directly to text on the right. For example, in Figure 12.5 the text in the right column explains what's in the left. They go together as a set and you want to make sure that the corresponding text is kept together.

```
                 Popular Computer Software Packages


Word Processing,          These are applications software
data management,          packages. They are designed to perform a
graphics,                 specific useful functions. For most
spreadsheet, project      users in business and academic areas,
planning                  applications software is the most
                          important to master.


COBOL, FORTRAN,           These are programming languages. They
BASIC, Pascal, C,         are used to write specific applications
PL/1, Assembly            for which appropriate or adequate
                          applications software is no available.


PC/DOS, MS/DOS,           These are disk operating systems. The
TRS/DOS, UNIX             operating systems is a very
                          sophisticated software package that
                          handles the interface between the
                          computer, devices that are attached to
                          it, and the user.
```

Figure 12.5: Parallel columns

This format is used often in job resumes, where the left column contains employment dates, and the right column includes the employer and job responsibilities.

These are called *parallel columns* and they must be defined and typed differently from newspaper columns. For instance, in newspaper columns you just continued typing and let WordPerfect run the text from column to column. With parallel columns, however, you enter the text in blocks: the first text on the left, then its corresponding text on the right; the second text on the left, then its corresponding text on the right, etc. You use the Ctrl-↵ key to end a block and move to the other column.

Use these techniques when the text in each column will not fit on one line. When creating numeric columns or tables, use the techniques shown in Chapter 6. But when typing paragraphs, use parallel columns.

Parallel columns can be regular or *block-protected*. Block-protected parallel columns are kept next to each other even if it means moving them all to a new page. Regular parallel columns, on the other hand, will span a page break.

In this lesson, you will create the text shown in Figure 12.5, two uneven parallel columns with 5 spaces between them. One column is 20 characters wide, the other 40.

For your own documents, plan how wide you want each column to be, making sure they are wide enough to contain the text. Columns that are too narrow are difficult to read.

Defining Parallel Columns

The procedures for parallel columns are almost exactly the same as for newspaper columns—define the layout, turn Column mode on, and enter the text.

The number and width of parallel columns must be defined, including the spacing between columns. Since the text in the right column refers to the text on the left, WordPerfect will use Block Protect to keep corresponding paragraphs on the same page.

Follow these steps to define two parallel columns:

1. Select **L**ayout **C**olumns **D**efine (Alt-F7 C D) to show the Text Column Definition menu (see Figure 12.3).

2. Select **T**ype. The prompt line changes to

   Column Type: **1** Newspaper; **2** Parallel;
   3 Parallel with **B**lock Protect:0

3. Select **P**arallel for regular parallel columns. The number of columns and the column spacing remain at the default 2. Now let's change the width of the two columns by using the Margin option.

4. Select **M**argins. The cursor moves to the left margin setting for the first column.

5. Press ◄─┘ to accept the default 1 inch setting. The cursor moves to the right margin setting for that column.

6. Type *3* for its right margin, then press ◄─┘. This creates a column 20 characters wide.

7. Type *3.5* for the second column's left margin, then press ◄─┘.

8. Press ◄─┘ to accept the default right margin of 7.5 inches and return to the prompt line.

9. Press ◄─┘ twice to return to the typing area.

Typing Parallel Columns

Now that the columns have been defined, you can turn on Column mode when you are ready to enter the text.

1. Select **Layout Align Center** (Shift-F6) and type

   Popular Computer Software Packages

2. Press ◄─┘ three times to add space between the heading and the columns.

3. Select **Layout Justify Left** (Shift-F8 L J L F7) to turn off justification.

4. Select **Layout Columns On** (Alt-F7 C O) to turn on Column mode. *Col 1* will appear on the status line.

5. Now type the text of the first column:

   Word processing, data management, graphics,
   spreadsheet, project planning

The text will conform to the column margins.

6. Press Ctrl-◄─┘. The cursor will move to the left margin of the next column. When the Column mode is on, Ctrl-◄─┘ ends one column and moves to the next. (With Column mode off, Ctrl-◄─┘ ends the page.)

   Use Ctrl-◄─┘ only when you are done typing the parallel text in one of the columns and you want to move to another to type corresponding text. When editing, do not try to use it as a cursor movement command to move from column to column. As with newspaper columns, move from column to column with the Ctrl-Home → and Ctrl-Home ← commands.

With regular parallel columns, WordPerfect uses the Ctrl-← codes to move from column to column. However, with block-protected parallel columns, special codes—[Block Pro:On] and [Block Pro:Off]—surround each column. WordPerfect uses these to determine which blocks will be kept on the same page. If the text in one column extends into the new page, both blocks will be carried over so they start on that page. If you select regular parallel columns, the longer column will span the page break.

7. Type

> These are applications software packages. They are designed to perform a specific useful function. For most users in business and academic areas, applications software is the most important to master.

8. Press Ctrl-← to end that column and move back to the first column.

9. Type the following:

> COBOL, FORTRAN, BASIC, Pascal, C, PL/1, Assembly

10. Press Ctrl-← , then type

> These are programming languages. They are used to write specific applications for which appropriate or adequate applications software is not available.

11. Press Ctrl-← , then type

> PC/DOS, MS/DOS, TRS/DOS, UNIX

12. Press Ctrl-←, then type

> These are disk operating systems. The operating system is a very sophisticated software package that handles the interface between the computer, devices that are attached to it, and the user.

13. Select **Layout Columns Off** (Alt-F7 C F) to exit Columns mode.

14. Select **File Print Full** (Shift-F7 F) to print the parallel columns, or Select **File Print View** (Shift-F7 V) to view them.

15. Select **File Exit** (F7) **No No** to clear the screen and remain in WordPerfect.

WordPerfect's automatic on-screen Column feature can save you hours of formatting. If you're unsure how to use it, first type your document using the default single column format and save it to your disk. Then place the cursor where you want the columns to begin and experiment with various column definitions. Remember, you can always delete the Column Definition code and try another format.

In the next chapter you'll learn another powerful yet simple word processing feature—how to create form letters.

Creating Personalized Form Letters

Featuring

Form letters

Merging to the screen

Merging to the printer

Lesson 54—How to Write the Form Letter

Form letters and junk mail just seem to go together, but that's because many form letters are obviously mass-produced and are as "personal" as the phone directory.

That doesn't have to be the case. You can use form letters yourself whenever you want to send the same message, or a similar one, to more than one person. For example, you might want to send a form letter as a response to an employment ad, a letter of complaint, a request for information, or an invitation to a party.

While there are many personal uses for form letters, there are many more business uses. They can serve as notices to customers, requests for proposals, or announcements. In fact, WordPerfect provides form document commands that can convert the word processor into a sophisticated data management system.

Every use of form letters requires certain basic steps:

- A form letter must be written that contains the text common to all copies of the document. This letter is written only once, no matter how many copies will be printed.

- A data file must be prepared, or be already available, that contains the variable information to be inserted into each letter. Once the data file is created, it can be used with other form documents.

- The two files must be merged for printing. They can be merged onto the screen, saved in a file and printed later on, or printed as they are merged.

This lesson will explain the first step, writing the form letter. Constructing the data file will be covered in Lesson 55, and the final step of merging and printing is in Lesson 56.

The Primary Document

The form letter is also called the *primary document*. In addition to the words or phrases that will be used in every copy of the letter, the primary document includes special *Field* codes that will insert variable information during the "personalization" process.

Each field stands for one item of personal information, such as a last name, an address, a telephone number, or a credit rating. When a letter is printed, the field will be replaced by an item of information. For instance, the Name field might be replaced by *Frederick Rogers*. The fields can be used in any order and the same field could even be used more than once in the same primary file. There are also special Merge codes in the primary document that tell WordPerfect how to merge the documents.

> The display of merge codes can be turned off using the File Setup (Shift-F1) menu.

Unlike other codes used by WordPerfect, the Field and Merge codes are displayed on the screen along with other text. You do not have to select Edit Reveal Codes (Alt-F3) to display them. As long as you print the documents through the special Merge feature, as explained in Lesson 56, the variable information, not the codes, will be printed.

In this lesson, you will create a form letter containing codes for seven fields: name, company, address, city, state, zip code, and salutation (Figure 13.1).

Follow these steps:

1. Start WordPerfect.

2. Select **T**ools **D**ate **C**ode to insert the date into the form letter. When the letter is merged, the system date will be inserted at this location.

3. Press ← twice to space between the date and the inside address.

> WordPerfect 5.1 recognizes the merge codes of version 5.0.

4. Select **T**ools **M**erge Codes (Shift-F9) to display the Merge Codes menu (Figure 13.2). These are all of the Merge codes that can be included in primary documents. Many of the codes are used for advanced merging and database functions that go beyond basic form letters.

5. Select **F**ield. The prompt shows

Enter Field:

Remember, each field stands for an item of information that will be merged into the document. Because you can have many fields, each must be given a number.

```
March 12, 1990

{FIELD}1~
{FIELD}2~
{FIELD}3~
{FIELD}4~, {FIELD}5~   {FIELD}6~

Dear {FIELD}7~:

       As a school project in financial management, we are analyzing
the annual reports from the nation's largest companies.
       We would like to include the annual report for {FIELD}2~ in
our study. Since your firm is known for sound fiscal policies and
strategic planning, we feel its report would contribute greatly to
our work.

                        Sincerely,

                        Alvin A. Aardvark
                        M.B.A. Candidate
```

Figure 13.1: The completed primary document

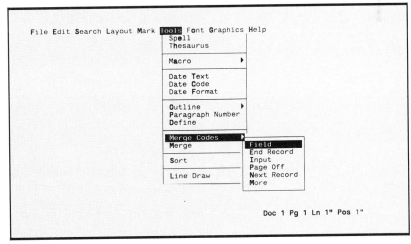

Figure 13.2: Merge Codes menu

6. Press *1* (the first field number), then ←⏎. The characters {FIELD}1 ˜ will appear in the text. In this case, field 1 will represent the name of the recipient, which will be inserted at the position of the {FIELD}1 ˜ code in the text.

7. Press ←⏎.

8. Select **Tools Merge Codes Field (Shift-F9 F)**.

9. Type *2*, then press ←⏎ twice to insert the {FIELD}2 ˜ code. This will represent the name of the company. It will be used twice in the letter, once in the address and once in the second paragraph.

10. Select **Tools Merge Codes Field (Shift-F9 F)**, type *3*, then press ←⏎ to insert the {FIELD}3 ˜ code for the street address.

11. Press ←⏎. The last address line will be a combination of three fields (city, state, and zip code) and will look like this:

    {FIELD}4˜, {FIELD}5˜ {FIELD}6˜

12. Select **Tools Merge Codes Field (Shift-F9 F)**, type *4*, then press ←⏎ to insert the {FIELD}4 ˜ code for the city.

13. Type a comma (,) then press the spacebar.

14. Select **Tools Merge Codes Field (Shift-F9 F)**, type *5*, then press ←⏎ to insert the {FIELD}5 ˜ code for the state.

15. Press the spacebar twice.

16. Select **Tools Merge Codes Field (Shift-F9 F)**, type *6*, then press ←⏎ to insert the {FIELD}6 ˜ code for the zip code.

17. Press ←⏎ twice to put space between the inside address and salutation.

18. Type *Dear*.

19. Press the spacebar.

20. Select **Tools Merge Codes Field (Shift-F9 F)**, type *7*, then press ←⏎ to insert the {FIELD}7 ˜ code for the salutation.

21. Type a colon (:), then press ←⏎ twice before typing the body of the letter.

22. Type

    As a school project in financial management, we are
    analyzing the annual reports from the nation's largest
    companies.

    We would like to include the annual report for

23. Press the spacebar once after typing the word *for.*

24. Select **Tools Merge Codes Field** (Shift-F9 F), type *2*, then
    press ◄━┙ to insert the {FIELD}2 ˜ code for the company
    name. A code can be used more than once in a document
    if you want the same information repeated. Since you want
    the name of the company to appear again here, you enter the
    same Field code again.

25. Press the spacebar, then continue typing:

    in our study. Since your firm is known for sound fiscal
    policies and strategic planning, we feel its report would
    contribute greatly to our work.

    Sincerely,

    Alvin A. Aardvark
    M.B.A. Candidate

26. Press ◄━┙.

    The form letter is now complete and the variable informa-
    tion that you enter in the next lesson will be inserted into each
    copy of the primary document. Everything will appear cor-
    rectly as long as you have seven bits of information to match
    the seven fields.

27. Select **File Exit** (F7) **Yes**, type *FORM*, and press ◄━┙ to save
    the primary file.

28. Select **No** to continue with the next lesson, or **Yes** to exit
    WordPerfect.

The primary form document is now complete.

Lesson 55—How to Assemble the Variable Information File

The variable information file, called the *secondary merge file* by WordPerfect, is entered as a series of *records*. Each record contains all of the individual items of information that can be merged into a letter. The order of the items must correspond to the field numbers representing them in the primary document. For instance, the recipient's name, which was assigned to Field 1 in our letter, must be the first item in the record. The item represented by Field 2 must be second, and so on. Thus if you are sending letters to 20 companies, there will be 20 records, each containing seven fields.

When the data file is entered, some means must be used to mark the end of each field and of each record. With WordPerfect, the end of each field is marked by the {END FIELD} code. The end of each record is shown by the {END RECORD} code. The placement of these codes is important, so let's practice by following these steps.

1. Start WordPerfect or make sure the screen is clear by selecting **File Exit (F7) No No**.

2. Type (but do not press ◄┘ when done)

   Frederick Rogers

3. Press F9. WordPerfect will display the code {END FIELD} next to the name and move the cursor to the next line.

4. Type *Rogers Motor Company* and press F9.

5. Type *431 Broad Street* and press F9.

   As you should see by now, you must press the F9 key immediately after each field. Do not press the ◄┘ key or you'll get extra lines in your letters.

6. Type *Philadelphia* and press F9.

7. Type *PA* and press F9.

8. Type *19101* and press F9.

9. Type *Mr. Rogers* and press F9. This is the last field for the first letter, so another code must be entered now to end the record.

10. Select **Tools Merge** Codes **End** Record (Shift-F9 E). The {END RECORD} code is placed at the end of the record and a hard page break is inserted. Do not press ⏎ after inserting the code or you will get an extra line at the beginning of the next record.

11. In the same manner, enter the next three records. Insert the {END RECORD} code after the last record.

Milford Wilson{END FIELD}
Wilson Widget Company{END FIELD}
42 East Broad Street{END FIELD}
Beuford{END FIELD}
PA{END FIELD}
19011{END FIELD}
Mr. Wilson{END FIELD}
{END RECORD}
Jean Kohl{END FIELD}
Kohl Scientific{END FIELD}
45th Street and Osage Avenue{END FIELD}
El Paso{END FIELD}
TX{END FIELD}
23123{END FIELD}
Mrs. Kohl{END FIELD}
{END RECORD}
Dr. Adam Chesin{END FIELD}
Northwest Drugs, Inc.{END FIELD}
401 Ocean Ave.{END FIELD}
Margate{END FIELD}
NJ{END FIELD}
71652{END FIELD}
Dr. Chesin{END FIELD}
{END RECORD}

The completed file should look like Figure 13.3.

12. Select **File Exit** (F7) **Yes**, type *LIST*, and press ⏎ to save the secondary document.

13. Select **No** to continue with the next lesson, or **Yes** to exit WordPerfect.

You can add or delete names from the secondary file as needed. Just remember to maintain the proper format with {*END FIELD*} after each

```
Frederick Rogers{END FIELD}
Rogers Motor Company{END FIELD}
431 Broad Street{END FIELD}
Philadelphia{END FIELD}
PA{END FIELD}
19101{END FIELD}
Mr. Rogers{END FIELD}
{END RECORD}
Milford Wilson{END FIELD}
Wilson Widget Company{END FIELD}
42 East Broad Street{END FIELD}
Beuford{END FIELD}
PA{END FIELD}
19011{END FIELD}
Mr. Wilson{END FIELD}
{END RECORD}
Jean Kohl{END FIELD}
Kohl Scientific{END FIELD}
45th Street and Osage Avenue{END FIELD}
El Paso{END FIELD}
TX{END FIELD}
23123{END FIELD}
Mrs. Kohl{END FIELD}
{END RECORD}
Dr. Adam Chesin{END FIELD}
Northwest Drugs, Inc.{END FIELD}
401 Ocean Ave.{END FIELD}
Margate{END FIELD}
NJ{END FIELD}
71652{END FIELD}
Dr. Chesin{END FIELD}
{END RECORD}
```

Figure 13.3: *The completed sample data file with page break lines dividing each record*

field, {*END RECORD*} after each record, and seven fields per record in the same order. Note that there is nothing in either file that links them. The primary file can be merged with any secondary file that has seven fields in each record. Likewise, the secondary file can be used with any form document needing name and address information.

So, for example, you can use the same secondary file to print envelopes for the form letters. Format a new primary document for printing envelopes (as explained in Lesson 41) and enter the following:

```
{FIELD}1~
{FIELD}2~
{FIELD}3~
{FIELD}4~, {FIELD}5~ {FIELD}6~
```

Using the techniques explained in the next lesson to merge and print the form letters, you can then print the envelopes.

Handling Missing Information

In the form letter and data file you just created, you coded seven fields (variables) in the form letter and seven in the data file. Each record in the data file must contain at least the same number of fields as in the form letter (it could contain more, with some just not being used).

But what if you don't have all of the same information for every letter? Say, for example, that you're writing to someone at a large company in a small town. Because the firm is so well known, they don't use any street address, such as

Mr. Word Perfect
WordPerfect Corporation
Orem, Utah 84057

Remember, the address in the form letter looks like this:

{FIELD}1 ~
{FIELD}2 ~
{FIELD}3 ~
{FIELD}4 ~ , {FIELD}5 ~ {FIELD}6 ~

Since the record must have at least the same number of fields, it would look like this, with an empty field line for the missing address:

Mr. Word Perfect{END FIELD}
Word Perfect Corporation{END FIELD}
{END FIELD}
Orem{END FIELD}
Utah{END FIELD}
84057{END FIELD}
Mr. Perfect{END FIELD}
{END RECORD}

Because of the missing data, the merged address would have an extra blank line:

Mr. Word Perfect
WordPerfect Corporation

Orem, Utah 84057

To avoid this if you think a certain field will be missing from some records, insert a question mark immediately after the field number, — {FIELD}3? ˜ . WordPerfect will not leave a blank line if the field is empty.

Lesson 56—How to Merge Files

By default, the results of merging primary and secondary files are displayed on the screen. The variable information from a record is inserted in the appropriate place in a form letter. A page break is inserted and another letter is created, until all of the records have been used.

Newly merged documents can be printed immediately, saved on disk, or edited. By merging them on the screen, you can add a large group of form letters to the queue and print them while you work on another document. You can also delete blank lines resulting from missing data.

If your mailing list is large, however, the resulting merged document may be too large for your computer's memory and available disk space. In this case you have two alternatives before you run out to the computer store for more memory.

- You can break the large mailing list down into smaller ones, then merge and save each set individually.

- You can direct the output of the merge to the printer, instead of to the screen. Each letter is printed as it is generated without saving it on the disk. But special codes have to be added to the end of the primary document for this type of output.

In this lesson you will merge the letters to both the screen and the printer.

Merging Form Documents to the Screen

Once both the primary and secondary files are completed, you can merge them. In this chapter the primary file is called FORM and the secondary file LIST.

You should still be in WordPerfect. If not, start the program before following these steps.

1. Select **Tools Merge** (Ctrl-F9 M) to display the prompt

    Primary file:

2. Type *FORM*.

3. Press ⏎ to display the prompt

    Secondary file:

4. Type *LIST.*

5. Press ⏎. The word *Merging* will appear on the status line as the letters are generated. The letters will be displayed on the screen only after all of the merging is completed (Figure 13.4). You can now save the merged letters as a new document or print them by selecting **File Print Full** (Shift-F7 F).

6. For now, select **File Exit** (F7) **No No** to clear the screen.

```
                              Alvin A. Aardvark
                              M.B.A. Candidate
==============================================================================
March 12, 1990

Dr. Adam Chesin
Northwest Drugs, Inc.
401 Ocean Ave.
Margate, NJ  71652

Dear Dr. Chesin:

     As a school project in financial management, we are analyzing
the annual reports from the nation's largest companies.
     We would like to include the annual report for Northwest
Drugs, Inc. in our study. Since your firm is known for sound fiscal
policies and strategic planning, we feel its report would
contribute greatly to our work.

                         Sincerely,


                         Alvin A. Aardvark
                         M.B.A. Candidate

                                    Doc 1 Pg 4 Ln 4.17" Pos 5.6"
```

Figure 13.4: A completed form letter

*M*erging Form Documents to the Printer

Let's merge the letters once more, but this time we'll print them at the same time. First you'll have to recall the primary file and add several new codes. Follow these steps:

1. Select **File Retrieve** (Shift-F10), type *FORM*, and press ←.

2. Press Home Home ↓ to reach the end of the document.

3. Select **Tools Merge Codes Page** Off (Shift-F9 P). The {PAGE OFF} code is inserted. This prevents extra form feeds, or blank pages from ejecting after each page.

4. Select **Tools Merge Code More** (Shift-F9 M). A box appears on the top right of the screen with merge and macro codes (Figure 13.5). Most of these codes are used for advanced macro operations and are beyond the scope of this book.

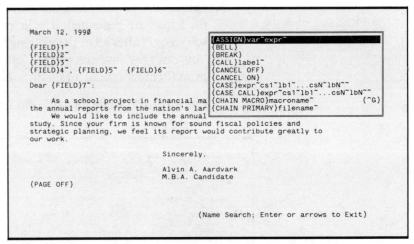

Figure 13.5: Advanced Merge and Macro codes

5. Press the ↓ key to scroll through the list until {PRINT} is highlighted, then press ←. The {PRINT} code directs the output to the printer.

    Notice that some codes show control keys on the right, such as (^T) for {PRINT}. These are equivalent commands that are used by earlier versions of WordPerfect and are still recognized by version 5.1.

6. Select **File Exit** (F7) **Yes**, press ←┘, then select **Yes No** to save the edited form letter and clear the screen.

7. Select **Tools Merge** (Ctrl-F9 M) to select the Merge option.

8. Type *FORM* at the Primary File prompt, then press ←┘.

9. Type *LIST* at the Secondary File prompt, then press ←┘. The records will be merged into the form letter and printed.

10. Select **File Exit** (F7) **No Yes** to exit WordPerfect.

You now know two ways to merge form letters: to the screen and directly to the printer. Each method has its advantages and disadvantages.

- Merging to the screen allows you to edit or save the merged letters; when you merge to the printer, no new document is created.

- Merging to the printer is appropriate when many copies of the letter must be generated. Otherwise you'd need enough disk space to hold all of the letters, and you'd still have to print them later.

Whichever method you select, merging can save a great deal of time and effort.

14

Adding Footnotes and Endnotes

Featuring

Lesson 57—How to Enter Footnotes

If you write academic or technical reports, you no doubt have been faced with the problem of footnotes. Placing footnotes on the bottom of appropriate pages can be a drudge using a typewriter or some word processing programs. If you later add or delete lines, the citation numbers may move to another page, which means you move a footnote.

WordPerfect, however, provides a feature known as *floating footnotes*. The program automatically places footnotes at the bottom of the appropriate page. If you delete or insert a footnote, the others will be renumbered automatically. The note is entered in a separate typing window, much like headers and footers, by selecting Layout Footnote (Ctrl-F7 F). While the footnote is stored in its own area, the Note code associated with it is inserted in the text of the document. When printing, WordPerfect will place the footnote on the same page as the code, automatically adding superscripted note references and adjusting the text. If the Note code moves to another page because text is added or deleted, the note will be printed on the new page.

In this lesson, you will enter several footnotes into a document called SYSTEM.

1. Start WordPerfect.

2. Type the SYSTEM document shown in Figure 14.1.

3. Place the cursor at the end of the first paragraph, the location of the first footnote citation.

4. Select **L**ayout **F**ootnote (Ctrl-F7 F) to see the footnote options (Figure 14.2).

```
Decision Support Needed

     With changing economic conditions the quality of management
is becoming crucial to the existence of clinical laboratories. No
longer should laboratory managers do without the decision support
systems necessary for setting and obtaining both short- and long-
term goals.

The Systems Approach

     The clinical laboratory is no different than any production
environment. Therefore the systems approach can be used to divide
this process into three basic steps: input, transformation, and
output.

     Input

     Resources of all types become the input to the system. In the
clinical laboratory, these resources include personnel, equipment,
supplies, and samples for testing.

     Transformation

     These resources are put through a conversion process in which
tests are performed, hardware maintained, and staff interacts.

     Output

     The results of this process are the output: results are
communicated to other systems in the organization and personnel
gains satisfaction and other rewards from participation in the
process.

The Flow of Resources

     To the informed manager, this flow of resources is critical,
since every action that takes place uses some resources. Each of
these "transactions" depletes the total pool of resources available
and should contribute to the output. When problems occur in any
organization, they can usually be traced to come problem in this
flow.
```

Figure 14.1: The SYSTEM sample document

5. Select **C**reate. The footnote screen, as shown in Figure 14.3, will appear with the first footnote number already displayed and indented ¹/₂ inch.

6. Type the text of the first footnote.

> Short-term goals are those aimed at objectives within four years.

7. Press F7. This "saves" the footnote and redisplays the document. The footnote number is next to the main text (Figure 14.4).

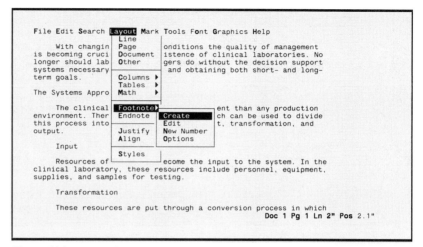

Figure 14.2: *Layout Footnote menu*

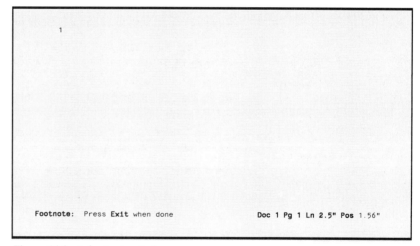

Figure 14.3: *A footnote window*

8. Place the cursor at the end of the last paragraph.

9. Select **Layout Footnote Create** (Ctrl-F7 F C). The footnote window appears, but with *2* for the second note.

10. Type the footnote.

> Some analysts consider all staff interactions as "transactions," even social ones that have no direct relationship to the job.

```
Decision Support Needed

     With changing economic conditions the quality of management
is becoming crucial to the existence of clinical laboratories. No
longer should laboratory managers do without the decision support
systems necessary for setting and obtaining both short- and long-
term goals.1

The Systems Approach

     The clinical laboratory is no different than any production
environment. Therefore the systems approach can be used to divide
this process into three basic steps: input, transformation, and
output.

   Input

     Resources of all types become the input to the system. In the
clinical laboratory, these resources include personnel, equipment,
supplies, and samples for testing.

   Transformation

     These resources are put through a conversion process in which
                                          Doc 1 Pg 1 Ln 2" Pos 2.16"
```

Figure 14.4: *A footnote citation number in the text*

11. Press F7. The number *2* is now in the text.

12. Select **F**ile **P**rint **F**ull (Shift-F7 F) to print the document (Figure 14.5).

The footnotes will be printed at the bottom of the appropriate page, using the following default format:

- Notes are single-spaced.

- Citation numbers run consecutively from page to page.

- A 2-inch line separates the notes from the text.

- Footnote and citation numbers are superscripted.

Like all default values, these can be changed to suit your own needs. With the footnotes added, the pagination automatically adjusts. The size of the footnotes will be taken into account and the page break line will reflect the end of the footnote text for that page.

*A*dding, Editing, and Deleting Footnotes

As documents are edited, footnotes often must be added or deleted from the text, moved around, or edited in some way. The process is a simple one with WordPerfect.

```
Decision Support Needed

    With changing economic conditions the quality of management
is becoming crucial to the existence of clinical laboratories. No
longer should laboratory managers do without the decision support
systems necessary for setting and obtaining both short- and long-
term goals.[1]

The Systems Approach

    The clinical laboratory is no different than any production
environment. Therefore the systems approach can be used to divide
this process into three basic steps: input, transformation, and
output.

    Input

    Resources of all types become the input to the system. In the
clinical laboratory, these resources include personnel, equipment,
supplies, and samples for testing.

    Transformation

    These resources are put through a conversion process in which
tests are performed, hardware maintained, and staff interacts.

    Output

    The results of this process are the output: results are
communicated to other systems in the organization and personnel
gains satisfaction and other rewards from participation in the
process.

The Flow of Resources

    To the informed manager, this flow of resources is critical,
since every action that takes place uses some resources. Each of
these "transactions" depletes the total pool of resources available
and should contribute to the output. When problems occur in any
organization, they can usually be traced to come problem in this
flow.[2]




                _____

    [1]Short-term goals are those aimed at objectives within four
years.

    [2]Some   analysts   consider   all   staff   interactions   as
"transactions," even social ones that have no direct relationship
to the job.
```

Figure 14.5: *The printed page with footnotes*

To edit a footnote, select **Layout Footnote Edit** (Ctrl-F7 F E), then the footnote number you want to edit, and press ◄─┘. The text of the note will be displayed. Make the desired changes and press F7.

Delete a footnote by deleting its citation number from the text. Add a footnote by positioning the cursor and inserting the note as usual. The subsequent notes will be renumbered automatically.

If you move a block of text containing a Note code, the citation numbers will change appropriately. In fact, to move a note, just move its code. You can do this by highlighting and moving the citation number that appears in the text.

Lesson 58—How to Change Footnote Options

If you are pleased with the default formats used for notes, you can just follow the steps in the last lesson. But if you want to change these formats, then you'll have to use the Footnote Options menu displayed by selecting **Layout Footnote Options** (Ctrl-F7 F O). Figure 14.6 shows this menu.

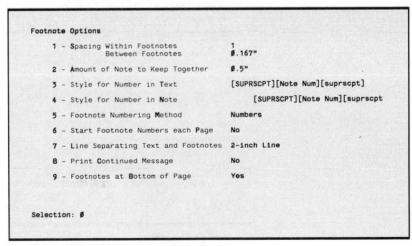

Figure 14.6: The Footnote Options menu

One reason to change formats is to print footnotes at the end of the document, a common academic style. But if you want both footnotes and endnotes in the document, you should also change default values. By default, both the footnote and endnote citations in the text are numbers. So with both in the document, there may be two number 1's, two 2's, etc. How will the reader know if a number 1 refers to a footnote or an endnote?

Using the Options menu, you can change the citations to either letters or special characters (such as asterisks). So instead of *1, 2, 3,* footnotes can be numbered *a, b, c* or **, **, ***.*

In this lesson, you will change the numbering style of footnotes to asterisks. Follow these steps:

1. Press Home Home ↑.

2. Select **Layout Footnote O**ptions (Ctrl-F7 F O) to display the Footnote Options menu.

   The options determine the location of footnotes and the format of the notes and citation numbers. Change an option by pressing the corresponding letter or number and entering the desired setting. For example, to restart footnote numbering on each page, rather than consecutively throughout the document, press *6,* then *Y.*

3. Select Footnote Numbering **Method**. The prompt line changes to

   1 Numbers; 2 Letters; 3 Characters:0

4. Select **C**haracters. The cursor moves to the prompt line in the menu.

5. Press ***. Now footnotes will be "numbered" with asterisks. The first footnote is marked by one asterisk, the second footnote by two, and so on.

6. Press ⏎ twice to return to the document.

7. Press Home Home ↓ to move the cursor to the end of the document. Notice that footnote citation numbers 1 and 2 changed to * and ** respectively.

If you want to make other format changes later, place the cursor after the [Ftn Opt] code in the text and select **Layout** **F**ootnote **O**ptions (Ctrl-F7 F O). Return the notes to the default format by deleting the [Ftn Opt] code.

Now that the numbering scheme for footnotes has been changed, you can enter the endnotes in the next lesson.

Lesson 59—How to Enter Endnotes

If you are putting expository comments or other informal notes in footnotes, you can use endnotes to include formal references. Rather than taking up text space, the endnotes appear as a group at the end of the document.

In this lesson, you will add two endnotes to the document on the screen. Since your footnotes are expository, the endnotes will be bibliographical. Follow these steps to enter the endnotes into the text:

1. Place the cursor at the end of the second paragraph.

2. Select **Layout Endnote** (Ctrl-F7 E) to see the endnote options.

3. Select **Create**. The screen will clear and display only

     1.

   By default, numbers in the endnotes themselves are not superscripted and are followed by a period. The endnote citation in the text is superscripted, as it was in footnote citations.

4. Press Tab, then type the endnote.

     Barbara Neibauer, The Systems Approach in Clinical Settings, Lockhart, California, 1981, p. 45.

5. Press F7. The number *1* appears in the text.

6. Place the cursor at the end of the paragraph subtitled "output," the location of the second endnote.

7. Select **Layout Endnote Create** (Ctrl-F7 E C).

8. Press Tab, then type the second endnote.

     Personnel Policy, October 1986, p. 2.

9. Press F7.

    When you print a document, the endnotes will start imme-
    diately after the text. If there is a footnote on the last page,
    however, WordPerfect will insert a page break and print end-
    notes on their own page.

    But to make sure endnotes appear on a separate page, let's
    insert our own page break.

10. Press Home Home ↓ to move to the end of the document.

11. Press Ctrl-← to insert the page break.

12. Select **F**ile **P**rint **F**ull (Shift-F7 F) to print the document and
    see how both footnotes and endnotes appear in the text. (In
    Figure 14.7, the location of the page break is indicated by a
    broken line.)

Unlike footnote numbers, endnote numbers or letters are not
indented. For that reason you pressed Tab in both endnotes to make
the text of the note stand out from the note numbers. Of course, you
can use the Endnote Options menu to format the citation numbers
any way you like.

For instance, to add spaces after the endnote number so you don't
have to press Tab every time, follow these steps:

1. Place the cursor at the start of the document.

2. Select **L**ayout **E**ndnote **O**ptions (Ctrl-F7 E O) to display the
    Endnote Options menu (Figure 14.8).

3. Select the Style for Numbers in **N**ote option. This allows you
    to change the format of the endnote number as it appears in
    the note. The status line displays

    Replace with: [Note Num].

4. Press End to place the cursor at the end of the prompt, where
    you want to insert spaces.

5. Press the spacebar five times. (Tab has no effect here.)

6. Press ← to accept the change. You'll see no change in option
    D. But now the text of the endnotes will start five spaces after
    the citation number.

Decision Support Needed

  With changing economic conditions the quality of management is becoming crucial to the existence of clinical laboratories. No longer should laboratory managers do without the decision support systems necessary for setting and obtaining both short- and long-term goals.[*]

The Systems Approach

  The clinical laboratory is no different than any production environment. Therefore the systems approach can be used to divide this process into three basic steps: input, transformation, and output.[1]

  Input

  Resources of all types become the input to the system. In the clinical laboratory, these resources include personnel, equipment, supplies, and samples for testing.

  Transformation

  These resources are put through a conversion process in which tests are performed, hardware maintained, and staff interacts.

  Output

  The results of this process are the output: results are communicated to other systems in the organization and personnel gains satisfaction and other rewards from participation in the process.[2]

The Flow of Resources

  To the informed manager, this flow of resources is critical, since every action that takes place uses some resources. Each of these "transactions" depletes the total pool of resources available and should contribute to the output. When problems occur in any organization, they can usually be traced to come problem in this flow.[**]

---

  [*]Short-term goals are those aimed at objectives within four years.

  [**]Some analysts consider all staff interactions as "transactions," even social ones that have no direct relationship to the job.

1.   Barbara Neibauer, <u>The Systems Approach in Clinical Settings</u>, Lockhart, California, 1981, p. 45

2.   <u>Personnel Policy</u>, October 1986, p. 2.

Figure 14.7: The completed document with footnotes and endnotes

```
Endnote Options

     1 - Spacing Within Endnotes          1
               Between Endnotes           0.167"

     2 - Amount of Endnote to Keep Together  0.5"

     3 - Style for Numbers in Text        [SUPRSCPT][Note Num][suprscpt]

     4 - Style for Numbers in Note        [Note Num].

     5 - Endnote Numbering Method         Numbers




Selection: 0
```

Figure 14.8: *Endnote Options menu*

7. Press ◄─┘ to return to the document.

This change inserts the [END OPT] code into the text, changing the endnote format only for this document, not the WordPerfect default.

To edit an endnote, select **Layout Endnote Edit** (Ctrl-F7 E E), then the endnote number (or letter) and press ◄─┘. The note will appear in its window. Make the changes needed, then press F7 to return to the document.

15

Advanced Printing
and Setup

Featuring

Customizing WordPerfect

Printing options

Print queue control

L*esson 60—How to Customize WordPerfect*

WordPerfect's default values let you start typing without having to worry about formatting. Well, there are other default values that determine how WordPerfect works. You can change these by selecting File Setup (Shift-F1) to display the Setup menu (Figure 15.1).

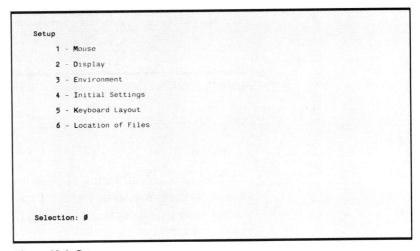

```
Setup

      1 - Mouse

      2 - Display

      3 - Environment

      4 - Initial Settings

      5 - Keyboard Layout

      6 - Location of Files




   Selection: 0
```

Figure 15.1: Setup menu

This menu contains a number of standard WordPerfect settings that you can modify. Some of these options are beyond the scope of this book, and changing them can be rather complicated. But several of them provide very useful and important features. Figure 15.2 summarizes all of the setup options, and Figure 15.3 outlines those available under Environment, some of the most commonly changed settings. But let's take a look in detail at the Backup and Fast Save options under the Environment menu.

Mouse	Determines the mouse type and port; double click interval rate; submenu delay time; acceleration factor; and whether you're using your mouse with the left or right hand.
Display	Sets the monitor and graphic board type; text screen type; the way text and menus are displayed on the screen; and view-document options.
Environment	Sets default values for the way WordPerfect operates.
Initial Settings	Determines the default settings for the format of the date, equations, and table of authorities; the number of repeats used for the ESC key; merge code delimiters; initial codes to be used as the default format; print options- -binding offset, how copies are generated, text and graphics quality, redline method, and the ratio of size attributes.
Keyboard Layout	Lets you redefine the purpose of functions keys.
Location of Files	Determines where WordPerfect expects to find files: the dictionary and thesaurus, style sheets, keyboard and macro files, document backups, printer, document, and graphic files.

Figure 15.2: Summary of Setup options

Backup

A *backup* is an extra copy of your document—the best insurance against disaster. You should make a backup of all important documents by copying them to another disk. This way all won't be lost if your disk becomes damaged. This type of backup, which has nothing to do with the Setup menu, is made using the Copy command, either from the DOS prompt or using the List Files (F5) command. I'll show you how soon.

But there are two other types of backup that can be made automatically—a timed backup and an original document backup. Let's look at these two first.

When you create or edit a document, WordPerfect stores it in the computer's memory. This memory is only temporary, so when you exit WordPerfect or turn off your computer, anything in it is erased.

Backup	Allows you to make automatic backup copies of the document you're editing.
Beep Options	Sets when WordPerfect sounds a warning beep: on errors, hyphenation prompts, and search failure.
Cursor Speed	Determines the speed at which the cursor moves if you hold down a directional or character key.
Document Management/Summary	Sets if summaries are automatically created when the document is saved, the subject search phrase (RE:), if long document names should appear in the List Files directory, and the default document type.
Fast Save	Allows you to save text formatted or unformatted. Formatted text takes longer to save but prints faster from List Files.
Hyphenation	Selects between use of the external dictionary or internal rules for automatic hyphenation.
Prompt for Hyphenation	Sets how frequently automatic hyphenation prompts for user input: never, when required, or always.
Units of Measure	Determines how certain measurements are entered: either as the default inches or centimeters, points, or as lines and columns.

Figure 15.3: Environment Setup options

As long as you've saved the document on the disk, everything is fine. But say someone accidentally pulls the plug, or something causes your computer to go haywire. What's on the screen will be lost forever. To guard against this possibility, WordPerfect by default makes timed backups—saving a special copy of your document every 30 minutes. So when disaster strikes, you'll only lose what you've typed since the last timed backup.

Of course, there are other ways to lose a document. Every semester I see students accidentally "save" one document with the same name as an existing one. They just select Yes at the Replace prompt without even thinking that the original document will be overwritten, or erased. Or they make extensive changes to a document, save it, then change their mind. Too late—the original is gone.

An original document backup protects against these losses. When you save a document that's already on the disk, WordPerfect first makes a copy of the original version. So you can always go back to the unedited document.

Timed Backups

Here's how to change the timed backup interval:

1. Select File Setup (Shift-F1) to display the Setup menu.

2. Select Environment to display the menu shown in Figure 15.4.

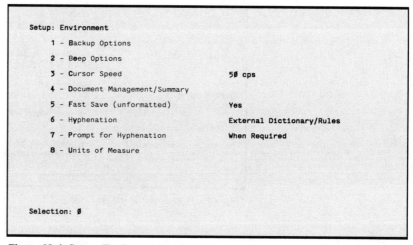

```
Setup: Environment

        1 - Backup Options

        2 - Beep Options

        3 - Cursor Speed                    5Ø cps

        4 - Document Management/Summary

        5 - Fast Save (unformatted)         Yes

        6 - Hyphenation                     External Dictionary/Rules

        7 - Prompt for Hyphenation          When Required

        8 - Units of Measure




Selection: Ø
```

Figure 15.4: Setup: Environment menu

3. Select Backup Options. The screen displays the Setup: Backup menu (Figure 15.5).

4. Select Timed Document Backup. The cursor moves to that option.

5. Select Yes (No turns off the feature). The cursor moves to the Minutes Between Backups option.

6. Type the number of minutes you'd like between backups.

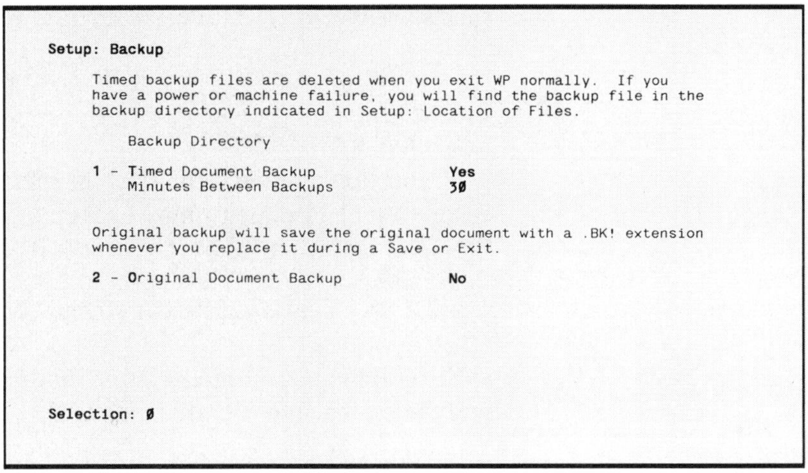

```
Setup: Backup

     Timed backup files are deleted when you exit WP normally.  If you
     have a power or machine failure, you will find the backup file in the
     backup directory indicated in Setup: Location of Files.

        Backup Directory

     1 - Timed Document Backup              Yes
         Minutes Between Backups            30

     Original backup will save the original document with a .BK! extension
     whenever you replace it during a Save or Exit.

     2 - Original Document Backup           No




Selection: 0
```

Figure 15.5: Setup: Backup menu

7. Press ⏎ to accept the changes.

8. Press ⏎ three times if you are ready to return to the document. You'll hear the disk drive spin as WordPerfect saves these new settings to the disk.

At these intervals, a backup copy of your document will be saved on the WordPerfect disk (floppy or hard). The backups are stored as WP{WP}.BK1 (document 1) and WP{WP}.BK2 (document 2). You can change this setting to another drive, say drive B, or to the hard disk directory using the Location of Files option on the Setup menu. I'll show you how shortly.

These files will be erased when you properly exit WordPerfect, but not if some machine failure or power problem occurs. In that case, you would start your computer again and use the DOS Rename command to change the name of the backup file to a document name. The *command syntax* (that is, the general form of the command) is

REN WP{WP}.BK1 *new-document-name*

So you might type

REN WP{WP}.BK1 OLDMEMO

then start WordPerfect. Before it starts you might see the prompt

Are other copies of WordPerfect currently running? (Yes/No)

Select **No**.

If you don't rename the backup file, then when WordPerfect is ready to make the first timed backup after the failure, you'll hear a beep and see

Old backup file exists. **1** Rename; **2** Delete:

Select **R**ename and enter a name for the backup file, or select **D**elete and the old backup file will be deleted.

Original Document Backups

1. Select **F**ile **S**etup **E**nvironment **B**ackup (Shift-F1 E B) to display the Setup: Backup menu.

2. Select **O**riginal Document Backup.

3. Select **Y**es (**N**o if you want to turn off this feature).

4. Press ⏎ three times to accept the changes and return to the document.

When you save a document that's already on the disk, WordPerfect first adds the extension *BK!* to the original version. So suppose you save a document called LETTER. The original version will be stored as LETTER.BK!, and the new version as LETTER.

You now have a copy of the document that existed before you made any changes.

Changing Backup File Location

Follow these steps to change the default directory in which backup files are stored:

1. Select **F**ile **S**etup (Shift-F1) to display the Setup menu (see Figure 15.1).

2. Select **L**ocation of Files to display the menu shown in Figure 15.6.

```
Setup: Location of Files

    1 - Backup Files

    2 - Keyboard/Macro Files              C:\WP51

    3 - Thesaurus/Spell/Hyphenation
                        Main              C:\WP51
                        Supplementary     C:\WP51

    4 - Printer Files                     C:\WP51

    5 - Style Files                       C:\WP51
            Library Filename              C:\WP51\LIBRARY.STY

    6 - Graphic Files                     C:\WP51

    7 - Documents




Selection: Ø
```

Figure 15.6: *Setup: Location of Files menu*

3. Select **B**ackup Files.

4. Type the path—the drive letter and directory name—in which you want to store backup files. Remember to end the drive in a colon, such as *B:*.

5. Press ←┘ twice to return to the Setup menu, then press it again if you're ready to return to the document.

Making DOS Backups

Even these automatic backups, however, won't help if the disk holding the document is destroyed. So the only real insurance is to save duplicates of important documents on another disk. If you have a hard disk, back up critical documents into a floppy. If you have floppy drives, back up copies onto another disk and store it in a separate location.

You can make copies of documents either from the DOS prompt or from the File List Files (F5) directory listing.

From the DOS prompt, use the following syntax:

COPY *name-of-document destination-disk*

Suppose you want to make a copy of the MEMO document from the hard disk onto drive A. Your command at the DOS prompt should look like this:

C>COPY MEMO A:

With floppy drives, place the disk containing your document in drive A and the disk you wish to copy it to (it must be a formatted disk) in drive B. Your command at the DOS prompt would look like

A>COPY MEMO B:

If you enter a name immediately after the destination drive letter, the copy will be given a new name.

If you are already in WordPerfect and want to copy a document, select **Files List Files** (F5) to display the directory listing. Use the arrow keys to highlight the document you wish to copy, then select **Copy**. The prompt changes to

Copy this file to:

Type the drive designation (such as *B:* or *C:\BACKUPS*), press ←, then press F1 to return to the document.

*F*ast Save

When you save a document, WordPerfect doesn't format it on the disk as it appears on the screen. Saving it unformatted this way speeds up the process. When you retrieve the document to the screen or print it from the disk, WordPerfect adds the formatting.

If you often print documents from the disk—using the Print option on the List Files menu—it may pay to save them formatted. This slows down the saving process but speeds up printing.

To save your documents formatted, you must turn off the Fast Save feature on the Files Setup Environment menu. To do this, select **Files Setup Environment**, then **Fast Save**. Select **No** (or **Yes** later if you want to turn it back on), then ← twice to return to the document.

Fast Save does not affect the appearance of a document on the screen or in View mode.

*L*esson 61—How to Set Print Options

So far you've printed all documents by selecting **F**ile **P**rint (Shift-F7), then either **F**ull for the full document or **P**age for the current page. Well, now it's time to look at some sophisticated printing options available on the Print menu (Figure 15.7).

```
Print

    1 - Full Document
    2 - Page
    3 - Document on Disk
    4 - Control Printer
    5 - Multiple Pages
    6 - View Document
    7 - Initialize Printer


Options

    S - Select Printer                    IBM PC Graphics Printer
    B - Binding Offset                    0"
    N - Number of Copies                  1
    U - Multiple Copies Generated by      WordPerfect
    G - Graphics Quality                  Medium
    T - Text Quality                      High




Selection: 0
```

Figure 15.7: Print menu

With these options you can control the way documents are printed, print documents directly from the disk, and more. Refer to the **P**rint menu displayed when you select **F**ile **P**rint (Shift-F7). You're already familiar with the Full Document, Page, View Document, and Select Printer options. Let's take a look at the other options. (Control Printer will be discussed separately in detail in Lesson 62.)

*D*ocument on Disk

Using the Document on Disk command, you can print a document that's stored on the disk without first displaying it on the screen.

Here's how to print a document:

1. Select **F**ile **P**rint **D**ocument on Disk (Shift-F7 D). The status line changes to

   Document name:

2. Type the name of the document you'd like to print, then press ←⏎. You'll see the prompt:

    Page(s): (All)

3. Press ←⏎ to print the entire document, or type a page number or range of pages (as you'll learn next), then press ←⏎.

    If your document is numbered consecutively, without a new page number set, print a range of pages according to these rules:

    - For a single page, type the number and press ←⏎.

    - For a range of pages, type the starting page, a hyphen, the ending page, and ←⏎. For example, to print pages 2 through 6, type *2-6* ←⏎.

    - From a given page to the end of the document, type the starting page number, a hyphen, and ←⏎. Type *8-*, then ←⏎ to print from page 8 to the end of the document.

    - From the first page of a document through a specific page, type a hyphen, the last page you want printed, and ←⏎. Type *-6*, then ←⏎ to print pages 1 through 6.

No spaces are allowed in any of these entries.

If you restarted page numbering in your document, thus dividing it into sections, you must specify what sections contain the pages to be printed. Type the section number and a colon before entering the page number.

Here are some examples:

RANGE	WILL PRINT
2:1–2:8	The second set of pages numbered 1 through 8.
1:1–3:1	The first page numbered 1 through the third page numbered 1.
2:8–	From the second page numbered 8 to the end of the document.
–3:1	From the start of the document through the third page numbered 1.

By the way, you can also print a document from the directory listing that's displayed by selecting **F**ile **L**ist **F**iles (F5). Highlight the name of a document then select **P**rint. The Pages prompt line will appear. Enter the range of pages you want to print, then press ←.

*M*ultiple Pages

The Multiple Pages option lets you print selected pages from the document shown on the screen. Select **F**ile **P**rint **M**ultiple Pages to see the prompt

    Page(s):

Enter the pages you want to print using the techniques just described. Remember that if you want to print just the page displayed, select **F**ile **P**rint **P**age.

*I*nitialize Printer

The Initialize Printer option clears your printer's memory and downloads soft fonts that you've marked as Initially Present.

*B*inding Offset

Documents normally start printing at the left margin, but if you plan to bind the pages into a book, you'll need some extra margin space or *binding width*. For instance, with a three-ring binder, you should insert extra space or else the holes might be punched too close to the text, if not directly on it! With the binding option, you can add extra space to the left margin of odd-numbered pages and to the right margin of even-numbered ones.

From the Print menu, select **B**inding Offset. Type the amount of extra space you want to add to the left margin, then press ←.

The value you enter stays in effect until you exit WordPerfect.

*N*umber of Copies

Change the Number of Copies option to print more than one copy of the text. With the Print menu displayed, select **N**umber of Copies, type the number of copies desired, then press ←⎯. Like binding, this option stays in effect until you exit WordPerfect. So change it back to 1 if you want to print a single copy later on.

Multiple Copies Generated By

The Multiple Copies Generated By option determines how multiple copies are generated. Select Multiple Copies Generated By to see the prompt:

Multiple Copies Generated By: **1** WordPerfect; **2** Printer: 1

Using the default setting, WordPerfect actually transmits the document once for each of the number of copies. So if you set the Number option to 10, WordPerfect treats the job as ten different documents. But some printers, such as Hewlett-Packard LaserJets, have their own built-in function for printing multiple copies. When you select Printer, WordPerfect transmits the printer code for multiple copies, then the document itself only one time. This can greatly increase printer speed, especially for complex documents combining fonts and graphics.

Graphics Quality

As you'll learn in Chapter 18, you can add graphics to your documents for maximum impact. The Graphics Quality option determines whether you want to print the graphics, and, if so, the quality of the final printout.

Select Graphics Quality from the Print menu to display the prompt

Graphics Quality: **1** Do Not Print; **2** Draft; **3** Medium; **4** High: 3

- Select Do Not Print to suppress printing the graphics and print only the text. Why would you want this option? Well, graphics take a long time to print, particularly on dot-matrix printers. So for a quick rough copy, turn graphics off and print the document. If you're using a laser printer, it might not have enough memory to print an entire page of text and graphics. So you can turn off graphics to print just the text. Then insert the same sheet of paper, turn off text printing (you'll see how soon), turn graphics printing back on by selecting any of the other options, and print the document a second time. Now the graphics will be printed.

- Select **D**raft to print the graphics in low resolution. This is the fastest way to print graphic images.

- Select **M**edium to print the graphics in medium resolution.

- Select **H**igh to print the graphics in high resolution, the slowest method.

*T*ext Quality

Select **T**ext Quality from the Print menu to display the prompt

Text Quality: **1** Do **N**ot Print; **2** Draft; **3** Medium; **4** High: 3

These options work just the same as described above for graphics, but they only affect the text. So to print only the graphic images, select Do Not Print from this prompt. Selecting any of the other options turns text printing back on and sets the quality.

All of the options discussed in this lesson are selected before your document is sent to the printer. In Lesson 62 you'll learn how to control the printing process after that has taken place.

*L*esson 62—How to Control Printing

WordPerfect uses a *print queue* to control your printing. A queue is a "waiting line" where WordPerfect stores the names of documents that you've sent to the printer. Because of this, you can give the command to print a document even while one document is still being printed. Each document will be stored in the queue until the previous one is completed. You can also create or edit a document while printing another.

The fact that you've added documents to the queue, however, doesn't mean that you've lost control over the printing process. On the contrary, you can control the queue and the order of documents in it from the Control Printer menu (Figure 15.8). You can also use this menu to check on the progress of a document and see which page is currently being printed.

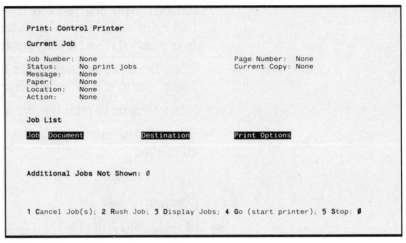

```
Print: Control Printer

Current Job

Job Number:  None                        Page Number:  None
Status:      No print jobs               Current Copy: None
Message:     None
Paper:       None
Location:    None
Action:      None


Job List

Job  Document                Destination           Print Options




Additional Jobs Not Shown: 0



1 Cancel Job(s); 2 Rush Job; 3 Display Jobs; 4 Go (start printer); 5 Stop: 0
```

Figure 15.8: Control Printer menu

To display this menu, select **F**ile **P**rint (Shift-F7) to reveal the Print menu, then select **C**ontrol Printer.

The top of the menu reports on the status of the queue and the current print job. The page being printed, and the copy number if you're printing more than one, is shown on the right. On the left is the job number, and a report of any problems encountered.

A numbered list of documents in the queue will be displayed in the Job List section. If you're printing a document from the disk, its name will appear. Documents being printed from the display are shown as *(screen)*.

If you have more documents that can be displayed on the job list, you'll see the number in the Additional Jobs Not Shown message.

Your queue control panel is the prompt line at the bottom of the screen. Here are the options:

1 Cancel job(s)	Select **C**ancel, type the number of the document shown in the job list, then press ←⎟. Cancel everything in the queue by entering an asterisk (*) in place of a number. Some printers have a built-in queue called a *print buffer.* Any text in the buffer waiting to be printed will still be printed even if you cancel the job. Turn your printer off then on again to stop printing what's in the buffer.

2 Rush job	Select **R**ush to move a document to the first spot in the queue. You'll be prompted to enter the number of the job you want to print next. This does not cancel the current job being printed.
3 Display jobs	This option lists the names of the documents in the print queue, if they cannot all be listed in the bottom of the menu.
4 Go	Select this option to resume printing after a Stop Print command or when using individual sheets of paper.
5 Stop	This option halts the printing process. Restart the current job with the **G**o command. Any text in your printer's buffer will continue to be printed.

If you try to exit WordPerfect while jobs are in the print queue, you'll see the warning

Cancel all print jobs? No (Yes)

Select **N**o to remain in WordPerfect and let the documents be printed. Select **Y**es to leave WordPerfect, cancelling any jobs in the queue including the one currently being printed.

The next chapter takes you one step further into fast and efficient word processing. You'll learn how to reduce long series of keystrokes to simple commands.

16

Automating Keystrokes with Macros

Featuring

Named, temporary, and Alt-key macros

A macro library

Lesson 63—How to Create and Use Macros

Do you ever find yourself writing the same word or phrase over and over? For instance, you're writing a history paper and have to write *World War II* at least twice on every page. Or do you end every letter with the same closing, or start every letter with your name and address centered at the top of the page?

Are there special formats that you use time and again? Each time you want that format you have to repeat the same keystrokes, go through the same menus.

These are occasions to use macros. A *macro* is a special command that you create to "remember" a number of keystrokes. You can then repeat the keystrokes automatically by just repeating that one command. Macros can be used to repeat text, such as *World War II* in the example just given, or complex formatting commands, such as changing to an odd size of paper or inserting a header or footer. While all macros work basically the same way, there are three distinct types of macro commands.

Alt-key macros	These are convenient to use because they can be recalled quickly. The remembered keystrokes are linked with an Alt-key combination, such as Alt-A. The macro is defined, then saved on the disk. Just press the same Alt-key combination to repeat the keystrokes.
Named macros	These macros are also stored on the disk but under a name from one to eight characters long. To repeat the keystrokes, select **Tools Macro Execute** (Alt-F10), type the macro name, then press ⏎. While this requires more keystrokes than Alt-key macros, it's easier to remember a macro with a descriptive name.

| Unnamed macros | You can create one macro that has neither a name nor an Alt-key assignment. This macro is stored on the disk as WP{WP}.WPM and is repeated by selecting Tools Macro Execute, then pressing ←⎯. |

Before using a macro, you must first define it by selecting **Tools Macro Define** (Ctrl-F10). This links the keystrokes to be repeated with either an Alt-key combination, a name, or assigns it to the one unnamed macro. Since all macros are stored on disk, you must have the correct disk in the drive when you recall or use the macro.

Defining Macros

Let's create macros of each type to speed everyday correspondence. Normally, you would define the macro when you first want to use the keystrokes in a document. In this case, however, you will define a series of macros, clear the screen, then use them in the next section. Follow these steps:

1. Start WordPerfect. The first macro will be a named macro to quickly insert your name, your address, and the date, centered on the page. Thus, this macro will include both text and formatting (Center Text) keystrokes. You can use it to place your address on letters.

If you're using the keyboard, make sure you press *A* for macro, not *M*.

2. Select **Tools Macro** (Ctrl-F10) to see the macro options (Figure 16.1).

3. Select **Define** to see the prompt

   Define Macro:

   This is the prompt where you must enter either the macro's name or the Alt-key combination to be linked with the keystrokes.

4. Type *HEAD* (the name of the macro) and press ←⎯. WordPerfect doesn't distinguish between uppercase and lowercase in macro names.

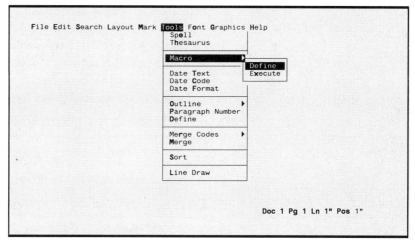

Figure 16.1: Tools Macro menu

The prompt changes to

Description:

5. If you want, type a brief description of the macro, up to 60 characters. This description is used for editing macro definitions, a function beyond the level of this book.

6. Press ←⎯.

   Now enter the keystrokes of the macro, following steps 7 through 11 below. While you enter the keystrokes, the words *Macro Def* will blink on the status line.

7. Select **Layout Align** Center (Shift-F6), type your name, then press ←⎯.

8. Select **Layout Align** Center (Shift-F6), type your street address, then press ←⎯.

9. Select **Layout Align** Center (Shift-F6), type your city, state, and zip code, then press ←⎯.

10. Press ←⎯ twice to insert a blank line between the address and the date.

11. Select **Layout Align** Center (Shift-F6), then **Tools Date Code** (Shift-F5 2) to center and insert the date function, then ←⎯ twice. The extra ←⎯ will leave a blank line following the date.

12. Select **T**ools **M**acro **D**efine (Ctrl-F10). This ends the macro and *Macro Def* disappears from the status line. This particular macro is stored on the disk under the name HEAD.WPM. WordPerfect adds the .WPM (for WordPerfect Macro) extension to all stored macros.

    Now let's create an Alt-key macro to store a single word.

13. Select **T**ools **M**acro **D**efine (Ctrl-F10) to begin the macro definition.

14. Press *Alt-D* as the macro's "name." You can name up to 26 Alt-key macros, one for each letter of the alphabet.

15. Press ← at the Description prompt.

16. Type *Dear* (the text of the macro), press the spacebar, then select **T**ools **M**acro **D**efine (Ctrl-F10) to end the macro definition and save it on the disk as ALTD.WPM. Now whenever you want the word *Dear* in a letter just press Alt-D.

    Since the word *Dear* will always be followed by a space, you included the space in the macro itself.

    Let's create another Alt-key macro. This one will contain the formatting commands to indent a paragraph 1 inch from both margins.

17. Select **T**ools **M**acro **D**efine (Ctrl-F10), then press Alt-Z ← to define a macro called *ALT-Z*.

18. Select **L**ayout **A**lign **In**dent (Shift-F4) twice, the keystrokes needed to indent 1 inch on both the left and right sides.

19. Select **T**ools **M**acro **D**efine (Ctrl-F10) to end the definition. The macro will be stored on the disk as ALTZ.WPM.

    Finally, let's create an unnamed macro.

20. Select **T**ools **M**acro **D**efine (Ctrl-F10) for the Define Macro prompt.

21. Press ← without entering a name or an Alt-keystroke combination.

22. Type *December 15, 1990*, then select **T**ools **M**acro **D**efine (Ctrl-F10) to end the definition.

23. Select **F**ile E**x**it (F7) **N**o **N**o to clear the screen.

You now have four macros defined and ready to use.

It is not always necessary to insert extra lines or spaces after the text of a macro as you did in several cases above. For example, the word *Dear* in the salutation will always be followed by a space. So inserting the space within the macro will save entering that keystroke in the letter. However, no extra space was inserted after the date in the temporary macro, just in case it ends a sentence and needs a period.

Using Macros

Now that the macros are defined, they can be used in any document. Remember, to use Alt-key or named macros, you must be using the disk that contains them.

You will now type a letter using the macros defined in the last section. When you want to repeat the keystrokes, just recall the macro. Here's how:

1. Select **T**ools **Ma**cro **E**xecute (Alt-F10) to display the prompt

   Macro:

2. Type *HEAD* (uppercase or lowercase) and press ⏎. The text and formats in the HEAD macro will be loaded from disk and displayed.

3. Type the inside address of the letter:

   Mr. Terry Dershaw
   153 Sampson Lane
   Willow Grove, PA 19011

4. Press ⏎ twice to leave a blank line between the inside address and the salutation.

5. Press *Alt-D*. The macro will be recalled and the word *Dear* displayed on the screen. Because you included a space in the macro, the cursor is positioned for the remainder of the salutation. Now complete the salutation.

6. Type *Mr. Dershaw:* and press ⏎ twice.

7. Now start typing the body of the letter:

   Thank you for your interest in renting offices in our
   building for your legal practice. However, if you wish to
   occupy the space by

   This is the point where you want to insert the text in the temporary macro.

8. Select **Tools Macro Execute** (Alt-F10), then press ←┘. The
   text of the temporary macro appears in the document.

9. Complete the sentence:

   please keep in mind the following:

10. Press ←┘ twice. You want the next sentence to be indented on
    both sides. Rather than select **Layout Align Indent** (Shift-F4)
    twice, use the ALT-Z macro you just created.

11. Press *Alt-Z*, then type:

    A two-month security deposit is required no later than
    one month prior to occupancy. The first three months of
    rent are due no later than seven days prior to occupancy.

12. Press ←┘ twice. Pressing ←┘ cancels the Indent commands.

13. Now finish the letter by typing

    Sincerely,

    Your Friendly Management

Using macros can streamline typing and formatting. As a
summary, here is how the three types of macros are recalled:

Alt-key macros	Press the Alt-key combination.
Named macros	Select **Tools Macro Execute** (Alt-F10), type the name, and press ←┘.
Unnamed macros	Select **Tools Macro Execute** (Alt-F10) then press ←┘.

14. Select File Exit (F7) **No Y**es to exit WordPerfect without saving the document.

　　The macros are on your disk and can be used, or deleted, at any time.

As you type, consider whether certain keystrokes should be saved as a macro. Most users create a macro for their name and address, their company name, and other frequently used words and phrases. You might also create macros for special paragraph and page formats.

If you enter the name of an existing macro at the Define Macro prompt, the status line will show

(macro name) Already Exists. **1** Replace; **2** Edit; **3** Description: 0

Select **R**eplace if you want to replace the macro with other keystrokes or ◄┘ to cancel the definition.

If you select **R**eplace, the prompt changes to

Replace (macro name)? **No (Yes)**

Select **Y**es to make the replacement, **No** to cancel.

The Edit and Description options let you change the macro definition or add special programming commands to it. This is a complex function that won't be of use to you until you've gained more experience with WordPerfect.

Lesson 64—A Macro Library

Macros are so useful that you should build libraries of them and store them on disk until needed. Floppy disk users should be prudent in the number of macros on their disks, since macros take room that may be needed for documents. If you have a floppy-disk system, you could create several libraries and store each on a different working copy of your system disk; use the disk containing the macros needed for that particular job. Hard disk users, however, can store an almost unlimited number of useful macros.

Let's look at some macros that many WordPerfect users find practical.

Go *Command for Hand-Fed Paper—Alt-G*

When using hand-fed paper, you must issue the Go command before printing each sheet. Rather than repeat all of the necessary keystrokes each time, create and use a macro.

1. Select **T**ools **M**acro **D**efine (Ctrl-F10).

2. Press *Alt-G* ←⌐.

3. Select **F**ile **P**rint **C**ontrol Printer **G**o (Shift F7 C G).

4. Press ←⌐ twice.

5. Select **T**ools **M**acro **D**efine (Ctrl-F10).

M*acro for Resetting to the Default Format—Alt-F*

This macro sets margins, tabs, line spacing, and font back to their default settings. After changing settings for a special format and typing the text, use this macro to resume typing with the default settings.

1. Select **T**ools **M**acro **D**efine (Ctrl-F10).

2. Press *Alt-F* ←⌐.

3. Select **L**ayout **L**ine Line **S**pacing (Shift-F8 L S).

4. Press *1*, then ←⌐.

5. Select **M**argins.

6. Press *1* ←⌐ *1* ←⌐.

7. Select **T**ab Set.

8. Press Home Home ← Ctrl-End *0,.5* ←⌐.

9. Press F7.

10. Select **F**ont **N**ormal (Ctrl-F8 N).

11. Select **T**ools **M**acro **D**efine (Ctrl-F10).

*M*acro to Center Text on the Page—*Alt-P*

This macro centers text between the top and bottom margins.

1. Select **T**ools **M**acro **D**efine (Ctrl-F10).
2. Press *Alt-P* ⏎.
3. Select **L**ayout **P**age **C**enter **Y**es (Shift-F8 P C Y).
4. Press F7.
5. Select **T**ools **M**acro **D**efine (Ctrl-F10).

*D*ouble Space Macro—*Alt-D*

This macro changes to double-spacing.

Since an Alt-D macro was already created in this chapter to type the word *Dear*, you will be prompted whether to replace it. Step 3 below confirms the replacement.

1. Select **T**ools **M**acro **D**efine (Ctrl-F10).
2. Press *Alt-D* ⏎.
3. Select **R**eplace, then **Y**es.
4. Select **L**ayout **L**ine **L**ine **S**pacing (Shift-F8 L S).
5. Press *2*, then ⏎.
6. Press F7.
7. Select **T**ools **M**acro **D**efine (Ctrl-F10).

*P*age Number Macro—*Alt-N*

This macro turns on page numbering at the bottom center of each page.

1. Select **T**ools **M**acro **D**efine (Ctrl-F10).
2. Press *Alt-N* ⏎.
3. Select **L**ayout **P**age **P**age **N**umbering (Shift-F8 P N).

4. Select Page Numbering **P**osition.

5. Press *6*, then F7.

6. Select **T**ools **M**acro **D**efine (Ctrl-F10).

Swap Words Macro—Alt-S

This macro transposes two words. Place the cursor anywhere in the word on the left, then execute the macro. Because it searches for a space to find the end of the word, this macro will not switch the last two words of a sentence.

1. Select **T**ools **M**acro **D**efine (Ctrl-F10).

2. Press *Alt-S* ←⏎.

3. Select **S**earch **F**orward (F2).

4. Press the spacebar once.

5. Press F2.

6. Press the ← key once, then Ctrl-Backspace.

7. Select **S**earch **N**ext (F2).

8. Select **E**dit **U**ndelete **R**estore (F1 R).

9. Select **T**ools **M**acro **D**efine (Ctrl-F10).

Save Named Text Macro—Alt-X

This saves the current document under an already given name and returns to the document. It can only be used for documents that have previously been saved, so make sure you are in a document that has already been saved before entering these keystrokes:

1. Select **T**ools **M**acro **D**efine (Ctrl-F10).

2. Press *Alt-X* ←⏎.

3. Select **F**ile **S**ave (F10).

4. Press ←⏎.

5. Select **Yes**.

6. Select **T**ools **M**acro **D**efine (Ctrl-F10).

*F*ont Change Macros

Use these macros for a quick change to a new printing font. The letters used are on the top row of the keyboard running in order from the fine font to extra large. For example, Alt-Q changes to the fine font, the smallest, while Alt-Y is used for extra large. Each macro first resets the font to normal to avoid conflicting formats. Alt-E selects the normal font alone.

Fine Font—Alt-Q

1. Select **T**ools **M**acro **D**efine (Ctrl-F10).

2. Press *Alt-Q* ←⏎.

3. Select **F**ont **N**ormal (Ctrl-F8 N).

4. Select **F**ont **F**ine (Ctrl-F8 S F).

5. Select **T**ools **M**acro **D**efine (Ctrl-F10).

Small Font—Alt-W

1. Select **T**ools **M**acro **D**efine (Ctrl-F10).

2. Press *Alt-W* ←⏎.

3. Select **F**ont **N**ormal (Ctrl-F8 N).

4. Select **F**ont **S**mall (Ctrl-F8 S S).

5. Select **T**ools **M**acro **D**efine (Ctrl-F10).

Normal Font—Alt-E

1. Select **T**ools **M**acro **D**efine (Ctrl-F10).

2. Press *Alt-E* ←⏎.

3. Select **F**ont **N**ormal (Ctrl-F8 N).

4. Select **T**ools **M**acro **D**efine (Ctrl-F10).

Large Font—Alt-R

1. Select **T**ools **M**acro **D**efine (Ctrl-F10).

2. Press *Alt-R* ⟵.

3. Select **F**ont **N**ormal (Ctrl-F8 N).

4. Select **F**ont **L**arge (Ctrl-F8 S L).

5. Select **T**ools **M**acro **D**efine (Ctrl-F10).

Very Large Font—Alt-T

1. Select **T**ools **M**acro **D**efine (Ctrl-F10).

2. Press *Alt-T* ⟵.

3. Select **F**ont **N**ormal (Ctrl-F8 N).

4. Select **F**ont **V**ery Large (Ctrl-F8 S V).

5. Select **T**ools **M**acro **D**efine (Ctrl-F10).

Extra Large Font—Alt-Y

1. Select **T**ools **M**acro **D**efine (Ctrl-F10).

2. Press *Alt-Y* ⟵.

3. Select **F**ont **N**ormal (Ctrl-F8 N).

4. Select **F**ont **E**xtra Large (Ctrl-F8 S E).

5. Select **T**ools **M**acro **D**efine (Ctrl-F10).

By planning your macros carefully, you can streamline the typing, editing, and formatting of your documents. In the next chapter, you'll learn about two other powerful tools, the Speller and the Thesaurus.

17

Word Tools:
The Speller
and Thesaurus

Featuring

Dictionary

Thesaurus

Lesson 65—How to Check Your Spelling

If you are as bad a speller as I am, you probably keep a dictionary near the computer at all times. But even if you win spelling bees, typing errors can still occur.

The WordPerfect spelling program will report if a word in your document is not found in its list of over 100,000 correctly spelled words. If the word is not found, it is reported as a possible misspelling. You can then tell WordPerfect that the word is properly spelled, correct it yourself, or select from a list of suggested spellings taken from the dictionary. The new word will automatically be inserted into the text.

Just like any dictionary, the list may omit some correctly spelled words. Many technical words and names, for instance, will be reported as possible misspellings. But if the word really is spelled correctly, you can add it to a supplemental dictionary of your own words so it will not be reported as incorrect again.

With a hard disk drive, the spelling dictionary and thesaurus will be installed on the same drive and directory as other WordPerfect programs. These programs don't require any special instructions.

Floppy Disk Systems

With floppy disk systems, however, there is no room for the spelling or thesaurus programs on the Program disk in drive A or the document disk in drive B. So you'll have to insert separate Dictionary or Thesaurus disks in drive B when they are needed. To do so, you must first set up WordPerfect so it expects to find the dictionary and thesaurus in that drive. Follow these steps:

1. Start WordPerfect.

2. Select File Setup Location of Files (Shift-F1 L).

3. Select Thesaurus/Spell/Hyphenation.

4. Type *B:*\ then press ←⏎.

5. Type *B:*\ then press ←⏎.

6. Press F7 to return to the typing screen.

You can now insert the Dictionary or Thesaurus disk in drive B when you want to use either program.

Checking Spelling

You can check the spelling of individual words, blocks of text, specified pages, or the entire document. All spelling tasks begin by selecting Tools Spell (Ctrl-F2). Here are the steps for checking your spelling:

1. Start WordPerfect and either retrieve a document or type a new one.

2. To check an individual word, place the cursor on or immediately following the word.
   To check a block of text, select Edit Block (Alt-F4) and use the cursor keys to highlight the block.
   To check a page, place the cursor anywhere on the page.
   To check an entire document, place the cursor anywhere in the document.

3. If you have a floppy disk system, place the Spell disk in drive B.

4. Select Tools Spell (Ctrl-F2). The message *Please Wait* will appear on the screen. If you are checking a highlighted block, skip to step 7. WordPerfect is now checking each word in the block.

5. If you do not have a block highlighted, the following prompt will appear:

    Check: **1** Word; **2** Page; **3** Document;
    4 New Sup. Dictionary; **5** Look Up; **6** Count:0

    Select **W**ord to check an individual word.

    Select **P**age to check all of the words on the current page.

    Select **D**ocument to check the entire document.

6. If you are checking a page or a document, the message *∗Please Wait∗* will appear in the status line while each word is compared with those in the dictionary.

    If you are checking an individual word and the cursor moves to the next word in the document, the word is spelled correctly. The prompt will remain on the screen so you can select another option to continue the checking process or press F1 to stop.

7. When a match is not found in the dictionary, a word will become highlighted and the screen will change as illustrated in Figure 17.1. The line across the screen and the prompt line will appear first. Then some suggested spellings will appear as they are found in the dictionary.

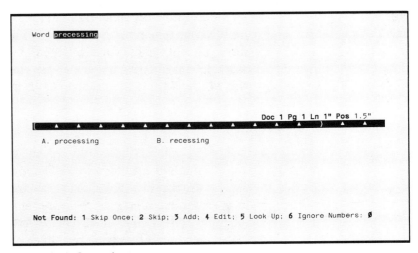

Figure 17.1: Correction screen

Notice that each of the suggested spellings is labeled with a letter. If the correct spelling appears among the suggestions, press the appropriate letter. That spelling will replace the one in the document.

If none of the suggested words is correct, or nothing was found in the dictionary, then select another option from the prompt line. Here are the options:

- **1** Skip Once tells WordPerfect that the word is spelled as you want it in this one instance. The program will look for the next misspelled word.

- **2** Skip tells WordPerfect you want it to accept the word as spelled for the remainder of the current checking session. The checking will continue but will not stop if this word is encountered again.

- **3** Add lets you add a word to the supplemental dictionary. If a word is spelled correctly and you use it regularly, you will want to use this option.

- **4** Edit lets you edit the word. If you select Edit, the cursor will appear on the word and a prompt appears

Spell Edit: Press Exit when done

You can now press the right and left arrow keys, use Backspace and Del, or type new characters to change the word. (The ↑ and ↓ keys, and other cursor-movement key combinations, will not work.) Press F7 to return to the spell checking after you have edited the word. If the edited word is still misspelled according to the WordPerfect dictionary, it will again be highlighted and you will have to select an option on the prompt line.

- **5** Look Up displays the prompt *Word or word pattern:* on the status line. Enter a word that you want to search for. You can use the wild-card characters * and *?*. A *wild-card* character is one that stands for an undetermined character or several characters. Each *?* will be replaced in the search by a single character, each * by any number of characters. For instance, looking up *f?r* will display *for* and *fur*, while *f*r* will result in words such as *fair, falter,* and *fascicular*. To stop the Look Up process, press F1 (Cancel) at any prompt to return to the Spelling selection line. Press F1 once more to exit the spelling checker and return to the document.

- **6** Ignore Numbers tells the program not to bother checking any words with numbers.

You can really use the wild cards to take advantage of Word-Perfect's dictionary. Say, for example, that you vaguely remember that the word you want to use starts with an *a* and ends with *gram*. Rather than taking a guess at the spelling, enter *a*gram* as the lookup phrase. The wild cards are also helpful to find related words based on the same root, such as entering *photo** or **meter.*

I hate to admit it, but I even use this feature for solving crossword puzzles. If you know some of the letters in the word, enter them but use the question mark for the blank boxes, such as looking for a "unit of measure" to fit in *l???r.*

In two instances a different prompt will appear on the status line. If WordPerfect finds the same word twice in a row, the prompt changes to

Double Word: **1 2** Skip; **3** Delete 2nd; **4** Edit;
5 Disable Double Word Checking

Enter the appropriate selection:

- **1 2** Skip keeps both words in the text.
- **3** Delete 2nd deletes one of the pair.
- **4** Edit moves the cursor to the text for editing.
- **5** Disable Double Word Checking ignores paired words throughout the document.

If a word is found with the first two letters capitalized, or just the second letter capitalized, the prompt changes to

Irregular Case: **1 2** Skip; **3** Replace; **4** Edit;
5 Disable Case Checking

Enter the appropriate selection:

- **1 2** Skip leaves the work as it appears.
- **3** Replace capitalizes only the first letter in the word.

- **4** Edit moves the cursor to the text for editing.

- **5** Disable Case Checking ignores cases throughout the document.

When the spelling check is completed, the number of words checked will be displayed in the status line with the prompt

Press any key to continue

You can now press any key to return to the document. To exit the spelling checker quickly at any prompt, press F1 twice.

Other Spelling Options

In addition to checking a word, a block, a page, or a document, there are three other options on the main Spelling prompt line displayed when you select **T**ools **S**pells (Ctrl-F2).

- **4** New Sup. Dictionary allows you to use a special supplemental dictionary. A *supplemental dictionary* is a list of your own words that are not found in WordPerfect's main dictionary. For example, say you often write articles containing technical words. To avoid having these words reported as misspellings, you add them to the supplemental dictionary using the Add option when you check spelling. The default supplemental dictionary is called WP{WP}US.SUP and it is normally used whenever you check spelling. But since searching this dictionary takes time, why use it when you're writing nontechnical documents that will not contain these words? In this case, create your own supplemental dictionary that you can use whenever you need it as a reference.

  To create or use your own supplemental dictionary, select New Sup. Dictionary to display the prompt

  Supplemental dictionary name:

  Type the name of the supplemental dictionary you'd like to use, or the name of a new dictionary you'd like to create, then press ◄─┘.

- **5 L**ook Up works in the same way as the Look Up option discussed earlier. Use it when you want to check the spelling of a word before typing it.

- **6** Count reports the number of words in the current document.

The spelling dictionary is a powerful aid in the writing process. While it is more convenient with a hard disk system, it can still be used to advantage with floppy disks.

Lesson 66—How to Use the Thesaurus

Sometimes the hardest part of writing is selecting just the right word. You know what you want to say but you're not sure of the best word. Other times, you find yourself repeating a word frequently in a paragraph and you'd like to find another way to say the same thing without sounding repetitious. These times call for the Word-Perfect thesaurus.

The thesaurus displays synonyms—words with similar meanings—and antonyms—words with opposite meanings. The WordPerfect thesaurus has over 10,000 words, called *headwords,* that can be looked up.

Like the spelling dictionary, the thesaurus requires its own floppy disk. So if you do not have a fixed disk system, you must insert the Thesaurus disk in drive B before using it.

To use the thesaurus, place the cursor on or immediately following the word you would like to replace with a synonym (or antonym) and select **Tools Thesaurus** (Alt-F1). Four lines of text will remain on the screen above a box of three columns containing the synonyms. Figure 17.2 shows the Thesaurus screen displaying synonyms for the word *help.*

Note that, in this case, synonyms are given for the word *help* in both the noun *(n)* and verb *(v)* form, along with several antonyms. The words are listed in subgroups having similar connotations. Words preceded by dots are themselves headwords that can be looked up to find additional possible substitutions. Press the letter next to a headword to see more selections. For example, pressing *H* (before *ease*) changes the screen as shown in Figure 17.3. Synonyms for the word *ease* now

```
I would like to help



 ┌help─(v)────────────────┬────────────────────────────────────┐
 │    1 A ·abet           │help─(n)───────────                   │
 │      B ·aid            │    5   ·assistance                   │
 │      C ·assist         │        ·relief                       │
 │      D ·serve          │        ·service                      │
 │                        │        ·succor                       │
 │    2 E ·extricate      │                                      │
 │      F ·rescue         │    6   laborers                      │
 │      G ·save           │        workers                       │
 │                        │                                      │
 │    3 H ·ease           │help─(ant)─────────                   │
 │      I ·expedite       │    7   ·hinder                       │
 │      J ·facilitate     │        ensnare                       │
 │                        │        ·worsen                       │
 │    4 K ·ameliorate     │                                      │
 │      L ·better         │    8   ·hindrance                    │
 │      M ·improve        │                                      │
 │                        │                                      │
 └────────────────────────┴──────────────────────────────────────┘
 1 Replace Word; 2 View Doc; 3 Look Up Word; 4 Clear Column: 0
```

Figure 17.2: Synonyms for the word "help"

```
I would like to help



 ┌help─(v)──────────┬ease─(n)───────────────────────────────────┐
 │    1   ·abet     │ 1 A ·composure         ·relax             │
 │        ·aid      │   B ·poise             ·slacken           │
 │        ·assist   │   C  spontaneity                          │
 │        ·serve    │                    6   ·allay             │
 │                  │ 2 D ·dexterity         ·alleviate         │
 │    2   ·extricate│   E ·expertise         ·assuage           │
 │        ·rescue   │   F ·facility          ·relieve           │
 │        ·save     │                                           │
 │                  │ 3 G ·comfort       7   ·calm              │
 │    3   ·ease     │   H ·leisure           ·pacify            │
 │        ·expedite │   I ·repose            ·quiet             │
 │        ·facilitate│                       ·soothe            │
 │                  │ 4 J ·affluence                            │
 │    4   ·ameliorate│  K ·luxury        8   ·maneuver          │
 │        ·better   │   L ·prosperity        ·slide             │
 │        ·improve  │ease─(v)───────────     ·slip              │
 │                  │ 5 M ·loosen                               │
 └──────────────────┴───────────────────────────────────────────┘
 1 Replace Word; 2 View Doc; 3 Look Up Word; 4 Clear Column: 0
```

Figure 17.3: Synonyms for "ease" from the first column

appear in the second and third columns, and the selection letters have
moved from the first column to the second.

You can continue to search for the proper word by pressing the letter next to another headword. If you want to select a word in another
column, you must first move the reference letters there by pressing the
→ or ← key.

The prompt line at the bottom of the screen can be used anytime. The four options are:

You cannot select options from this prompt with the mouse. Clicking right cancels the Thesaurus and returns to the document.

- **1** Replace Word—When you find the word you want to use, make sure it is preceded by a letter. If not, press the → or ← key until letters appear in that column. Press *1* to display the prompt

  Press letter for word

Press the letter preceding your selection.

- **2** View Doc—This option returns the cursor to the document at the top of the screen and displays the prompt line

  View: Press EXIT when done

Use the arrow keys to scroll through the text, then press F7 when you want to return to the thesaurus.

- **3** Look Up Word—Use this option to look up synonyms for words not listed on the screen.

- **4** Clear Column—The Thesaurus screen holds a maximum of three columns. To erase synonyms that you know are irrelevant, use the arrow keys to place the letters in the column you no longer need, then press *4*.

Press ← to select the default *0* option and leave the thesaurus. If the word you are looking up is not a headword, the message

Word Not Found

will appear on the status line for a few seconds and then change to

Word:

Type another word with a similar meaning that may be a headword, or press F1 to display the prompt line.

You'll notice that the thesaurus also shows some words with opposite meanings—antonyms. Here's how you can use them.

There may be times when you're trying to find the correct word but can't even think of where to start. Or every word you try to find in the

Thesaurus results in the Word Not Found message. In these instances, try to think of a word with the opposite meaning. If that is a headword, the suggested antonyms would be just what you're looking for.

This is particularly useful when you want to find synonyms for phrases. For example, perhaps you want to find a synonym for the phrase *put all your eggs in one basket.* Looking up synonyms for *put, eggs,* or *basket* certainly wouldn't help.

So try looking up a word with the opposite meaning, *diversify.* The antonym *consolidate* will be listed, and you can extend the search from that point on. Figure 17.4 shows how your screen would look.

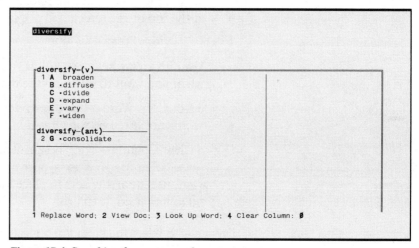

Figure 17.4: *Searching for synonyms by antonyms*

Of course, you'll have to use caution and judgement when selecting synonyms from the thesaurus. Not all synonyms are interchangeable in every context. Many words have connotations that make them unsuitable replacements for one in the text.

The next chapter will take you the last step into desktop publishing, as you learn how to add graphics to your WordPerfect documents.

18

Enhancing
Your Documents
with Graphics

Featuring

Adding horizontal and vertical lines

Enclosing text in boxes

Merging graphics and text

Warning! If you're like me, you may find the topics covered in this chapter to be habit-forming. But they are also interesting and powerful, enabling you to create finished-looking documents complete with drawings. If you produce newsletters, flyers, mail-order literature, or any document that can be improved with graphics, then this chapter is for you—especially if you have a high-quality dot-matrix or laser printer.

In this chapter, you'll learn the fundamentals of WordPerfect's potent graphics commands. I'll show you how to add vertical and horizontal lines to your documents, enclose text in a box, and add drawings and graphic images to your documents.

Because these commands are so powerful, you'll just get the basics here. But you'll learn enough to take advantage of these commands in a variety of documents. Go through this chapter, following each instruction carefully. Then, when you have time, return to the graphics menus that are shown here and experiment a little.

But first the small print. Your ability to print graphics, just like type sizes and fonts, is based entirely on your printer. If you have a daisywheel printer, or a dot-matrix printer without graphics capabilities, then many of the features in this chapter will not be very useful to you.

How can you tell what your printer can do? Just follow the lessons here and print out each of the examples. You'll see which features your printer supports.

Lesson 67—How to Add Vertical and Horizontal Lines

You can use horizontal and vertical lines to separate text on the page or simply to add some visual perspective. Using the Graphics Line (Alt-F9 L) command, you insert lines before and after text, between columns, or along the margins. You won't see lines on the editing screen, but they will appear when the document is printed or displayed in View mode.

Let's use the command to create two different documents. First, we'll use a simple 2-inch horizontal line to separate two parts of the MEMO document, which you created in Chapter 4. This was a short memorandum followed by a brief list of items. Of course, you can add horizontal lines to any document.

Horizontal Lines

1. Recall the MEMO document.

2. Place the cursor where you want to insert a line, in this case between the memorandum and the list of items.

3. Select **Graphics** (Alt-F9) to see the Graphics menu, as in Figure 18.1. For now, ignore the submenu that shows. You'll learn how to use these options in the next lesson.

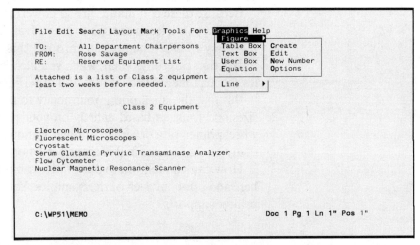

Figure 18.1: Graphics menu

4. Select **Line** to display the Graphics Line menu (Figure 18.2).

5. Select Create **Horizontal**. The screen will show the Graphics Horizontal Line menu (Figure 18.3).

   These options are used to set the position and size of the line. The default settings call for a single solid horizontal line

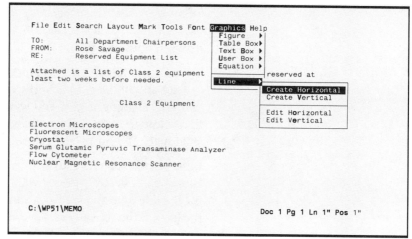

Figure 18.2: Graphics Line menu

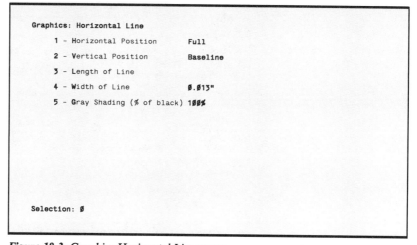

Figure 18.3: Graphics Horizontal Line menu

extending from the left margin to the right margin. But let's change this to a 2-inch line in the center of the page.

6. Select **Horizontal Position.** The prompt line changes to

Horizontal Pos: **1** Left **2** Right **3** Center **4** Full
5 Set Position:0

7. Select **Center.**

8. Select **Length of Line**. Selecting this option has no effect if the horizontal position is set at Full, in which case the line extends between both margins.

9. Type *2* for a 2-inch line, then press ←.

   Let's accept the default vertical position, width (thickness), and gray shading. But if you wanted, you could position the line below the text, print a thicker line, or a line other than solid black if your printer allows.

10. Press ← to return to the document. The code [HLine:Center, Baseline,2", 0.013", 100%] will be inserted in the text, showing the line type and specifications. Remember, you won't see the line on the screen.

11. Select **File Print** (F7) **Full** to print the memo (Figure 18.4).

12. Select **File Exit** (F7) **No No** to clear the screen.

```
MEMORANDUM

TO:        All Department Chairpersons
FROM:      Rose Savage
RE:        Reserved Equipment List

Attached is a list of Class 2 equipment that must be reserved at
least two weeks before needed.

                        _____
                         Class 2 Equipment


Electron Microscopes
Fluorescent Microscopes
Cryostat
Serum Glutamic Pyruvic Transaminase Analyzer
Flow Cytometer
Nuclear Magnetic Resonance Scanner
```

Figure 18.4: Memo with horizontal line

To remove a line from the document, select **Edit Reveal Codes** (Alt-F3) to reveal the codes and then delete the Line code. If you want to edit the line, select **Graphics Line** (Alt-F9 5), then either Edit **Horizon**tal or Edit **Vertical**. WordPerfect will search back through the text to locate the closest line code, and then display the Graphics Line menu. Make your changes and press ←.

Vertical Lines

Vertical lines are used to separate columns on the page or to high-light the left or right margin. They can provide a pleasing visual effect that breaks up large sections of text, particularly in bound books.

Let's see how easy it is to add vertical lines. In this case, you'll insert a line along the left margin.

1. Select **Graphics Line Create Vertical** (Alt-F9 L V) to display the Vertical Line menu.

    The options on the menu are the same as for Horizontal lines but with some important differences. The Length of Line setting determines the height of the line, not the width. Use the Horizontal Position option to place the lines either at the right or left margin, between columns, or at some specific position. The Vertical Position option controls where at that position the line appears: along the full length of the page, near the top, center, or bottom, or at a specific position that you can set.

    You can only enter a line length if the vertical position is something other than full page.

2. Press ◀— to accept the default settings and return to the document.

3. Select **File Print** (F7) **View Document** to view the document (Figure 18.5).

    Any text you enter on the page will appear to the right of the vertical line.

4. Select **File Exit** (F7) **No No** to clear the screen.

Vertical Lines in Columns

To print a line separating columns, start by defining the columns as you did in Chapter 12. Then create the line by selecting the Horizontal Position option to see the prompt

Horizontal Position: **1** Left; **2** Right; **3** Between Columns;
4 Set Position: 0

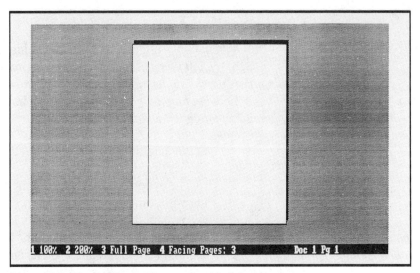

Figure 18.5: *Vertical line in View mode with default settings*

Select **B**etween Columns for the prompt

Place line to the right of column: 1

Press ⏎ if you want the line down the center of the page between two columns, then ⏎ again to return to the document. Turn Columns on and enter your columns.

By adjusting the vertical position and length, you can insert lines anywhere on the page, even between uneven parallel columns surrounded by regular paragraphs, as shown in Figure 18.6.

For complex lines, such as lines between columns as shown in Figure 18.6, first print a copy of the document and draw in the lines by hand. Then measure the vertical and horizontal positions, and the length of the lines you want to add. Place the cursor at the start of the document and enter the appropriate measurements on the Line menu.

Lesson 68—How to Enclose Text in a Box

Let's now take lines one step further into complete boxes. Surrounding text in a box calls attention to it and draws the reader's eye to

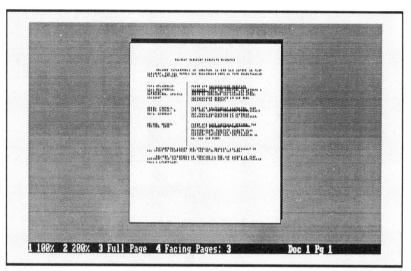

Figure 18.6: *Vertical lines in columns*

important points. Figure 18.7 shows the CLASSES document enhanced with a text box. The text in the box has been formatted as extra large to grab the reader's attention.

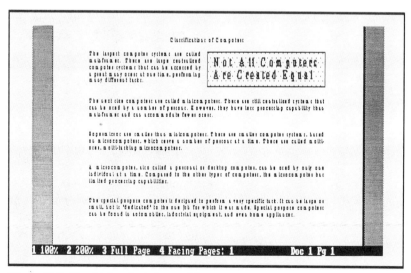

Figure 18.7: *Combining font sizes and boxes*

You can enclose any amount of text in a box, and even retrieve a document from disk into a box. Like all graphics, however, boxes are seen only when viewed or printed. But you can edit and format the text in the box easily.

In this lesson, I'll show you how to create the eye-catching announcement shown in Figure 18.8. (Of course, your own printout will depend on your printer.) The text will be enclosed in a box centered on the page.

Figure 18.8: Announcement using text box

1. Select **G**raphics (Alt-F9) and notice the options other than Line. Each of these represents a type of graphic box that can be included in your document.

   Except for Equations, which you'll learn about in the next chapter, the option names really have nothing to do with the type of text or graphics you place in the box. For example, you can have a table in a text box and text in a figure box. The names are just there to help you plan and control your document.

   The options in the submenu will be the same for all of the selections other than Line.

For consistency, however, let's use the text box to hold text. But before creating a box, you should set any specific options you want.

2. Select Text **B**ox **O**ptions to display the Text Box Options menu (Figure 18.9).

```
Options: Text Box

    1 - Border Style
            Left                            None
            Right                           None
            Top                             Thick
            Bottom                          Thick
    2 - Outside Border Space
            Left                            0.167"
            Right                           0.167"
            Top                             0.167"
            Bottom                          0.167"
    3 - Inside Border Space
            Left                            0.167"
            Right                           0.167"
            Top                             0.167"
            Bottom                          0.167"
    4 - First Level Numbering Method        Numbers
    5 - Second Level Numbering Method       Off
    6 - Caption Number Style                [BOLD]1[bold]
    7 - Position of Caption                 Below box, Outside borders
    8 - Minimum Offset from Paragraph       0"
    9 - Gray Shading (% of black)           10%

Selection: 0
```

Figure 18.9: Text Box Options menu

The menu shows the default values used for text boxes—thick border lines on the top and bottom, nothing on the sides, and a ten percent shade. To make it a complete box, you have to add lines on the sides.

3. Select **B**order Style. The cursor moves to highlight the word *None* next to the left border style and the prompt line changes to

   1 None; 2 Single; 3 Double; 4 Dashed; 5 Dotted; 6 Thick; 7 Extra Thick:0

4. Select **E**xtra Thick for the left border.

5. Select **E**xtra Thick three more times to select the extra thick border for the remaining sides.

   Take a moment to review the other options. They determine the space between the text and the border, and the numbering used to reference the boxes. The last option is used to shade the inside of the box, such as the light shading in the sample figure. On dot-matrix printers, shading takes a long time to print. So if you didn't want any shading you would select Gray shading, type *0,* then press ←.

6. Press F7 to return to the document.

You have just set certain characteristics that all text boxes now defined will have—an extra thick border and the default 10 percent shading. All text boxes from this position on will have that format until you select new options or delete the [Txt Opt] code in the text.

Now that you've selected the optional format characteristics, you must describe the contents and position of the box itself.

1. Select **G**raphics Text **B**ox **C**reate (Alt-F9 B C) to display the Text Box Definition menu (Figure 18.10).

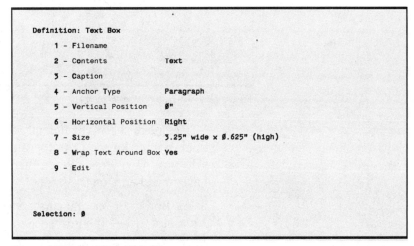

Figure 18.10: *Text Box Definition menu*

Graphics can be a complicated process, as you've seen by the many options in the menus. So I'll just briefly explain the purpose of these options.

- **Filename** allows you to recall a document or graphic image to be inserted into the box.

- **C**ontents allows you to specify one of four types of graphics boxes:

Graphic	A graphic file is merged into the document and saved along with it
Graphic on Disk	The graphic is linked with the document rather than merged within. When printed, the graphic file is located and used.
Text	The box will contain text and formatting codes. Any codes used to format box text do not affect other characters in the document.
Equation	Allows you to create an equation graphic, as explained in Chapter 19.

- **C**aption allows you to enter a caption to print under the box.

- **A**nchor **T**ype gives you a choice of Paragraph, Page, or Character. Paragraph boxes align with the paragraph where the box is defined; Page boxes can be placed anywhere on the page; Character boxes can be placed within lines.

- **V**ertical Position allows you to change the position of the box in relation to the text or the top margin.

- **H**orizontal Position allows you to position the box where desired between the right and left margins.

- **S**ize allows you to change the size of the box.

- **W**rap Text Around Box (with text wrapped around the box, the default mode) prevents text outside of the box from printing over the box and its contents.

- **E**dit allows you to add, edit, or format text in the box. With graphic boxes, this allows you to scale, move, or invert the image. With Equation types, the equation editor appears as explained in Chapter 19.

2. Select Anchor **T**ype to change the type of the box. The prompt line changes to

   Anchor Type: **1** Paragraph; **2** Page; **3** Character:0

3. Select **P**age. The prompt line changes to

   Number of pages to skip: 0

   This option allows you to place the box on a specific page. To place the box on the third page, for example, enter 2.

4. Press ← to accept the default 0.

   The vertical position automatically changes to Top, the horizontal position to Margin, Right. These are the default page box settings.

5. Select **V**ertical Position to change the vertical position and display

   Vertical Position: **1** Full Page; **2** Top; **3** Center; **4** Bottom;
   5 Set Position:0

6. Select **C**enter.

7. Select **H**orizontal Position. The prompt line changes to

   Horizontal Position: **1** Margins; **2** Columns;
   3 Set Position:0

8. Select **M**argins to align the box between the margins and display

   Horizontal Position: **1** Left; **2** Right; **3** Center; **4** Full:0

9. Select **C**enter.

   Finally, let's enter text into the box. You could insert the text of an existing document by entering its name at the Filename option. The box size will adjust automatically to accommodate the text. In this case, we're going to enter the text directly through the Edit menu.

10. Select **E**dit. The screen clears except for the status line and the prompt

    Box: Press Exit when done, Graphics to rotate text

    The length of the line you'll be able to type is controlled by the box width. The height will automatically adjust to fit the text that you enter. You can make the box larger than the text by using the Size option on the Text Box Definition menu.

If you want the boxed text to print in anything other than the default base font, you must change base fonts within this screen. Changing the base font of the document itself will not effect text entered in boxes.

11. Select **F**ont **E**xtra Large (Ctrl-F8 S E).

12. Select **L**ayout **A**lign **C**enter (Shift-F6) to center the cursor, then type

    ATTENTION

13. Select **F**ont **N**ormal (Ctrl-F8 N), then press ↵ twice.

14. Now type

    All members of Faculty Council are requested to submit their nominations for Student of the Year by Tuesday, May 24. Deliver nominations to room 205.

15. Press F7 to accept the text and display the Box menu. Figure 18.11 shows the completed menu.

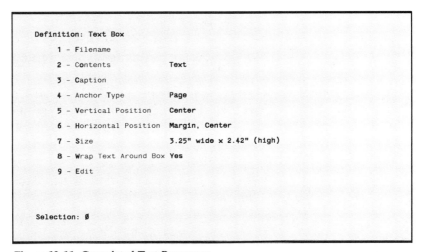

Figure 18.11: Completed Text Box menu

16. Press F7 again to return to the document. The appropriate codes are in the text, but nothing appears on the screen. That's because the box is centered on the page.

17. Press ⏎ until a box appears on the screen. The exact position depends on your printer fonts.

Notice that a box, with no text inside, appears on the screen to indicate the presence of a text box (Figure 18.12).

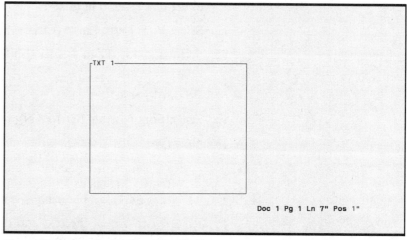

Figure 18.12: *Text box indicated on the screen*

18. Select **File Print** (F7) **Full** to print the document, or select **File Print** (F7) **View** to view it.

19. Select **File Exit** (F7) **No No** to clear the screen.

Text boxes can be any size, so you can create a full-page border by selecting Full Page for the vertical position of a page type box. To divide the page into a number of smaller boxes, define each box with coordinated positions—one each on the top, center, and bottom.

Text boxes can add impact to any document if not overused. Plan your documents and reserve boxes for those elements that you want to emphasize.

Lesson 69—How to Add Graphics to Your Documents

This final lesson also creates a box. But in this case you'll insert a graphic image. WordPerfect supplies a number of sample drawings, which are stored as files ending with the extension WPG (for Word-Perfect Graphic). You can merge any of these into your document as well as graphics files from many other programs, such as Lotus 1-2-3 or PC Paintbrush, a drawing program.

The techniques are almost identical to creating a text box, so most of the steps will be familiar to you.

In this lesson, you'll add a graphic image to the CLASSES document (Figure 18.13). Follow these steps to create that document:

Classifications of Computers

The largest computer systems are called mainframes. These are large centralized computer systems that can be accessed by a great many users at one time, performing many different tasks.

The next size computers are called minicomputers. These are still centralized systems that can be used by a number of persons. However, they have less processing capability than mainframes and can accommodate fewer users.

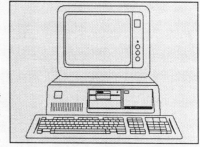

Supermicros are smaller than minicomputers. These are smaller computer systems, based on microcomputers, which serve a number of persons at a time. These are called multi-user, multi-tasking microcomputers.

A microcomputer, also called a personal or desktop computer, can be used by only one individual at a time. Compared to the other types of computers, the microcomputer has limited processing capabilities.

The special purpose computer is designed to perform a very specific task. It can be large or small, but is "dedicated" to the one job for which it was made. Special purpose computers can be found in automobiles, industrial equipment, and even home appliances.

Figure 18.13: Sample document with graphics

1. Recall the CLASSES document. The document contains a number of paragraphs, each indented farther to the right.

2. Remove the indentations using the Replace command.

   a. Select **S**earch **R**eplace (Alt-F2) **No** for unconfirmed replacement.

   b. Press F4, the Indent key.

   c. Press F2 twice to perform the replacement.

All of the [->Indent] codes will be deleted, aligning each of the paragraphs at the left margin.

3. Format the title to extra large printing.

    a. Place the cursor at the start of the title.

    b. Select **Edit B**lock (Alt-F4) to turn on Block mode.

    c. Press End to highlight the entire line.

    d. Select **F**ont **E**xtra Large (Ctrl-F8 S E).

4. Place the cursor at the start of the first paragraph.

5. Select **G**raphics **F**igure (Alt-F9 F) to select a Figure box. Remember, any box type could actually be used.

6. Select **O**ptions to display the Figure Options menu. It is just like the Text Box Options menu shown in Figure 18.9 except for some different default values: figure boxes are already formatted for a single line border but with no shading. So let's add a 10 percent shading to really make it stand out on the page.

7. Select **G**ray Shading.

8. Type *10,* then press ⏎ twice to return to the document. Now let's define the box itself.

9. Select **G**raphics **F**igure **C**reate (Alt-F9 F C). The Figure Box Definition menu appears. It includes the same options as the Text Box Definition menu shown in Figure 18.10. The Contents options says *empty* because no graphics or text has yet been inserted.

10. Now insert the graphics file PC-1.WPG, supplied on the WordPerfect Graphics disk if you're using 5-inch disks. If you have a floppy drive system, insert this disk in drive B.

    a. Select **F**ilename. The prompt changes to

       Enter filename:

    b. Type *PC-1.WPG* (or *B:PC-1.WPG* if you have floppy disks and did not change the default drive), then press ⏎. You'll see the message

       Please wait - Loading WP Graphics File

11. Press F7 to accept the box and return to the document, accepting the default paragraph type and other options.

12. Press Ctrl-F3 ↵ to rewrite the screen. It will appear as in Figure 18.14.

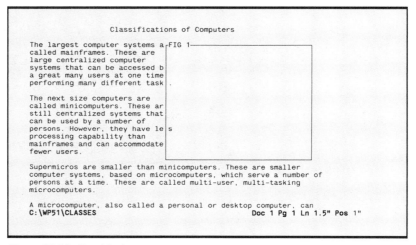

Figure 18.14: Graphic document

Even though some text characters appear in the box on the screen, they will not when printed.

13. Select **File** **P**rint (F7) **F**ull to print the document or select **File** **P**rint (F7) **V**iew to view it on the screen, then F7 to return to the document.

14. Select **File** **E**xit (F7) **N**o **Y**es to exit WordPerfect.

As you become more familiar with WordPerfect's graphics commands, you'll see that you can do some rather sophisticated formatting.

For example, you could use the Vertical Position option on the Definition menu to lower the position of the box. Figure 18.15 shows the box with a vertical position of 0.25". This lowers the box just enough so the top line of text runs across the page. You can also rotate, mirror-image, and scale the size of graphics.

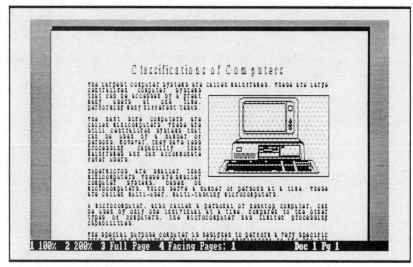

Figure 18.15: Position of box changed vertically

Here's a closing idea. If you have a painting or drawing program, use it to sign your name. Save the file, then merge it into your document using the graphics commands, placing the drawing at the end of a letter. When you print the document, your name will be signed for you (as in Figure 18.16). Think of how much time this will save if you produce form letters!

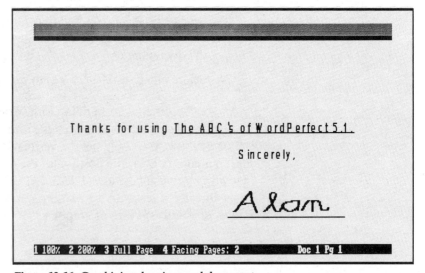

Figure 18.16: Combining drawings and documents

19

Printing Special Characters and Equations

300

Featuring

Foreign Language Characters

Mathematical and Technical Symbols

Graphic Characters

Equations

Lesson 70—How to Print Special Characters

As the world grows smaller, the use of foreign language characters in business and academic documents becomes more commonplace. Likewise, more documents require special typographical symbols and icons.

There was a time when printing these characters, symbols and icons required sophisticated printers and special fonts. If you have these printers and fonts, WordPerfect can take full advantage of them. If you don't have them but you have a printer capable of printing graphics, WordPerfect can create and print these characters, symbols, and icons for you.

A twelfth character set is available for storing user-defined characters.

To help you, WordPerfect has defined eleven character sets and included them in a file called WP.DRS. Figure 19.1 lists these characters sets. Character "positions" will be explained shortly. Using these character sets, you can construct characters not available in your printer's own font set and print them as graphic images along with your text.

These characters are created by selecting **Font Character (Ctrl-V)**.

Inserting Special Characters

Look at the sample character sets in Figure 19.2. Each character is identified by the set in which it is located, and by its position number within the set. To find the position of a character, add the number at the far left of the row in which it is located to the number along the top. Notice that the top numbers are in sets of ten.

For example, find the trademark symbol (™) in set number 4. It is located in row number 030 under column 11. (The 1 in 11 is located on the top row.) Add the two numbers to get 41. So the trademark symbol is in set 4, number 41.

Set	Positions	Name	Purpose
0	32-126	ASCII	The same characters available from the regular keyboard keys
1	0-233	Multinational 1	Common international characters
2	0-27	Multinational 2	Rarely used international characters
3	0-87	Box Drawing	Graphics, single and double lines
4	0-78	Typographical	Typographic symbols
5	0-34	Icons	Picture symbols
6	0-225	Math/Scientific	Regular size math and scientific characters
7	0-224	Math/Scientific Extension	Extensible and oversized math and scientific characters
8	0-226	Greek	Greek characters, both ancient and modern
9	0-40	Hebrew	Hebrew characters, vowel signs and punctuation
10	0-101	Cyrillic	Cyrillic characters, both ancient and modern
11	0-99	Japanese Kana	Hiragana or Katakana characters

Figure 19.1: WordPerfect Character Sets

You can also press Ctrl-2 to include a special character, although no prompt appears on the screen.

When you want to use any of these special characters, select Font Character (Ctrl-V) to see the prompt

Key =

Type the set number, a comma, then the position number. For example, find the star character (★) in set number 6. It's in row 180, under column 4—position 184.

To print this character:

1. Select Font Character (Ctrl-V).

2. Type *6,184*.

3. Press ←⊸.

Figure 19.2: Sample character sets in View mode

In most cases, depending on your hardware, you'll see a small box rather than the character. But if you view the document (again depending on your hardware) the special character will appear on the screen.

*P*rinting Special Characters

The size of the character is determined by the base font and size attribute. If you're using a 12-point font, the characters will be approximately 12 points large. If you select Font Extra Large before entering the character, or by blocking it afterward and then enlarging it, the character will be sized at 24-points (Figure 19.3).

Figure 19.3: Printer's fists (5,21 and 5,22) in different sizes

Because WordPerfect actually forms these characters as small graphic elements, it may take longer to display them in the View mode. In addition, with File Print Graphic Quality set to high, printing special characters may take considerably longer.

One caution for Laser printer users. Some of these character sets require a great deal of printer memory. With 512K of memory, for example, I was unable to print the entire seventh character set, even though it was the only thing on the page.

*L*esson 71—How to Print Equations

Just like foreign characters and graphic symbols, mathematical equations require special attention. These include mathematical symbols as well as various levels of subscripts and superscripts.

The Equation Editor is only used to form and print equations, not to perform the actual calculations.

WordPerfect's Equation Editor lets you enter equations using special instructions, then translate the equation into a graphic element that you can print. However, your printer must support graphic elements to do this.

The Equation Editor is a sophisticated feature that requires knowledge of mathematical terms and concepts. If you have this background, creating even complex equations is a simple process.

To get you started, let's create and print the equation shown in Figure 19.4. In case you've forgotten, the formula in the figure is for computing the attenuation in decibels per foot of concentric transmission lines.

$$a = \frac{4.6\sqrt{f}\,(d_1 + d_2)}{d_1 d_2 \left(\log \dfrac{d_1}{d_2}\right)} \times 10^{-6}$$

Figure 19.4: *The sample equation*

1. Select **Graphics Equation** (Alt-F9 E).

2. Select **C**reate to show the Graphic Equation menu. The menu is identical to those used to create figure and text boxes, except the Contents field is automatically set at Equation.

3. Select **E**dit. The Equation Editor screen is displayed (Figure 19.5).

You can also create an equation after selecting one of the other four graphics types on the Graphics menu. Just select **C**reate **C**ontents, and Equation will appear on the prompt line.

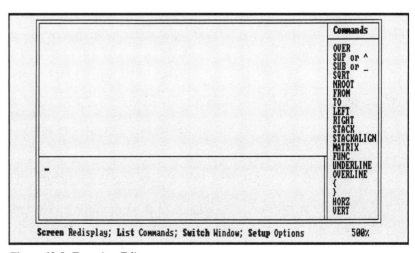

Figure 19.5: *Equation Editor screen*

On the Equation Editor screen, the pointer appears as an arrow.

The Equation Editor screen contains three parts.

- The Display Window at the top shows a graphic representation of the equation.

- The Editing Window, along the bottom, is where you create the equation by entering characters, symbols, and equation commands.

- The Equation Palette, along the right of the screen, shows the commands, functions, and symbols that are available. (You'll soon learn how to scroll the palette to display additional selections.)

When working on equations, use the commands below. You can select them either by clicking on the option with the mouse, or by pressing the keystroke combination.

- Select Screen Redisplay (Ctrl-F3) to update the graphic image in the Display Window without leaving the Editing Window.

- Select List Commands (F5) to enter the Equation Palette for selecting commands.

- Select Switch Window (Shift-F3) to move between the Editing and Display windows. When you switch to the Display window, the equation is updated to conform to any changes you made in the Editing Window.

- Select Setup Options (Shift-F1) to change the horizontal and vertical alignment, the default font size, or to change between graphic and text printing of the final equation.

The 500% shown at the bottom right means that the graphic image shown in the Display Window is five times the actual size.

4. Type $a =$. You'll soon see that the Equation Editor will ignore the space between the two characters. However, entering spaces in the Editing Window makes complex equations easier to read.

   Nothing yet appears in the Display Window. Let's take care of that now.

5. Select Screen Redisplay (Ctrl-F3). The characters in the Editing Window now appear enlarged in the Display Window (Figure 19.6).

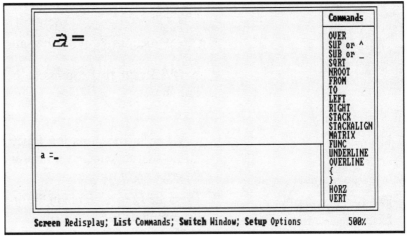

Figure 19.6: Partial equation shown in the Display Window

The Display Window is not updated automatically as you form the equation in the Editing Window. To see how the equation in the Editing Window looks, select either Screen Redisplay (Ctrl-F3) or Switch Windows (Shift-F3).

We're ready to enter the characters and symbols that appear above the large division line (see Figure 19.4). However, we need some way to tell WordPerfect that the characters $a =$ should not be included in the formula to the right of the equal sign.

We'll do this by enclosing the characters on the right side in brackets ({ and }).

6. Choose Select List Commands (F5) to enter the Equation Palette. You can see the first of 8 sets of options on the Equation Palette by pressing PgDn. These options are:

- Commands   Common formats and symbols
- Large   Popular math symbols from character set 7
- Symbols   Miscellaneous symbols from character sets 3, 4, 5 and 6

You cannot enter the Equation Palette from the Display window. You can only enter it from the Editing Window. If you're in the Display Window, you must select Switch Window (Shift-F3) before attempting to use the palette.

- Greek   Greek characters from set 10
- Arrows   Arrows, triangles, squares, and circles
- Sets   Set symbols, relational operators, Fraktur and hollow letters
- Other   Diacritical marks and ellipses
- Functions   Mathematical functions

OVER, the first command, is highlighted and the prompt line shows

> Fraction: x OVER y

When in the Equation Palette, the prompt line lists the name of the selected command and shows a sample or description of its use.

7. Press the ↓ key to highlight the open bracket character ({). The prompt line shows

> Start group: {x + 2}

The open and close brackets are used to surround groups, or parts, of the equation. Like parentheses in formulas, every open bracket must be evenly matched by a close bracket. If you have more of one than the other, the message

> ERROR: Incorrect format

will appear when you try to update the Display Window.

8. Press ←⎤. The bracket appears in the Editing Window. The Equation Editor automatically places a space before and after the bracket to improve readability.

9. Type *4.6*.

10. Now insert the square root.

     a. Select List Commands (F5) in order to enter the Equation Palette.

     b. Select SQRT.

     c. Press ←⎤.

The characters SQRT appear in the Editing Window. If you tried to select Screen Redisplay or Switch Windows, the

> You can select commands by pointing and clicking.

ERROR: Incorrect format message would appear. That's because you have a starting bracket but no ending one.

11. Now we want to place the letter *f* under the square root sign. Since only the *f* belongs there, not the following characters, we'll enclose it in its own set of brackets—creating a group within a group.

   a. Select List Commands (F5)

   b. Select {.

   c. Press ◄┘.

   d. Type *f*.

   e. Select List Commands (F5).

   f. Select }.

   g. Press ◄┘.

12. Type *(d*.

13. Enter the subscripted 1.

   a. Select List Commands (F5).

   b. Select SUB.

   c. Press ◄┘.

   d. Type *1*.

14. In the same manner, complete the rest of that group.

   a. Type + *d*.

   b. Select List Commands (F5).

   c. Select SUB.

   d. Press ◄┘.

   e. Type *2)*.

   f. Select List Commands (F5).

   g. Select }.

   h. Press ◄┘.

While the entire equation is not complete, we now have a matching number of opening and closing brackets. So let's see how the equation will appear when printed.

15. Select Screen Redisplay (Ctrl-F3). Figure 19.7 shows the screen at this point.

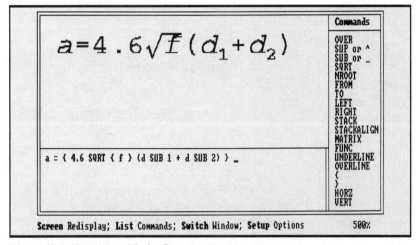

Figure 19.7: Equation with the first two groups

16. We are now ready to enter the next group, the part that comes under the large division line. We'll do this by telling WordPerfect that the previous group must appear over the next one.

   a. Select List Commands (F5).

   b. Select OVER.

   c. Press ◄─┘.

17. Enter the start of the next group.

   a. Select List Commands (F5).

   b. Select {, then press ◄─┘.

   c. Type *d*.

   d. Select List Commands (F5).

   e. Select SUB, then press ◄─┘.

   f. Type *1 d*.

g. Select List Commands (F5).

h. Select SUB, then press ◄─┘.

i. Type *2*.

18. Enter the next part of that group.

You could also select log from the Function menu in the Palette.

a. Type *(log*.

b. Select List Commands (F5).

c. Select {, then press ◄─┘.

d. Type *d*.

e. Select List Commands (F5).

f. Select SUB, then press ◄─┘.

g. Type *1*.

h. Select List Commands (F5).

i. Select OVER, then press ◄─┘.

j. Type *d*.

k. Select List Commands (F5).

l. Select SUB, then press ◄─┘.

m. Type *2*.

n. Select List Commands (F5).

o. Select }, then press ◄─┘. This "closes" off the opening bracket entered in step c.

p. Type *)*.

q. Select }, then press ◄─┘. This "closes" off the opening bracket entered in step 17.

19. Select Screen Redisplay (Ctrl-F3) to see how the equation appears at this point (Figure 19.8).

20. Now complete the equation. The final characters *-6* (see Figure 19.4) will have to be placed in their own group so both are superscripted at the same level.

a. Select List Commands (F5).

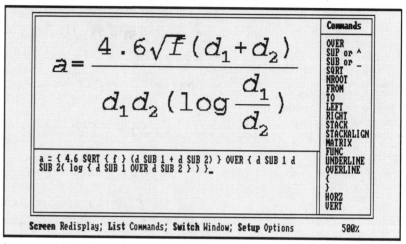

Figure 19.8: *Equation with three groups entered*

b. Press PgDn to see the next screen of commands (Figure 19.9). When in the Palette, use PgDn and PgUp to scroll between the 8 available sets of options.

c. Press PgDn again and notice that the times (×) sign is the first character in the second row.

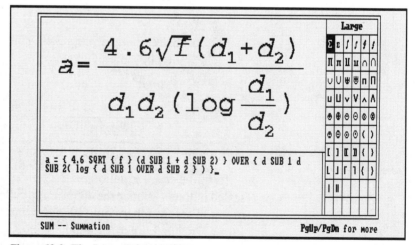

Figure 19.9: *The Large Palette options*

    d. Use the mouse or arrow keys to select the $\times$ character, then press ◄─┘. The word *Times* appears in the equation.

    e. Type *10*.

    f. Select List Commands (F5).

    g. Press PgUp twice to display the first listing of commands.

    h. Select SUP, then press ◄─┘.

    i. Select List Commands (F5).

    j. Select {, then press ◄─┘.

    k. Type *-6*.

    l. Select List Commands (F5).

    m. Select }, then press ◄─┘.

21. Select Screen Redisplay (Ctrl-F3) to see the final equation (Figure 19.10).

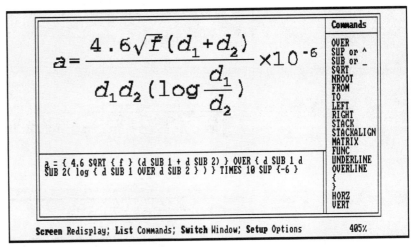

Figure 19.10: Completed equation

To fit the entire equation on the screen, WordPerfect automatically scaled it down—notice the 405% on the status line (depending on your monitor, this number could be different). This scaling doesn't effect the final printed size of the equation, just the scale at which it is shown in the Display Window.

You can also adjust the scale and position of the equation by switching to the Display Window itself. Lets try that now.

22. Select Switch Window (Shift-F3) to redisplay the image and show the prompt line

    Arrow Keys Move; **PgUp/PgDn** Scale; **GOTO** Reset; **Switch** Window.

    These commands are used to manipulate the image in the Display Window. For example, Figure 19.11 shows the equation after it was scaled down pressing the PgDn key three times. Each time, the equation was scaled 25 percent less, so the status line now shows that it is displayed 330% of its actual printed size (this number could be different depending on your monitor).

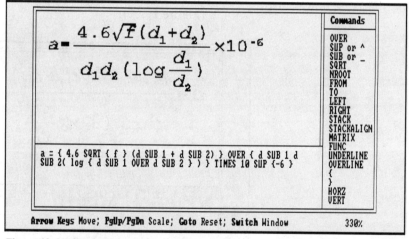

Figure 19.11: Equation scaled to 330%

23. Select Switch Window (Shift-F3) to return to the Editing Window.

    Before leaving this screen, look carefully at the final form of the equation:

    a = { 4.6 SQRT { f } (d SUB 1 + d SUB 2) } OVER { d
    SUB 1 d SUB 2(log { d SUB 1 OVER d SUB 2 }) }
    TIMES 10 SUP {-6}

Spaces inserted in the equation were ignored when Word-Perfect compiled it into its graphic form as shown in the Display Window.

24. Press F7 to accept the equation and return to the Equation Definition menu.

Use the options here to adjust the size and position of the equation just as you would a figure or text box. If you want, review the menu options explained in Chapter 18.

25. Press F7 to return to the document.

26. Select **File** **P**rint (Shift-F7) **F**ull or **File** **P**rint (Shift-F7) **V**iew to see the final equation.

Saving and Retrieving Equations

While you're working on an equation, you can save it in its own file separate from the document. This is useful when you are constructing complex equations and you don't want to exit the equation function to save the file.

From within the Equation Editor, press the F10 key to see the prompt:

Equation file to save:

Type the name of a file, then press ◄─┘. If a file with that name already exists you'll be asked to confirm replacement.

To recall the file into the Equation Editor, press Shift-F10 for the prompt

Equation file to retrieve:

Type the name, then press ◄─┘.

The Equation Editor is a powerful tool if you write technical or academic documents.

How to Make Backups

It is unethical and illegal to distribute copies of your WordPerfect disks or manual to anyone. You should, however, make a copy of all your WordPerfect disks before attempting to install the program. Because disks can wear out from use, an extra set of disks is simply a precaution against losing this valuable program.

You'll need a DOS or OS/2 disk, all of your WordPerfect disks, and a number of blank disks, either 5¼-inch or 3½-inch depending on your computer. Make sure you have a blank disk for each disk supplied with WordPerfect. If you have two floppy disk drives, and no hard disk, you'll need an extra blank disk. This will be used to hold your own documents.

First, *write-protect* your WordPerfect disks as a precaution against accidentally erasing your WordPerfect program. With 5¼-inch disks, place a write-protect tab over the small notch on the edge of each disk. The write-protect tabs are the small rectangular stickers that are packaged with blank diskettes. If you have 3½-inch disks, protect the disk by pushing the small tab toward the end of the disk. If the small square is blocked, then the disk is unlocked and the files can be erased. Lock the disk by pushing the tab so the hole is uncovered.

Do not lock or write-protect the blank disks that you will be copying onto. You want these disks free so that you can transfer WordPerfect to them.

Systems with Two Floppy Disks

You will first *format* the blank disks according to the instructions below, allowing them to accept the WordPerfect programs. Then you will copy WordPerfect onto these new disks. Check with your DOS manual if you have any problems with the following procedure.

In this procedure, NEVER place one of your original WordPerfect disks in drive B. If you tried to copy with a WordPerfect disk in drive B and without a write-protect tab on, the WordPerfect program would be destroyed.

1. Insert a DOS disk in drive A, turn on your computer, and respond to the date and time questions, if they appear.

   Type the date in MM-DD-YY format—such as *10-19-90*—and press ←.

   Type the time in HH:MM format—such as *10:16*—and press ←. Past noon, use military time by just adding 12 to the hours. For example, if it is 2:30, enter *14:30*.

   The disk drive prompt *A >* will appear.

2. Type *FORMAT B:/* and press ←. DOS and OS/2 commands can be entered in either uppercase or lowercase.

   The screen will display

   Insert new diskette for drive B:
   and strike ENTER when ready

3. Place a blank disk in drive B and press ←. It will take a few minutes, but the blank disk will be formatted.

   On some MS-DOS systems, the message

   Volume Label (11 characters, ENTER for none)?

will be displayed. Press ←.

A *volume label* is a disk name that is displayed when you list the directory. By pressing ← you didn't name this disk. We're only skipping the names here to save time. Since each disk will be labeled on the outside, and each will have different programs on it, a name is not needed. However, later you might want to give your disks volume labels that identify their contents so when you display the directory listing its name will appear. The volume label could be "School Papers," "Annual Report," or any name that will quickly identify the nature of the documents on that disk.

The screen will now display

Format another (Yes/No)?

4. Press *Y*.

    Remove the disk from drive B. Label it with the name of your first WordPerfect disk.

5. Place another *blank* disk in drive B, then press ◄─┘. When the formatting is complete, the *Format another (Yes/No)?* message will appear again.

6. Replace the disk in drive B with another blank disk.

7. Press *Y* to format another disk, then ◄─┘ to start the process.

8. Complete steps 6 and 7 until all of the blank disks have been formatted.

9. Press *N* to stop formatting.

Copying WordPerfect

Now that the disks are formatted, you must copy the WordPerfect programs. Remember, *never place one of your original WordPerfect disks in drive B.*

1. Remove the DOS disk from drive A.

2. Insert the original WordPerfect disk in drive A.

3. Insert the newly formatted disk in drive B.

4. Type *COPY A:*.** B:* and press ◄─┘. All of the programs from the original disk will be copied onto the working disk in drive B.

5. When the *A >* prompt reappears, remove both disks.

6. Place another original WordPerfect disk in drive A.

7. Place one of your formatted disks in drive B.

8. Type *COPY A:*.* B:* and press ⏎.

9. When the *A* > prompt appears, remove both disks and immediately label the disk in drive B to match the one in drive A.

10. Now repeat steps 6 to 9 until you have copied all of the WordPerfect disks and labeled all of the copies.

    You should have one blank formatted disk left. Label this "Document Disk."

    Place the original WordPerfect disks in a safe location and use the copies for your installation.

Hard Disk Systems with One Floppy

During this procedure, you must be very careful to follow the instructions displayed on the screen. Remember to install write-protect tabs on your WordPerfect disks as a precaution against accidentally erasing them.

1. Turn on the computer and respond to the date and time prompts if they appear. (See Step 1 of "Systems with Two Floppy Disks" if you need instructions.) Wait until the drive prompt appears. It will usually be *C*>.

2. Make sure the DOS program DISKCOPY.COM is on the current directory. If not, move to the appropriate subdirectory with the CD\ command. If you know that DISKCOPY.COM works on your computer, skip to step 3.

   a. Type *DIR* then press ⏎ to display the programs on the main, or root, directory. If DISKCOPY.COM is not there, make a note of the subdirectory names (marked with <DIR>).

   b. Move to each subdirectory by entering *CD* followed by the subdirectory's name, then use the DIR command again to check for the copying program, DISKCOPY.COM. ·

   c. If you can't find it, insert the DOS or OS/2 disk that contains DISKCOPY.COM into your floppy drive and continue below.

3. Type *DISKCOPY A: A:* and press ◄──┘. DOS and OS/2 commands can be entered in either uppercase or lowercase.
   The screen will display

   Insert source diskette in drive A:
   Strike any key when ready

   You will be making a copy using only one disk drive. During the process, you will be instructed to insert either the *source* diskette or the *destination* diskette into drive A. The *source* diskette is the original WordPerfect disk that you will be copying from. The *destination* disk is the blank diskette that you are copying onto. *Never* insert the original WordPerfect disk when you are asked to insert the *destination* disk. If the write-protect notch was not covered, the WordPerfect program would be erased.

4. Place one of your WordPerfect disks in drive A. This will be one of the original disks supplied with WordPerfect. You should have a write-protect notch on it, or with 3½-inch disks the tab should be moved to the locked position.

5. Press any key. Soon the message

   Insert destination diskette in drive A:
   Strike any key when ready

   will appear.

6. Remove the WordPerfect disk and insert a blank disk in drive A.

7. Press any key to begin the copy.
   You will be told several times to switch disks until all of the information on the WordPerfect disk has been copied onto the blank disk. Be certain that the original WordPerfect disk is in the drive only when the screen requests the source diskette.
   When the copy is completed,the message

   Copy Another (Yes/No)?

   will appear.

8. Remove the disk and immediately label the copy accordingly. Write the name of the disk on the label before sticking it on the disk. If you write on the disk itself, the impression of a pen or

pencil could damage the recording surface. If you must write on a disk, use a felt-tipped pen and write very lightly.

9. Press **Yes** and repeat this process for all of your disks.

Place the original WordPerfect disks in a safe location and use the copies for everyday work.

Installing
WordPerfect

When you *install* a program, you get it ready for use with your own computer. WordPerfect 5.1 comes with a comprehensive installation program that takes care of this for you.

Preparing WordPerfect for Use

To run the installation program, just follow these steps.

1. Turn on your computer, respond to the time and date questions, then wait until the drive prompt (*C>* or *A >*) appears.

2. Place the Install/Learning/Utility 1 diskette in drive A.

3. If you have a hard disk system, log onto drive A by typing *A:*, then pressing ←⎯.

4. Type *Install* and press ←⎯. You'll see the message

   Continue? Yes (No)

5. Select **Yes**. You'll see the message on the hard disk,

   Yes (No)

   If you have a floppy disk system, select **No**. You'll be warned that WordPerfect will not operate on low-density 360K 5¼-inch disks, and that you'll need nine blank formatted disks available. If you have the disks, continue with the installation, starting with step 6. While these steps are designed for hard disk systems, follow the prompts as they appear on your screen, using the instructions here as a guide.

6. Select **Yes**. The main installation screen will appear, as in Figure B.1. Figure B.2 summarizes the options on this menu. Since this is the first time you're installing WordPerfect, however, we'll use the Basic installation procedure.

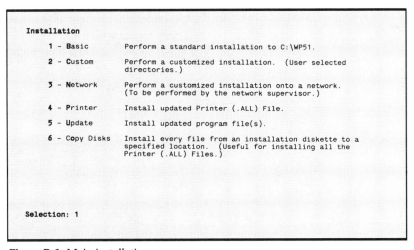

```
Installation

    1 - Basic          Perform a standard installation to C:\WP51.

    2 - Custom         Perform a customized installation.  (User selected
                       directories.)

    3 - Network        Perform a customized installation onto a network.
                       (To be performed by the network supervisor.)

    4 - Printer        Install updated Printer (.ALL) File.

    5 - Update         Install updated program file(s).

    6 - Copy Disks     Install every file from an installation diskette to a
                       specified location.  (Useful for installing all the
                       Printer (.ALL) Files.)




Selection: 1
```

Figure B.1: Main installation menu

Option	Purpose
Basic	For installing WordPerfect on your system for the first time.
Custom	For installing WordPerfect on a hard disk directory other than C:\WP51, for installing individual parts of WordPerfect at a later date, or for installing additional printers.
Network	For installing a network version of WordPerfect.
Printer	From time to time, WordPerfect releases additional printer files. Use this option to install these files onto your hard disk.
Update	Periodically, WordPerfect provides interim releases that enhance or improve basic program features. Use this option if you receive a program update and wish to install the new features on your system.
Copy Disk	For making copies of the files on your WordPerfect disks.

Figure B.2: Installation options

7. Select **B**asic installation. You'll see the prompt

   Do you want to install the Utility Files? Yes (No)
   The files will be installed to C:\WP51\

8. Select **Y**es to see the prompt

   Insert the Install-Learn-Utility 1 master diskette into drive A:\
   (Enter = Continue   F1 = Cancel)

9. Insert the Install-Learn-Utility 1 disk into drive A, then press ◄─┘.
   The necessary files will be copied onto the hard disk. After the files are copied, you'll be asked in a series of screens if you want to install other WordPerfect modules. Their names are summarized below.

FILE NAME	PURPOSE
Learning	Using the tutorials
Help	Displaying line help screens
Keyboard	Using alternate function keys
Style libraries	Using sample stylesheets
WordPerfect	Using the program itself
Speller	Checking the spelling of documents
Thesaurus	Looking up synonyms and antonyms
PTR program	Modifying printer files
Graphic drivers	Using WordPerfect with graphic monitors
Graphic images	Importing supplied graphic images

10. Follow the directions on the screen, selecting **Y**es for each of the modules you want to install, **N**o for those you don't. You must install the WordPerfect module. You'll be prompted to insert specific disks in drive A.
    When all of the files have been copied, WordPerfect will check your system configuration file—CONFIG.SYS. This file is checked everytime you start your computer and must include a special command that allows the disk operating system to handle all of the special files that WordPerfect uses.
    If your configuration file doesn't have the proper commands, you'll see a screen like the one in Figure B.3. Select **Y**es.

```
Check C:\CONFIG.SYS file

This file contains information about your system configuration.

Your CONFIG.SYS file allows for only 5 files.
It needs to allow for at least 20 files for WordPerfect to run.
Would you like to have it changed? Yes (No)
```

Figure B.3: *Warning that the configuration file must be updated*

WordPerfect then checks your system for an AUTOEXEC-.BAT file, and inserts a path command for the WP51 directory.

You'll then be prompted to insert Printer 1 disk in drive A to select a printer.

If WordPerfect had to modify the CONFIG.SYS file, you will be prompted to reboot your computer. Press Alt-Ctrl-Del, then start the Install program again. Select **B**asic, but answer **N**o to all of the installation modules until you return to this point.

11. Insert the Printer 1 disk in drive A, then press ⏎. You'll see a list of available printers (Figure B.4.).

12. Look for the name and model of your printer. If you don't see it, press the PgDn key until your printer is listed.

```
   1  Acer LP-76                          Printers marked with '*' are
   2  AEG Olympia Compact RO              not included with shipping
   3  AEG Olympia ESW 2000                disks.  Select printer for
   4  AEG Olympia Laserstar 6             more information.
   5  AEG Olympia Startype
   6  Alphacom Alphapro 101
   7  Alps Allegro 24
   8 *Alps Allegro 24 (Additional)
   9  Alps ALQ200 (18 pin)
  10  Alps ALQ200 (24 pin)
  11  Alps ALQ224e
  12 *Alps ALQ224e (Additional)
  13  Alps ALQ300 (18 pin)
  14  Alps ALQ300 (24 pin)
  15  Alps ALQ324e
  16 *Alps ALQ324e (Additional)
  17  Alps P2000
  18 *Alps P2000 (Additional)
  19  Alps P2100
  20 *Alps P2100 (Additional)
  21  Alps P2400C
  22  Amstrad DMP 4000

N Name Search; PgDn More Printers; PgUp Previous Screen; F3 Help; F7 Exit;
Selection: 0
```

Figure B.4: *Printer list*

13. Type the number corresponding to your printer, then press ←┘. You'll see the prompt

    Select printer (*your printer name*) Yes (No)

14. Select **Yes** to see the prompt

    Do you want to install the Printer (.ALL) File? Yes (No)

15. Select **Yes**. At this point you may be asked to insert one of the other Printer diskettes. After the printer information is installed, you'll see

    Do you want to install another printer? No (Yes)

    If you have more than one printer, select **Yes**, then repeat steps 12 through 14. Select **No** when all of your printers have been installed. You'll be prompted to enter your registration number.

16. Type your registration number, then press ←┘. In a moment you'll see a Printer Helps and Hints screen, as shown in Figure B.5.

17. Read the information, then press any key. The installation process finishes and the *A* > prompt reappears.

You're now ready to start WordPerfect 5.1.

Figure B.5: *Printer Helps and Hints screen*

Customizing Printer Information

In most cases, the printer information copied to your disk during the installation process is complete. But if you're using a laser printer with soft fonts, or have a special hardware configuration, then you might have to edit the printer information in order to take full advantage of your printer's features.

If you're unfamiliar with WordPerfect, then skip this section for now. But if you have trouble printing documents, or want to use your soft fonts, refer to this section after you've had a chance to get to know WordPerfect a little better.

1. Start WordPerfect. (If you're not sure how, go to Chapter 1, Lesson 1, follow the step-by-step instructions, and return here for step 2.)

2. Select **File Print** (Shift-F7) to see the Print menu shown in Figure B.6.

```
Print

        1 - Full Document
        2 - Page
        3 - Document on Disk
        4 - Control Printer
        5 - Multiple Pages
        6 - View Document
        7 - Initialize Printer


Options

        S - Select Printer                      HP LaserJet+
        B - Binding Offset                      0"
        N - Number of Copies                    1
        U - Multiple Copies Generated by        WordPerfect
        G - Graphics Quality                    Medium
        T - Text Quality                        High




Selection: 0
```

Figure B.6: *Print menu*

The printer listed at the Select Printer option is the one you selected during the installation process. Even if you installed more than one printer, only the first one will be shown at this prompt.

3. Select **Select Printer**. The screen changes to the Print: Select Printer menu (Figure B.7).

All of the printers you installed during the installation process will be listed here. If you later want to change printers to one of these printers, use the arrow keys to highlight the printer you want, then press F7.

4. Select Edit to display the Select Printer: Edit menu (Figure B.8).

    Look at the Port option. This refers to the plug where your printer is attached to your computer. LPT1: refers to a standard parallel printer port, the most common in use with PCs. Chances are you're using a printer attached to that port. If you have a parallel printer and the port listed on the menu

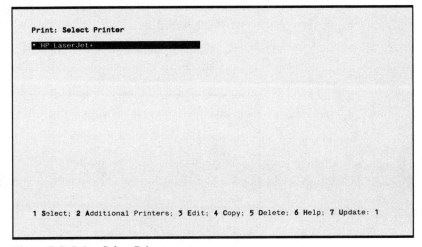

Figure B.7: *Print: Select Printer menu*

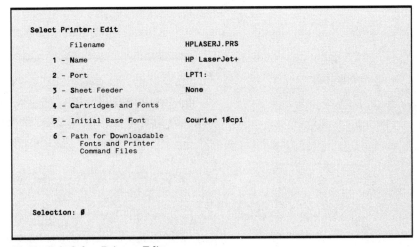

Figure B.8: *Select Printer: Edit menu*

says LPT1:, then just skip to step 7. If you have a serial printer and the port says COM1:, then press ⏎ and skip to step 7.

If you're not quite sure, read the explanation following the next step.

5. Select **P**ort to display the prompt line

    Port: 1 LPT 1; 2 LPT 2; 3 LPT 3; 4 COM 1; 5 COM 2;
    6 COM 3; 7 COM 4; 8 Other: 0

    You can't tell a serial printer from a parallel one just by looking at it. But you might tell by seeing where it's connected to the back of your computer. You'll see a plug—called a *port*—where the printer's cable is attached. If the plug is labelled *Printer, LPT 1,* or *Parallel,* then your printer is a parallel printer. If it's the only port on the back of the computer, then it's probably a parallel port as well.

    If the port is labelled *COM 1* or *Serial* you're using a Serial printer, so enter *4.* However, if you do have a serial printer, you'll have to read your manual for complete instructions.

    By the way, if you have more than one port of a type, they are called LPT 2, LPT 3, or COM 2. You would use these if you had more than one printer attached, say a dot-matrix printer for quick rough copies and a letter-quality printer for the final draft. If you do have this type of hardware, repeat this entire procedure for each printer you have.

6. Press the number corresponding to your printer's port.

    If you don't have a laser printer, then skip to step 15.

7. Select **C**artridges and Fonts to see the menu shown in Figure B.9.

    The Quantity column indicates how many cartridge slots you have, or the amount of memory your printer has to hold downloaded fonts. You can change the amount by using option 2 on the prompt line. The Available column shows how many slots or how much memory is still available.

8. Designate the cartridge(s) you are using. The Built-In selection should be highlighted.

    a. Press the ↓ key to select Cartridges, then press ⏎ to display a list of cartridges available for your printer (Figure B.10).

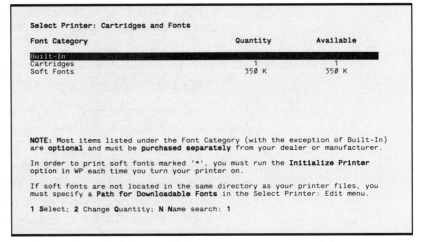

Figure B.9: *Cartridges and Fonts menu*

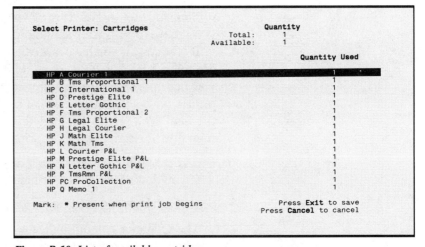

Figure B.10: *List of available cartridges*

b. Use the arrow keys to highlight the cartridge you will be using.

c. Type *.

d. Repeat this procedure if your printer accepts more than one cartridge at a time.

e. Press F7 to return to the previous menu.

Now it's time to designate the downloadable fonts you wish to use.

9. Highlight the Soft Fonts option on the Cartridges and Fonts menu (see Figure B.9), then press ⏎. You'll see a list of font groups available (Figure B.11).

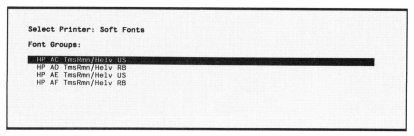

```
Select Printer: Soft Fonts

Font Groups:

  HP  AC  TmsRmn/Helv  US
  HP  AD  TmsRmn/Helv  R8
  HP  AE  TmsRmn/Helv  US
  HP  AF  TmsRmn/Helv  R8
```

Figure B.11: *Soft Font groups*

You can designate soft fonts as *Present* or *Can be Loaded*. WordPerfect assumes that all fonts marked Present (with an asterisk) have already been downloaded when you start to print a document. (You can download them yourself or have WordPerfect download them for you.) Fonts marked with a plus sign (+) will be downloaded by WordPerfect when you start to print a document.

10. Use the arrow keys to highlight the font group you will be using, then press ⏎. You'll see a list of soft fonts available (Figure B.12). It might take a few seconds for this list to appear.

11. Scroll through the list and mark each of your fonts with either * a (Present) or a + (Can be loaded).

   When you mark a font as Present, WordPerfect subtracts the amount of printer memory it requires from the Available Quantity amount on the top of the menu.

12. Press F7 three times when all of your fonts have been marked. You'll see the message

   Updating font:

at the prompt line followed by a font number while Word-Perfect loads the appropriate printer codes onto your disk. The Select Printer: Edit menu (see Figure B.8) will reappear.

```
    Select Printer: Soft Fonts                    Quantity      * Fonts
                                          Total:     350 K         32
                                      Available:     350 K         32

    HP AC TmsRmn/Helv US                                     Quantity Used

     (AC) Helv  6pt                                               8 K
     (AC) Helv  6pt (Land)                                        8 K
     (AC) Helv  6pt Bold                                          8 K
     (AC) Helv  6pt Bold (Land)                                   8 K
     (AC) Helv  6pt Italic                                        8 K
     (AC) Helv  6pt Italic (Land)                                 8 K
     (AC) Helv  8pt                                               9 K
     (AC) Helv  8pt (Land)                                        9 K
     (AC) Helv  8pt Bold                                         11 K
     (AC) Helv  8pt Bold (Land)                                  11 K
     (AC) Helv  8pt Italic                                       10 K
     (AC) Helv  8pt Italic (Land)                                10 K
     (AC) Helv  10pt                                             13 K
     (AC) Helv  10pt (Land)                                      13 K
     (AC) Helv  10pt Bold                                        13 K
     (AC) Helv  10pt Bold (Land)                                 13 K

    Mark:  * Present when print job begins          Press Exit to save
           + Can be loaded/unloaded during job      Press Cancel to cancel
```

Figure B.12: *Soft Font list*

13. Select Path for **D**ownloadable Fonts.

14. Enter the complete path (disk and directory) where the downloadable fonts are stored, then press ←⏎.

15. Press F7 three times to return to the document.

*C*hanging Printer Definitions

If you purchase a new printer, you must add its definition to the list and select it. Just follow steps 1 through 3 shown above, then select **A**dditional Printers from the Print: Select Printer menu. A list of printers will appear similar to those shown during the installation process.

Select the printer desired, press ←⏎, then complete the Edit menu as shown above.

*Q*uitting WordPerfect

You are now prepared to use WordPerfect, and since you have already started WordPerfect you are ready to continue with Lesson 2. But if you want to stop now, select File Exit No Yes. If you're using the keyboard, press the F7 (Exit) key, then select No to the *Save Document?* prompt and Yes to the *Exit WP?* prompt.

Just turn to Lesson 1 when you want to start WordPerfect again.

Using a Mouse
with WordPerfect

All of the command functions that can be performed using the keyboard keys can be accomplished by moving the mouse and pressing its buttons. These functions include simple tasks, such as cursor movement and blocking text, as well as pulling down and selecting from menus.

This appendix reviews the basic functions that the mouse performs.

Installing the Mouse

To use your mouse with WordPerfect, you must have its driver program (such as MOUSE.SYS or MOUSE.COM) on the disk that you use to boot your computer.

See if the driver is on your disk by typing from the DOS prompt

```
DIR MOUSE.*
```

If your mouse driver is MOUSE.COM, then just type MOUSE and press ⏎ before starting WordPerfect.

But if the driver is called MOUSE.SYS, then you'll need a special entry in the CONFIG.SYS file. This is the configuration file discussed in Appendix B. The file must include the entry

```
device = mouse.sys
```

To see if the mouse driver is already set up on your hardware, type

```
TYPE CONFIG.SYS
```

If the device command is shown, then you are ready to start WordPerfect. Otherwise, you must add the command to the file with these steps:

1. Make sure you are on the boot directory that contains the MOUSE.SYS file. Type *cd*, then press ⏎ to make sure.

2. Type *copy config.sys + con: config.sys*, then press ↩. The screen will display

   CONFIG.SYS
   CON

3. Type *device = mouse.sys*, then press ↩.

4. Hold down the Ctrl key and press *Z*. Let go of them both. The characters ^Z will appear.

5. Press ↩.

6. Make sure your mouse is plugged into the computer, then press Ctrl-Alt-Del to reboot. You're now ready to use the mouse.

Using the Mouse

When dealing with the mouse, you'll see instructions to click, double-click, and drag.

- Click means to press and release the mouse button. For example, the instruction

  Click the left button

  means to quickly press and release the left mouse button.

- Double-clicking means to click the mouse button twice within the double-click interval. This is set at about one-third of second by default.

- Drag means to press and hold down the button while moving the mouse pointer. So the instruction

  Hold down the left button and drag the mouse

means to keep the left button held down while you move the mouse pointer.

The instructions given assume you're using all of the default mouse values. That is, with the mouse set at right-handed operation. See the section "Changing Mouse Defaults" if you are left-handed.

The Pointer Shape

The mouse pointer appears on the WordPerfect screen when you move the mouse, and disappears as soon as you press any key. When you're working on a document, the pointer will appear as a small rectangle. In the Equation Editor, which has a graphics mode screen, the mouse will be a small hollow pointer.

Cursor Movement

To move the cursor with the mouse, place the pointer where you want to position the cursor, then click the left button. The cursor will appear at that position.

Scrolling

You can use the mouse for both vertical and horizontal scrolling. To scroll the mouse vertically, move the mouse pointer to the left edge of the screen, hold down the right mouse button, then drag the mouse in the direction you wish to scroll.

To scroll the mouse hortizontally, place the mouse pointer at the far edge of the screen, on the line you wish to scroll, hold down the right button, then drag the mouse towards the edge of the screen.

Blocking Text

To block text, place the mouse pointer at one end of the text, press and hold down the left button, then drag the pointer to the other end of the text. Click the left button to unblock the text.

Selecting Commands and Options

The mouse can be used with the pull down menus, and most prompts, selection lines, and other menus.

- To display the menu bar, click the right mouse button. Click the button again to remove the menu bar.

- To pull down a menu or submenu, place the pointer on the option, then click the left button.

- To select an option, place the pointer on the option, then click the left button.

- Drag with the left button to move along the menu bar and sub-menus to display options. If an option is selected—highlighted—when you release the button, that option will be performed.

- In selection lines and menus, place the pointer on the option you wish to select, then click the left button.

- In selection lines and prompts, clicking the right button is like pressing the ← key—it accepts the default value shown at the prompt line.

- In List menus, select an option by clicking it with the right button. Double-click with the right button to select an option and accept the default option at the same time. In List Files, for example, double-click on a file name to look at its contents.

Changing Mouse Defaults

You can adjust some features of the mouse through the Setup menu. Select File Setup from the pull down menu, or press Shift-F1, then select Mouse. You'll see options for changing:

- Mouse Type   Designates the manufacturer of your mouse and its type.
- Port   Designates the port to which the mouse is attached.

- Double
  Click
  Interval

Sets the amount of time you have between clicks when double-clicking. Setting the rate too fast might make it difficult to double-click within the interval; setting it too slow might result in two separate clicks being interpreted as a double-click.

- Sub-Menu
  Delay
  Time

Sets the amount of time before a submenu is displayed when you highlight an option that has a submenu. This also sets the amount of time the submenu is displayed before you can select an item on the menu.

- Acceleration
  Factor

Sets how responsive the mouse pointer is to the movement of the mouse. A higher acceleration factor makes the mouse pointer more responsive to movement. A factor too high, however, might make it difficult to make small and concise pointer movements.

- Left-
  Handed
  Mouse

Lets WordPerfect know if you're using your left hand for mouse movements. If you set this option to Yes, then all button functions are the reverse as those listed above. For example, clicking the left button displays the menu bar.

- Assisted
  Mouse
  Pointer
  Movement

Moves the mouse pointer directly to the menu bar or the selection line menu. Normally the mouse pointer remains in its current position when you display the menu bar or selection line menu.

Index

Selections from The SYBEX Library

graphics, high-speed recalculation techniques, and spreadsheet linking available with Release 2.2.

The Complete Lotus 1-2-3 Release 3 Handbook
Greg Harvey
700pp. Ref. 600-6

Everything you ever wanted to know about 1-2-3 is in this definitive handbook. As a Release 3 guide, it features the design and use of 3D worksheets, and improved graphics, along with using Lotus under DOS or OS/2. Problems, exercises, and helpful insights are included.

Lotus 1-2-3 Desktop Companion
SYBEX Ready Reference Series
Greg Harvey
976pp. Ref. 501-8

A full-time consultant, right on your desk. Hundreds of self-contained entries cover every 1-2-3 feature, organized by topic, indexed and cross-referenced, and supplemented by tips, macros and working examples. For Release 2.

Advanced Techniques in Lotus 1-2-3
Peter Antoniak/E. Michael Lunsford
367pp. Ref. 556-5

This guide for experienced users focuses on advanced functions, and techniques for designing menu-driven applications using macros and the Release 2 command language. Interfacing techniques and add-on products are also considered.

Lotus 1-2-3 Tips and Tricks
Gene Weisskopf
396pp. Ref. 454-2

A rare collection of timesavers and tricks for longtime Lotus users. Topics include macros, range names, spreadsheet design, hardware considerations, DOS operations, efficient data analysis, printing, data interchange, applications development, and more.

Lotus 1-2-3 Instant Reference Release 2.2
SYBEX Prompter Series
Greg Harvey/Kay Yarborough Nelson
254pp. Ref. 635-9, 4 3/4" × 8"

The reader gets quick and easy access to any operation in 1-2-3 Version 2.2 in this handy pocket-sized encyclopedia. Organized by menu function, each command and function has a summary description, the exact key sequence, and a discussion of the options.

Lotus 1-2-3 Instant Reference
SYBEX Prompter Series
Greg Harvey/Kay Yarborough Nelson
296pp. Ref. 475-5; 4 3/4" × 8"

Organized information at a glance. When you don't have time to hunt through hundreds of pages of manuals, turn here for a quick reminder: the right key sequence, a brief explanation of a command, or the correct syntax for a specialized function.

Mastering Symphony (Fourth Edition)
Douglas Cobb
857pp. Ref. 494-1

Thoroughly revised to cover all aspects of the major upgrade of Symphony Version 2, this Fourth Edition of Doug Cobb's classic is still "the Symphony bible" to this complex but even more powerful package. All the new features are discussed and placed in context with prior versions so that both new and previous users will benefit from Cobb's insights.

The ABC's of Quattro
Alan Simpson/Douglas J. Wolf
286pp. Ref. 560-3

Especially for users new to spreadsheets, this is an introduction to the basic concepts and a guide to instant productivity through editing and using spreadsheet formulas and functions. Includes how to print out graphs and data for presentation. For Quattro 1.1.

Mastering Quattro
Alan Simpson
576pp. Ref. 514-X
This tutorial covers not only all of Quattro's classic spreadsheet features, but also its added capabilities including extended graphing, modifiable menus, and the macro debugging environment. Simpson brings out how to use all of Quattro's new-generation-spreadsheet capabilities.

Mastering Framework III
Douglas Hergert/Jonathan Kamin
613pp. Ref. 513-1
Thorough, hands-on treatment of the latest Framework release. An outstanding introduction to integrated software applications, with examples for outlining, spreadsheets, word processing, databases, and more; plus an introduction to FRED programming.

The ABC's of Excel on the IBM PC
Douglas Hergert
326pp. Ref. 567-0
This book is a brisk and friendly introduction to the most important features of Microsoft Excel for PC's. This beginner's book discusses worksheets, charts, database operations, and macros, all with hands-on examples. Written for all versions through Version 2.

Mastering Excel on the IBM PC
Carl Townsend
628pp. Ref. 403-8
A complete Excel handbook with step-by-step tutorials, sample applications and an extensive reference section. Topics include worksheet fundamentals, formulas and windows, graphics, database techniques, special features, macros and more.

Excel Instant Reference
SYBEX Prompter Series
William J. Orvis
368pp. Ref.577-8, 4 3/4" × 8"
This pocket-sized reference book contains all of Excel's menu commands, math operations, and macro functions. Quick and easy access to command syntax, usage, arguments, and examples make this Instant Reference a must. Through Version 1.5.

Understanding PFS: First Choice
Gerry Litton
489pp. Ref. 568-9
From basic commands to complex features, this complete guide to the popular integrated package is loaded with step-by-step instructions. Lessons cover creating attractive documents, setting up easy-to-use databases, working with spreadsheets and graphics, and smoothly integrating tasks from different First Choice modules. For Version 3.0.

Mastering Enable
Keith D. Bishop
517pp. Ref. 440-2
A comprehensive, practical, hands-on guide to Enable 2.0—integrated word processing, spreadsheet, database management, graphics, and communications—from basic concepts to custom menus, macros and the Enable Procedural Language.

Mastering Q & A (Second Edition)
Greg Harvey
540pp. Ref. 452-6
This hands-on tutorial explores the Q & A Write, File, and Report modules, and the Intelligent Assistant. English-language command processor, macro creation, interfacing with other software, and more, using practical business examples.

Mastering SuperCalc5
Greg Harvey/Mary Beth Andrasak
500pp. Ref. 624-3
This book offers a complete and unintimidating guided tour through each feature. With step-by-step lessons, readers learn about the full capabilities of spreadsheet, graphics, and data management functions. Multiple spreadsheets, linked spreadsheets, 3D graphics, and macros are also discussed.

ACCOUNTING

Mastering DacEasy Accounting
Darleen Hartley Yourzek
476pp. Ref 442-9
Applied accounting principles are at your fingertips in this exciting new guide to using DacEasy Accounting versions 2.0 and 3.0. Installing, converting data, processing work, and printing reports are covered with a variety of practical business examples. Through Version 3.0

DATABASE MANAGEMENT

The ABC's of Paradox
Charles Siegel
300pp. Ref.573-5
Easy to understand and use, this introduction is written so that the computer novice can create, edit, and manage complex Paradox databases. This primer is filled with examples of the Paradox 3.0 menu structure.

Mastering Paradox (Fourth Edition)
Alan Simpson
636pp. Ref. 612-X
Best selling author Alan Simpson simplifies all aspects of Paradox for the beginning to intermediate user. The book starts with database basics, covers multiple tables, graphics, custom applications with PAL, and the Personal Programmer. For Version 3.0.

Quick Guide to dBASE: The Visual Approach
David Kolodney
382pp. Ref. 596-4
This illustrated tutorial provides the beginner with a working knowledge of all the basic functions of dBASE IV. Images of each successive dBASE screen tell how to create and modify a database, add, edit, sort and select records, and print custom labels and reports.

The ABC's of dBASE IV
Robert Cowart
338pp. Ref. 531-X
This superb tutorial introduces beginners to the concept of databases and practical dBASE IV applications featuring the new menu-driven interface, the new report writer, and Query by Example.

Understanding dBASE IV (Special Edition)
Alan Simpson
880pp. Ref. 509-3
This Special Edition is the best introduction to dBASE IV, written by 1 million-reader-strong dBASE expert Alan Simpson. First it gives basic skills for creating and manipulating efficient databases. Then the author explains how to make reports, manage multiple databases, and build applications. Includes Fast Track speed notes.

Mastering dBASE IV Programming
Carl Townsend
496pp. Ref. 540-9
This task-oriented book introduces structured dBASE IV programming and commands by setting up a general ledger system, an invoice system, and a quotation management system. The author carefully explores the unique character of dBASE IV based on his in-depth understanding of the program.

dBASE IV User's Instant Reference SYBEX Prompter Series
Alan Simpson
349pp. Ref. 605-7, 4 ¾" × 8"
This handy pocket-sized reference book gives every new dBASE IV user fast and easy access to any dBASE command. Arranged alphabetically and by function, each entry includes a description, exact syntax, an example, and special tips from Alan Simpson.

dBASE IV Programmer's Instant Reference
SYBEX Prompter Series
Alan Simpson

544pp. Ref.538-7, 4 ¾" × 8"

This comprehensive reference to every dBASE command and function has everything for the dBASE programmer in a compact, pocket-sized book. Fast and easy access to adding data, sorting, performing calculations, managing multiple databases, memory variables and arrays, windows and menus, networking, and much more. Version 1.1.

dBASE IV User's Desktop Companion
SYBEX Ready Reference Series
Alan Simpson

950pp. Ref. 523-9

This easy-to-use reference provides an exhaustive resource guide to taking full advantage of the powerful non-programming features of the dBASE IV Control Center. This book discusses query by example, custom reports and data entry screens, macros, the application generator, and the dBASE command and programming language.

dBASE IV Programmer's Reference Guide
SYBEX Ready Reference Series
Alan Simpson

1000pp. Ref. 539-5

This exhaustive seven-part reference for dBASE IV users includes sections on getting started, using menu-driven dBASE, command-driven dBASE, multiuser dBASE, programming in dBASE, common algorithms, and getting the most out of dBASE. Includes Simpson's tips on the best ways to use this completely redesigned and more powerful program.

The ABC's of dBASE III PLUS
Robert Cowart

264pp. Ref. 379-1

The most efficient way to get beginners up and running with dBASE. Every 'how' and 'why' of database management is demonstrated through tutorials and practical dBASE III PLUS applications.

Understanding dBASE III PLUS
Alan Simpson

415pp. Ref. 349-X

A solid sourcebook of training and ongoing support. Everything from creating a first database to command file programming is presented in working examples, with tips and techniques you won't find anywhere else.

Mastering dBASE III PLUS: A Structured Approach
Carl Townsend

342pp. Ref. 372-4

In-depth treatment of structured programming for custom dBASE solutions. An ideal study and reference guide for applications developers, new and experienced users with an interest in efficient programming.

Also:
Understanding dBASE III
Alan Simpson

300pp. Ref. 267-1

Advanced Techniques in dBASE III PLUS
Alan Simpson

454pp. Ref. 369-4

A full course in database design and structured programming, with routines for inventory control, accounts receivable, system management, and integrated databases.

Simpson's dBASE Tips and Tricks (For dBASE III PLUS)
Alan Simpson

420pp. Ref. 383-X

A unique library of techniques and programs shows how creative use of built-in features can solve all your needs—without expensive add-on products or external languages. Spreadsheet functions, graphics, and much more.

dBASE III PLUS Programmer's Reference Guide
SYBEX Ready Reference Series
Alan Simpson

1056pp. Ref. 508-5

Programmers will save untold hours and effort using this comprehensive, well-organized dBASE encyclopedia. Complete technical details on commands and functions, plus scores of often-needed algorithms.

dBASE Instant Reference
SYBEX Prompter Series
Alan Simpson

471pp. Ref. 484-4; 4 ¾" × 8"

Comprehensive information at a glance: a brief explanation of syntax and usage for every dBASE command, with step-by-step instructions and exact keystroke sequences. Commands are grouped by function in twenty precise categories.

Understanding R:BASE
Alan Simpson/Karen Watterson

609pp. Ref.503-4

This is the definitive R:BASE tutorial, for use with either OS/2 or DOS. Hands-on lessons cover every aspect of the software, from creating and using a database, to custom systems. Includes Fast Track speed notes.

Power User's Guide to R:BASE
Alan Simpson/Cheryl Currid/Craig Gillett

446pp. Ref. 354-6

Supercharge your R:BASE applications with this straightforward tutorial that covers system design, structured programming, managing multiple data tables, and more. Sample applications include ready-to-run mailing, inventory and accounts receivable systems. Through Version 2.11.

Understanding Oracle
James T. Perry/Joseph G. Lateer

634pp. Ref. 534-4

A comprehensive guide to the Oracle database management system for administrators, users, and applications developers. Covers everything in Version 5

from database basics to multi-user systems, performance, and development tools including SQL*Forms, SQL*Report, and SQL*Calc. Includes Fast Track speed notes.

GENERAL UTILITIES

The ABC's of the IBM PC (Second Edition)
Joan Lasselle/Carol Ramsay

167pp. Ref. 370-8

Hands-on experience—without technical detail—for first-time users. Step-by-step tutorials show how to use essential commands, handle disks, use applications programs, and harness the PC's special capabilities.

COMPUTER-AIDED DESIGN AND DRAFTING

Visual Guide to AutoCAD
Genevieve Katz

325pp. Ref. 627-8

A visual step-by-step tutorial for AutoCAD beginners, this book gives the reader at a quick glance, the graphically presented information needed to understand and respond to commands. It covers more than 90 commands, from getting started to drawing composites using multiple commands. Through Release 10.

The ABC's of AutoCAD (Second Edition)
Alan R. Miller

375pp. Ref. 584-0

This brief but effective introduction to AutoCAD quickly gets users drafting and designing with this complex CADD package. The essential operations and capabilities of AutoCAD are neatly detailed, using a proven, step-by-step method that is tailored to the results-oriented beginner.

SYBEX®

TO JOIN THE SYBEX MAILING LIST OR ORDER BOOKS
PLEASE COMPLETE THIS FORM

NAME _____ COMPANY _____

STREET _____ CITY _____

STATE _____ ZIP _____

☐ PLEASE MAIL ME MORE INFORMATION ABOUT **SYBEX** TITLES

ORDER FORM (There is no obligation to order)

PLEASE SEND ME THE FOLLOWING:

TITLE	QTY	PRICE
_____	____	____
_____	____	____
_____	____	____
_____	____	____

TOTAL BOOK ORDER _____ $_____

CUSTOMER SIGNATURE _____

SHIPPING AND HANDLING PLEASE ADD $2.00 PER BOOK VIA UPS _____

FOR OVERSEAS SURFACE ADD $5.25 PER BOOK PLUS $4.40 REGISTRATION FEE _____

FOR OVERSEAS AIRMAIL ADD $18.25 PER BOOK PLUS $4.40 REGISTRATION FEE _____

CALIFORNIA RESIDENTS PLEASE ADD APPLICABLE SALES TAX _____

TOTAL AMOUNT PAYABLE _____

☐ CHECK ENCLOSED   ☐ VISA
☐ MASTERCARD   ☐ AMERICAN EXPRESS

ACCOUNT NUMBER _____

EXPIR. DATE _____ DAYTIME PHONE _____

CHECK AREA OF COMPUTER INTEREST:

☐ BUSINESS SOFTWARE

☐ TECHNICAL PROGRAMMING

☐ OTHER: _____

THE FACTOR THAT WAS MOST IMPORTANT IN YOUR SELECTION:

☐ THE SYBEX NAME

☐ QUALITY

☐ PRICE

☐ EXTRA FEATURES

☐ COMPREHENSIVENESS

☐ CLEAR WRITING

☐ OTHER _____

OTHER COMPUTER TITLES YOU WOULD LIKE TO SEE IN PRINT:

_____

_____

OCCUPATION

☐ PROGRAMMER   ☐ TEACHER

☐ SENIOR EXECUTIVE   ☐ HOMEMAKER

☐ COMPUTER CONSULTANT   ☐ RETIRED

☐ SUPERVISOR   ☐ STUDENT

☐ MIDDLE MANAGEMENT   ☐ OTHER:

☐ ENGINEER/TECHNICAL   _____

☐ CLERICAL/SERVICE

☐ BUSINESS OWNER/SELF EMPLOYED

CHECK YOUR LEVEL OF COMPUTER USE   OTHER COMMENTS:

☐ NEW TO COMPUTERS   _____

☐ INFREQUENT COMPUTER USER   _____

☐ FREQUENT USER OF ONE SOFTWARE   _____

   PACKAGE: _____

   NAME _____   _____

☐ FREQUENT USER OF MANY SOFTWARE   _____

   PACKAGES   _____

☐ PROFESSIONAL PROGRAMMER   _____

PLEASE FOLD, SEAL, AND MAIL TO SYBEX

SYBEX, INC.
2021 CHALLENGER DR. #100
ALAMEDA, CALIFORNIA USA
                              94501

SEAL

SYBEX Computer Books are different.

Here is why . . .

At SYBEX, each book is designed with you in mind. Every manuscript is carefully selected and supervised by our editors, who are themselves computer experts. We publish the best authors, whose technical expertise is matched by an ability to write clearly and to communicate effectively. Programs are thoroughly tested for accuracy by our technical staff. Our computerized production department goes to great lengths to make sure that each book is well-designed.

In the pursuit of timeliness, SYBEX has achieved many publishing firsts. SYBEX was among the first to integrate personal computers used by authors and staff into the publishing process. SYBEX was the first to publish books on the CP/M operating system, microprocessor interfacing techniques, word processing, and many more topics.

Expertise in computers and dedication to the highest quality product have made SYBEX a world leader in computer book publishing. Translated into fourteen languages, SYBEX books have helped millions of people around the world to get the most from their computers. We hope we have helped you, too.

For a complete catalog of our publications:

SYBEX, Inc. 2021 Challenger Drive, #100, Alameda, CA 94501
Tel: (415) 523-8233/(800) 227-2346 Telex: 336311
Fax: (415) 523-2373

Function-Key	Pull-Down Menu Function	Function-Key	Pull-Down Menu Function
Ctrl-F1	File Goto DOS	Ctrl-F2	Tools Spell
Shift-F1	File Setup	Shift-F2	Search Backward
Alt-F1	Tools Thesaurus	Alt-F2	Search Replace
F1 Alone	Edit Undelete	F2 Alone	Search Forward
Ctrl-F3	Edit Window	Ctrl-F4	Edit Select
	Tools Line Draw		Edit Append
Shift-F3	Edit Switch Documents		Edit Move
Alt-F3	Edit Reveal Codes		Edit Copy
F3 Alone	Help		Edit Paste
Ctrl-F5	File Text In/Out	Shift-F4	Layout Align Indent -> <-
	File Password	Alt-F4	Edit Block
	Edit Comment	F4 Alone	Layout Align Indent ->
Shift-F5	Tools	Ctrl-F6	Layout Align Tab Align
Alt-F5	Mark	Shift-F6	Layout Align Center
F5 Alone	Files List Files	Alt-F6	Layout Align Flush Right
		F6 Alone	Font Appearance Boldface
Ctrl-F7	Layout Footnote		
	Layout Endnote	Ctrl-F8	Font
Shift-F7	File Print	Shift-F8	Layout Line
Alt-F7	Layout Columns		Layout Page
	Layout Tables		Layout Document
	Math		Layout Other
F7 Alone	File Exit (Save)	Alt-F8	Layout Styles
		F8 Alone	Font Appearance Underline
Ctrl-F9	Tools Merge		
	Tools Sort	Ctrl-F10	Tools Macro Define
Shift-F9	Tools Merge Codes	Shift-F10	File Retrieve
Alt-F9	Graphics	Alt-F10	Tools Macro Execute
F9 Alone	Tools Merge Codes More {End Field}	F10 Alone	File Save